The Daily

A–Z GUIDE TO
PROPERTY

Ann Morris is a journalist, magazine editor and media consultant. She has written about property for twelve years and is a regular contributor to the *Daily Telegraph* property section. Ann was previously property columnist for *Harpers and Queen* and for the *Observer*. She has also written articles on a wide variety of other subjects and is the author of *The Adoption Experience: Families Who Give Children a Second Chance*.

The Daily Telegraph

A–Z GUIDE TO
PROPERTY

ANN MORRIS

MACMILLAN

First published 2001 by Macmillan
an imprint of Macmillan Publishers Ltd
25 Eccleston Place, London SW1W 9NF
Basingstoke and Oxford
Associated companies throughout the world
www.macmillan.com

In association with the *Daily Telegraph*

ISBN 0 333 90482 6

1 3 5 7 9 8 6 4 2

A CIP catalogue record for this book is available from
the British Library.

Typeset by SetSystems Ltd, Saffron Walden, Essex
Printed and bound in Great Britain by
Mackays of Chatham plc, Chatham, Kent

Contents

Acknowledgements

Thanks are due to many staff at the *Daily Telegraph* who have supported this book and helped put it together. In particular Susannah Charlton of Telegraph Books for her encouragement, patience and making her own research resources available to me; Mark Edmonds and Angela Pertusini, the two property editors I have worked with at the *Daily Telegraph*; Sue Ryan, the managing editor, for her support and friendship; and the unsung heroes of the Telegraph Library.

Special thanks are due to Ian Cowie for checking through the financial section of the book and to Justin Sidnick of solicitors William Heath for checking through the legal aspects of buying and selling. Their patience and expert knowledge has been invaluable.

On a more personal note, many thanks are due to my family who have given me much needed support, space and time to complete the book. Without them it would not have been possible.

Introduction

Experts might tell you that you are about to embark on one of the most stressful periods of your life: moving home. But it is also one of the most exciting times. A move heralds change – and usually for the better – whether we are moving in or out of town, upsizing or downsizing: the four walls we call home no longer suit our needs.

Moving is a stimulating opportunity not just to swop properties, but to consider entirely changing the way we live: to exchange a listed manor house on the edge of nowhere for a city loft apartment with every modern convenience from infra-red security to underfloor heating – or vise versa. The possibilities are endless. Every move is an opportunity to enhance, develop and change your life style.

The thrill of purchasing your first home is unforgettable. It doesn't matter where it is or how small it is, it is yours and you are finally free to impose your own taste and style on it; however bizarre or conventional that may be. 'Style is the dress of thought,' said Samuel Wesley, the eighteenth-century clergyman and poet, and in that sense our homes speak for us.

But why do we move? According to a recent national survey over 66 per cent of people move because they are upsizing, downsizing or relocating to another area: others move to recoup needed funds or because of a divorce, a death or bad neighbours. Whatever the reason, the move itself is the cathartic moment. Times change and we must change with them, and the physical move from our home forces us out of the past and into the future.

It is a moment when we can get things right if they were not so right before. The longed for big kitchen, second bathroom, large garden or separate study are all on the agenda of possibilities. It is important to think about your needs and priorities (not what everyone else thinks are your needs) both in terms of the size and style of the property you are going to buy and in terms of the surrounding area. A not so perfect house in the right area is usually better than a perfect house in the wrong one.

But finding even that not so perfect house can be stressful. Any excitement about moving is too often dampened or drowned by the effort involved in chasing unobtainable properties and the physical, financial and emotional energy needed to effect the move.

The aim of this book is to take away some of that stress by giving you the information you need to make the process easier. We have avoided long-winded chapters on the mechanics of buying and selling. Instead subjects are listed in a cross-referenced A to Z format covering everything from solicitors and surveys to bats and bathrooms so you can pick what you want from it. However, if you want a starting point look under P for preparing your home for sale and H for home hunting.

We have also put together a clutch of buyers and sellers checklists that should help you to organize your sale and purchase efficiently and effectively: they cover everything from finding a mortgage and choosing an estate agent to preparing your home for sale and clinching the best deal.

First tuck this book under one arm, get a fresh notepad and a pen, pour yourself a cup of tea, coffee or a glass of wine and sit down and ponder. You are going to move – why? Where do you want to live, how much money have you got to spend and how much space do you need?

Happy hunting.

A

ACCESS AND EASEMENTS

> All the world's a stage,
> And all the men and women merely players:
> They have their exits and their entrances.
>
> William Shakespeare, *As You Like It*

Access to your property is normally not a problem as long as you know where your exits and entrances are and they are clearly marked – not just for you but also for the post, deliveries and any guests. But beware; unclear access rights to a property or across a property can be some of the most tedious and expensive problems to sort out.

There are several typical problems:

- Shared access. This is where part of a driveway is shared between two or more properties, or most commonly when flat dwellers share a hallway and stairs.

- Access to other properties. This happens when someone else needs to access their property across yours. Very typical is an access clause concerning a local farmer who has converted the old barn you live in and sold it – but wants to retain a right of access into his fields.

- Easements are short cuts across your property to a neighbour's garden, orchard, garage or house which they may or may not use. It is also a term used to describe the right of a neighbour to access drainage systems, water supply, etc. used by them but running under your land. If there is a problem they will have a right to sort it out from your side of the fence.

Selling

Ensure that there is a clear formal agreement in place about any easements, shared access or access rights to other properties. If the agreement is informal, prepare for the sale by getting this formalized. You may not have minded being the one who always weeded the shared path but a buyer might not be so generous. Equally you might trust the farmer next door whose children go to school with yours and who has only accessed his fields through your property once in the three years you have lived there – but a new owner may not.

Remember:

Don't try to hide the fact that an access is shared or there is an easement of some sort running across your property. It will all come out once the sale is in the hands of solicitors.

Buyers are always on the lookout for problems waiting to happen. If you provide your buyer with something to worry about you could well find the sale falling through.

Any sale that falls through for whatever reason leaves

behind that 'no smoke without fire' feeling and the next potential buyer will almost inevitably be more cautious.

Buying

Don't let shared access or easements put you off but do insist early in negotiations on clear documentation about your rights and the rights of the others concerned. Never assume anything.

One *Telegraph* reader bought a barn near her home from a roofing contractor who had used it as a depot; access had always been clear down a mutually used lane. But the minute the roofing contractor moved out, another neighbour started to block the lane with cars and vans. Her problem was that she had not established who the owner of the lane was.

Legally, as long as a lane or path has been used for access to a property for twenty years or more then you have an established right of way.

When you are buying confirm:

- who is the owner of the access

- whether the access is an established right of way

- who is responsible for the upkeep of the access

You need to know if you will be expected to gravel the lane or clean a shared hall, or if you are expected to pay someone else to do this. Ask if there is any legally binding agreement about upkeep and costs. Ensure you know exactly what your part in this deal will be.

Remember:
If you share any access, you have to be considerate of others' needs and wishes. Nobody is going to object if you take it upon yourself to weed the shared drive or vacuum the hallway daily but don't *expect* to be thanked or overstep your rights by changing anything without full consultation with the person with whom you share access. You might think the hedge is too wild or the hallway light fitting incredibly ugly – your co-owner might not.

(See also **Boundaries, Common Parts, Footpaths and Rights of Way, Neighbours**.)

ACCESSIBILITY

Science is built up of facts, as a house is built
of stones; but an accumulation of facts is no more
of a science than a heap of stones is a house.
Henri Poincaré, *Science and Hypothesis*

Don't ever underestimate the importance of accessibility – whether you are looking for a bachelor pad in London, a family home in the country or a weekend cottage in the wilds of Wales. We all have mental travel barriers and it is best to know where they lie.

Almost every estate agent will tell tales of families that fell in love with a house just that extra ten or twenty miles away, and then sold it two years later because they couldn't stand the commute to work, the school run or the isolation.

The accessibility of any property is important: if it is near a good main route to the city, within easy reach of good schools and a local town but not on a motorway, under a flight path or next to a railway line its value will be higher than its less convenient neighbours. Expect to pay 15 per cent more for a property with good accessibility – and it is worth it.

For many, accessibility to work is the key factor when deciding on where to live. Before you start house hunting:

- check out commuter routes

- work out your commuting limits – some commuters are prepared to let the train take the strain for a two-hour commute each way but many are not

- sort out your family's commuting needs and limits, particularly if you are all going in different directions

- remember that the oddities of train, tube and bus routing and timetabling may mean that the physical distance between your workplace and home doesn't always relate to the commuting effort involved

A friend who works in the City of London recently moved from Clapham to Oxted in Surrey and swears it takes him no longer to get to work because the train service is so efficient. Whatever city you live and work in or around – from Bristol to Brighton, from Liverpool to Loughborough – the message is the same. The eccentricities of our road and public transport systems mean that you can sometimes get to work as quickly and easily when you live fifteen miles away as when you live five miles away.

For commuters to London help in working out commuting timetables is available in *The Daily Telegraph Commuter Guide*. For others a good source of information on stations and timetables is British Rail's website www.railtrack.co.uk.

The golden rule is to never move north of a city if you work south of it, and vice versa. Despite the ring roads it is a hard slog driving from Solihull (west of Birmingham) to Walsall (east of Birmingham) on a daily basis and public transport is generally far too city-centric. If you live and work in a city then make sure you live in the right part of it. There is nothing more annoying than having to change trains twice and take an hour to get to work when you live only a handful of miles away.

Another relentless routine to be taken into the accessibility equation for some families is the commute to school. As a rule of thumb day schools should be within 20 minutes of your home and not much more than 30 minutes away. It's a sad fact that if you go beyond a six-mile radius of the school, you are unlikely to find a school bus so you are committed to well over two hours a day driving your children back and forth.

One fair way to work out where you should live is to draw circles at one-mile intervals around the different places members of the family have to get to. Start at five miles from each place and finish at ten miles. Where the circles intersect is a good place to start looking.

Accessibility is slightly less important when you are looking for a second home or country cottage for weekends – but not entirely. If you live in the south that little stone croft on the Isle of Skye or cottage in the shadow of Snowdon in North Wales sounds wonderful – but without a personal helicopter it's a good day's drive which will ensure that weekending is a rare occurrence and you won't enjoy its delights as much as you might if it was accessible within three or four hours.

Selling

Make sure that any buyer knows all the good access routes from your home and the available services. Highlight:

- Convenient public transport – distance from bus stop/ train station; how to get there and how often services run to the nearest major centre. This is information well worth having to hand. Even if you don't commute on public transport, most people do.

- Back routes by road into local centres.

- Good schools of all types in the area. Find out about these even if you don't have children of your own if you are selling a three-bedroom-plus property.

- Distance from shops, churches, doctor's surgery and garage, and from recreation facilities, i.e. swimming pool, golf course, riding stables and community centre.

Buying

Think clearly about where you ideally need to be. Consider:

- How you are going to get to work. Work out the routes – consult train and bus timetables, test the car or bike ride. Add in the walk to the station, etc.

- How you are going to get to work. Work out the routes – consult train and bus timetables, test the car or bike ride. Add in the walk to the station, etc.

- Nearness to friends and family. A move, whether to a bachelor pad in Camden or to a country house in Kent is always that much more pleasant if you have good friends or close family reasonably near.

- Access to shops and entertainment that interests you (cinemas, restaurants, golf club, etc.).

- Schooling (if part of your current life equation). Check with the school the routes of school buses. Can you get on the school bus (there are often waiting lists)? Ask if there are other families coming from your area with whom you could share a run and if the school will put you in touch with them.

(See also **Home Hunting**, **Location**, **Schools**, **Second Homes**.)

ADJACENT LAND AND PROPERTY

By avarice and selfishness, and a grovelling habit,
from which none of us is free, of regarding the soil
as property . . . the landscape is deformed.
Henry David Thoreau, 'The Bean Field'

Many of us dream of a pastoral view of green fields
dotted with rhythmically chewing black and white cows
or flocks of fluffy white sheep. In our built-up lives any
open space around our homes is welcomed with a gasp of
delight.

Be warned – the grass or concrete on the other side of
the fence could be someone else's financial opportunity
and, before you know it, you might find yourself living at
best next to a new housing development, at worst next to
an all-night lorry park.

Selling

If you know about plans to develop adjacent land it is in
your interests to tell the estate agent and those interested
in buying your property. They will undoubtedly find out
when their solicitor carries out the necessary local authority searches. But you can take the sting out of the situation
by pointing out that:

- Under current planning laws all development is
  constrained in order to keep within the needs of the
  surroundings.

- The building's 'protection' – for instance any fencing that protects your view. This might seem obvious but is worth doing as the person viewing the property will have difficulty taking everything in at once.

If there is unused land adjacent to your property it is worth finding out if it is for sale. Potential buyers could find your property more attractive if they think extra land is available where they could extend the garden, build a double garage or accommodate Polly the pony.

Buying

Always ensure that searches are thoroughly carried out. The most innocent piece of grazing land one month can be a mud field of ongoing development the next.

Look at any plans for development in detail. If the property is just what you want and all safeguards have been taken to protect your privacy and light then consider going ahead.

Don't forget the opportunities that the land around you offers, but equally don't assume that an uncultivated field must be for sale. Do track down the owners and ask them what they intend to do with the land. You might find that they will sell to you or that they have put in their own plans for development.

Remember:
Even if one set of plans is turned down an owner is within his rights to rethink ideas for the property. I know one farmer who was so cross when the local authority turned down his plans for building a group of houses on a field

that he put up three hulking ugly modern steel barns on the site which, as a farmer, he could erect as 'permitted development' without planning permission. Locals and the council who had wanted to preserve the green open space were shocked and angry but helpless and could merely nickname the monstrosities 'revenge barns'.

(See also **Boundaries, Land, Paddocks, Permitted Development Rights**.)

ADVERTISING

Advertising may be described as the science of arresting
human intelligence long enough to get money from it.
Stephen Leacock, 'The Perfect Salesman' from *Garden of Folly*

There is one universal way of selling your home and of finding the property you want to buy: advertising. The property pages of local paper supplements from Cardiff to Carlisle, from Brighton to Birmingham and from Land's End to John O'Groats are packed with grainy postage-stamp-sized pictures of mansions and maisonettes of all sizes and at all prices. And at the top end of the market the postcard-perfect pictures in magazines like *Country Life* can make otherwise satisfied home owners salivate at the thought of still greener pastures.

An advert is a quick clue as to what is for sale but is never totally reliable. A wider angle picture might show that the property backs on to a bus station and fronts on to a main road. No one buys sight unseen but the important facts should be there – price, position and size – to catch the eye of both the desperately seeking or vaguely interested reader.

Advertising can be cheap – a handwritten note and weekend snapshot pinned on to the school or office notice board – or expensive – a page in a magazine or display advert in a national newspaper. All can be effective.

Most memorable were the irreverent property ads penned by London agent Roy Brooks in the 60s and his successor Tony Halstead in the 70s and 80s which appeared in the Sunday newspapers. When selling Desmond Morris's house in 1969 Roy Brooks wrote: 'Attracted by the cover, read 'The Naked Ape' & am pleased to offer residence of decadent descendant. D*sm*nd M*rr*s going Oxford. Forced sell 100-yr-old det family house (Barnet) reconstructed regardless of cost, retaining period features. An immaculate conception, high, healthy, gorgeous views across to Hadley Woods and Barnet Church.'

Today the Internet cannot be ignored as an advertising medium. Most agents with a website will put your property up as part of their sales service package. On other independent sites you can place your own advert; fees for these are usually much lower than fees for adverts in any newspaper and are often waived altogether.

Selling

Ads are a useful guide to what you might expect to get for your property. A good estate agent will suggest where and when to market your property. A local agent will often offer free:

- a prime spot in their shop window

- a 'For Sale' board outside your house

- one or two inserts on an advertising page they take in the local newspaper or magazine

You usually have to pay for advertisements in a national newspaper or magazine and more than two ads in the local paper (unless the agent's stock of properties is very low). But who pays is often negotiable. If you push for a sale price that the agent thinks your property is unlikely to achieve, he or she is unlikely to give you very much advertising space for free as the odds on selling are considerably lowered.

Advertising is also one way to find a buyer if you decide to sell privately. You can take out an ad in the local or national press, in school or parish magazines, on notice boards in a shop or at work. Remember, the wider the readership the more you will pay: a card on the notice board at your tennis club or gym might cost you nothing; a national newspaper small ad, for instance in the *Daily Telegraph*, will cost between £11.50 and £15.50 per line per day; a display ad just five centimetres long and one column wide with a picture costs approximately £330 plus VAT. Regional newspapers are cheaper – small ad lineage in the *Yorkshire Post* is £2.70. Glossy colour magazine adverts are the most expensive – a quarter page advert in *Country Life* costs just under £1,000 plus VAT.

In your advert remember to include: type of house, location, number of bedrooms, number of reception rooms, number of bathrooms, garage, garden, price and a telephone number for appointments. Emphasize special features – Grade 1 listed, thatched, adjacent to a park, etc.

If your first run of adverts doesn't produce a buyer you might find you have to rethink your strategy – and pay again.

Remember:
The picture tells the story and you must ensure that the best possible shot is taken of your house. If the garden is going to feature ensure hedges and lawns are clipped and that it looks colourful; a tray of annuals from the local garden centre can be a real boon. Move pot plants into the picture and take dustbins out to improve the look of the property – and keep it that way until the property is sold.

Buying

Ads give you a very good idea of what properties are costing in the area where you want to buy. They also give you a taste of who is selling what and which agents are most likely to sell the property you are looking for, whether it's a bedsit in Streatham or a country mansion in Suffolk. But they do not give you all the information you will need before viewing.

Remember:
The ad only tells part of the story. Don't immediately call up and ask to view. Save yourself some wasted journeys by first asking the agent:

- what state the property is in

- how long it has been on the market

- any conditions attached to its sale

- Whether it is near a main road, village, train station, etc.

- what is next door

- if it is overlooked

(See also **Do-it-yourself Buying and Selling, Estate Agents, Internet Buying and Selling, Preparing Your Home for Sale.**)

ARCHITECTS

The physician can bury his mistakes, but the
architect can only advise his client to plant vines.
Frank Lloyd Wright, *New York Times*, 1953

The word architect is Greek for builder, but architects are rather more than that. The greats of the past, from Christopher Wren to Frank Lloyd Wright, and the greats of the present, from Peter Palumbo to Quinlan Terry, all combine a sense of design and style with practical building knowledge. They create the built environment, one of man's greatest contributions to the landscape.

Although we admire the work of the best, we tremble at the thought of accidentally employing someone whose vision is too extreme for our day-to-day lives or whose skills are rather less than adequate. So how do you find the architect you need for the house you want to build from scratch or, more usually, for imaginative ideas about extending the home you own or are buying? Most architects are members of the Royal Institute of British Architects (RIBA), which produces two free leaflets: 'Engaging an Architect' and 'Guide to the Standard Form of Agreement'. The leaflets also give details of architects' services and fees – which are usually based on a percentage of the overall building contract. This percentage varies and is usually dependent on the scale of the work to be carried out. RIBA's website – www.architecture.com – provides you with a mass of information including 'Find an architect', a directory of members and a list of '103 things architects do'. The RIBA library can give you names and information about British architects and their buildings. Information from the library is also available on the RIBA website.

Information in Scotland is provided by the Royal Incorporation of Architects in Scotland who also have a website: www.rias.org.uk. The Royal Society of Architects in Wales provides similar information for that area, as does the Royal Society of Ulster Architects for Northern Ireland.

Another useful organization is the Architects and Surveyors Institute which recommends surveyors and architects and answers specific queries from members of the public. They also provide an advisory service to help people find the type of architect they need. It is worth drawing up a clear brief of what you are looking for before you call them. The final brief to the architect will need to include everything from how many people will live in the house to the type of materials you want used in building it and how much money you have to spend.

Most architects are insured against things going wrong but check this with them first.

Selling

If you are selling a house that needs a lot of updating and is on a large plot of land it might be worth approaching a local architect about ways in which it could be enlarged or improved. You can sometimes attract a better price and certainly a wider number of potential buyers if the details say, for example, 'with planning permission for a two-bedroom extension/conversion of the old dairy'.

Possible buyers then have a clearer idea of the real potential of the house, something which can add enormously to its value.

Buying

There are several reasons why you might want to call in an architect.

Building your own home

It has become increasingly popular in the overcrowded landscape of Britain either to buy a plot of land and build your own home or to buy a rather unattractive house on your ideal country acre, pull it down and build something more beautiful and more suited to your needs.

In either case it is probably worth spending a lot of time thinking about exactly what you want. A Georgian or Victorian reproduction? Something very sleek and modern? Lots of rooms or lots of open space? You also have to consider your future family needs. It is not worth getting involved in a building project unless it is part of a long-term plan and you are prepared to spend the money and take the time to ensure you end up with the home you have always dreamed of.

Building your own home takes time. On the most basic level you have to:

- find the plot and purchase it

- get planning permission for your proposed house

- find and hire an architect

- find and hire builders

If you complete the project in a year from start to finish you have been extraordinarily lucky; expect it to take at least two years.

Building an extension

In the competitive housing market in which we live you might find the perfect spot with the perfect house which is just too small for your family needs – but this can be changed with sympathetic extension and development of the house. It might be as simple as building out the kitchen or putting on a conservatory, or as complicated as a two- or three-storey rear extension and complete remodelling of the internal space.

Before you buy:

- Assess whether you are likely to get the necessary planning permission.

- Consult an architect about just what can be done to create the space you need in a sympathetic way.

- Be aware that few local authorities like to see the overdevelopment of a plot. If you need to increase the size of the house by more than half perhaps you should be looking elsewhere.

(See also **Builders, Extensions, Listed Buildings and Conservation Areas, Permitted Development Rights, Planning Permission, Surveyors**.)

ASSETS AND LIABILITIES

Procrastination is the art of keeping up with yesterday.

Don Marquis, American post and journalist, *archy and mehitabel*

Almost every property has them: assets that add pounds to the purchase price and liabilities that just as quickly take them away. The magnificent fireplace and beautiful stained-glass door are assets in a Victorian terraced property within a fashionable square, but the lack of a downstairs cloakroom and the flightpath roaring overhead are liabilities. You can put in the cloakroom and fireplace but you can't reorganize Britain's airspace. Before selling and when buying a property it is worth evaluating the assets and liabilities, and considering whether you can do anything to change them.

Assets include:

- easy access to main commuting routes +15%

- within twenty minutes of good schools +15%

- fashionable village situation +10%

- well sited (edge of village) with right amount of land for property size +5%

- good views +5%

- extra accommodation (granny flat) +5%

- well decorated / good structural order +5%

    Liabilities include:

- structurally unsound − 30 to 40%

- motorway, flight path or railway noise − 20 to 30%

- close to industrial/council estate − 15 to 20%

- large house with inadequate land − 10 to 15%

- no view / overlooked by other property / poor situation − 10%

- poor decorative order − 10%

(See also **Adjacent Land and Property, Conservatories, Flight Paths, Ghosts, Land, Listed Buildings and Conservation Areas, Location, Neighbours, Swimming Pools, Tennis Courts, Views.**)

AUCTIONS

That Europe's nothin' on earth
but a great big auction, that's all it is.
Tennessee Williams, *Cat on a Hot Tin Roof*

Auction rooms are filled with anticipation and excitement, peppered by nervous tension. It's on-the-edge buying and selling, an organized competitive scramble with all the delights of an Egyptian bazaar – whether you are buying an antique Ming vase, second-hand washing machine or a house. Auctions are a traditional way of getting the best price for all kinds of personal property. The first auction king was James Christie who in the eighteenth century would entice buyers by telling them, 'the inexhaustible munificence of your superlatively candid generosity must harmonize with the refulgent brilliance of this little jewel . . .'

Auctioneers today are more to the point. Descriptions are short and the bidding can be fast. Some find them exhilarating, others feel beads of sweat trickling down their spine before they push their way through the auction room door.

Although the vast majority of properties are sold by private treaty, property auctions are regularly held all over Britain and now also take place on the Internet. At least two websites have been set up to auction properties: www.homes4living.co.uk and www.propwatch.com. On the first site some properties are viewable on line with 360-degree pictures and floor plans. At propwatch.com buyers search for a property online and then view it in person by contacting the seller via email. Auctions take place over several days or weeks until a set closing date; you can up your bid as often as you like until that moment. At homes4living.co.uk exchange must take place within forty-eight hours of the auction ending but, unlike physical auctions, the successful bidder is not obliged to proceed. Both sites are trying to make auctioning property a more effective and usual sales practice.

Although for most people selling by auction on or off

the net is not usually a first option as it is more expensive for the seller, there are five significant reasons why a property finds itself under the auctioneer's hammer:

- Following repossession by a bank or mortgage company.

- The property is difficult to sell because there is a sitting tenant, it has been badly damaged by fire, or it suffers from some sort of blight – anything from siting on a main road to subsidence.

- To satisfy the legal requirements of beneficiaries or executors of a will. A sale by auction is considered proof that every effort has been made to obtain the best price.

- The owner wants to sell quickly to realize capital.

- The property is unusual and difficult to value – a converted millhouse or windmill – or so 'prime' that the agent suggests selling by auction might be the best way of getting the highest price.

More properties are sold for the first two reasons during a bust or stagnant market; more for the last reason during a buoyant market. The third and fourth reasons keep property auctioneers in business.

Auctions are a fast fair-chance option, but once the hammer goes down the sale is legally binding. Making a mistake is very expensive. It's no good bidding for lot 66, a former newsagents premises on the edge of the A12 in east London, when you had meant to bid for lot 88, a two-bedroom flat in Bristol. It is a tragedy for both buyer and seller if the person who wants a particular property most is caught in traffic on the M25, can't get their mobile to work, or misses the sale at the Horse and Hound in Upper Bumble by two minutes. It's no good complaining that they would have paid another £25,000 for the property. When the hammer goes down, the deal is legally done, as long as the property has passed its reserve price.

Selling

This is not a cheap option. At auction you are responsible for a large proportion of the costs. Most significant is the percentage of the auction price that the auctioneer will expect you to pay, usually 2.5 per cent.

Think about selling by auction if:

- You need to capitalize on the equity in your property quickly, for whatever reason. After the sale there is usually a maximum completion time of twenty-eight days.

- You have witnessed massive interest in properties like yours in the area and believe or are advised that this is the best way of getting the best price. An auction can take the seller away from the awkward situation of getting involved in gazumping. Many sellers find it hard to stick by an agreed offer if others with an extra £5,000, £10,000 or £15,000 come forward.

- Your property hasn't sold because of a downturn in the market, because it's too near a main road or seems blighted for some other negative reason, and you have reached a point where you just want to get rid of it.

If you decide to go ahead, then before an auction:

- Choose your agent/auctioneer carefully and discuss at length the costs of advertising the auction, where and when it is going to be held, what preparations for the sale you should make and the percentage the agent is charging for handling the auction.

- Decide on a reserve price and whether you want to include in the auction particulars the clause 'unless previously sold' so that you can accommodate a keen buyer who would never attend or bid at an auction. (There are quite a number of these about.)

- Appoint a solicitor and apprise him fully of your plans so that he can deal with requests for title deeds, etc. from prospective buyers.

- Prepare your property for sale.

- Ensure you have somewhere to live within a month of the auction.

- To facilitate a sale it is wise, and may soon be law, to provide potential buyers with a survey.

On the day of the auction be ready to sign over your property or, if the property doesn't reach its reserve price, be prepared to go away and think again or negotiate with the highest bidder.

Remember:

Once a property is sold at auction the sale is legally binding. On the positive side that means as a seller you are not going to be let down. On the negative side it means you can't change your mind even if someone offers you twice the price the following day.

If your property fails to sell for the reserve price, the auctioneer will still expect to be paid a fee.

You don't choose the buyer; a developer or your arch enemy are just as entitled to buy as the young couple, first-time buyer or family you had hoped to see in your home.

Buying

Auctions are fun and can be addictive but property auctions are not the sort to get addicted to unless you have serious cash.

Buying a house through private treaty you can do all the groundwork as you go along, even after you have made a bid for a property. But if you are buying at auction a lot of work has to be put in by you before the day of the sale. Against that is the possibility that you won't get the property anyway.

Advantages are:

- You could get a bargain as everything hangs on who turns up – a flat or house being sold by someone who wants to quickly realize some capital can often go for less than it would if the owner was prepared to smarten the property up and put some effort into selling it. But be prepared; these properties are often stripped of everything, quite literally including the kitchen sink.

- You could get a real dream property, the house you have always wanted and never thought you would have.

If you decide to go ahead, before the auction:

- Appoint a solicitor and ask him to get the title deeds of the property you are interested in, carry out a search and advise you on any special conditions of sale.

- Make sure you have the funds to pay for the property; arrange finance through a bank or mortgage company. Ten per cent of the purchase price has to be put down at the auction. This can be done with a banker's draft but has to be arranged beforehand.

- Ensure that the property is actually going to auction. If the details have the proviso 'unless previously sold' it could be sold before auction. Check the price the buyer is looking for. If you are prepared to pay that price it may be worth making an offer rather than hoping you succeed at the auction.

- Have a survey done of the property you intend to purchase; this will probably be necessary if you are borrowing funds to buy but is a wise precaution in any event.

- Ask why the property is being sold at auction. Is there something wrong with it?

- Decide firmly on the absolute top price you are prepared to pay.

  On the day of the auction:

- Arrive early. Get a good seat and be clear about which lot you are bidding for. If the auction is more than an hour's journey from your home, arrange to stay with friends or at a hotel nearby the night before.

- Take your solicitor with you if possible.

- If you are nervous about bidding ask your solicitor to bid for you; he might charge you for this but it could be worth it. Do *not* get carried away by the excitement of the auction and bid beyond your top price; you could seriously regret this later on.

- If you are successful be ready to sign the auction contract and hand over a ten per cent deposit to the auctioneer who becomes the stakeholder until the deal is completed.

Remember:
Once the hammer goes down you are legally bound to buy the property knocked down to you, even if you walk out of the auction room without signing the contract.

You must have your funds ready.

You must be prepared to lose – bring the tissues with you.

If in doubt, don't bid.

As one auctioneer sagely warns his audience of potential buyers before starting the bidding, 'If you're unsure, I suggest you leave now. But if you are sure then I suggest you stay and buy because tomorrow will be too late.'

(See also **Advertising, Completion, Estate Agents, Internet Buying and Selling, Negotiating, Preparing Your Home for Sale, Private Treaty, Solicitors, Surveys, Title Deeds.**)

B

BANKS AND BUILDING SOCIETIES

> Long ago, the Englishman's castle was his home;
> then that went, and his home became his castle. Now his
> castle is the nation's and his home is the bank's.
> Leon Garfield, *Children's Literature in Education*

Until quite recently almost all mortgages for home buyers were from building societies who would fund the loan with other people's investments. The situation has changed dramatically in the last fifteen years: now most banks also offer mortgages and many building societies also offer banking facilities.

It is worth having several options; banks and building societies compete for business just like anyone else so it is worth knowing what deals are available and what the conditions are for different loans.

The bank or a building society that you have had an account with for some time should probably be your first port of call when you decide to get a mortgage, a second mortgage or a home improvement loan of some sort. There are sometimes advantages to be had because you have been a loyal customer and it is worth checking these first. Study the literature provided carefully; evaluate the various types of mortgage or loan they offer. Decide which is probably most suitable and then make sure that you can't get a better deal from another organization offering a similar package.

Although the easy route is to take the advice of the bank or building society you know, it is always worth shopping around. There are more than 200 institutions in the money-lending mortgage business and the packages on offer change and become more inventive almost daily. Make sure you get the best deal for you.

If you want to find out more about what different banks are offering, the quickest way is to access them through the Internet. All major banks and building societies now have websites. A lot of these websites have information about finding estate agents and offer tips for buying, selling and moving. Or you could look at 'Borrower's Choice' in the 'Your Money' section of the *Daily Telegraph* on Saturday. You could also look under banking in the personal finance section of the *Telegraph* site: www.money.telegraph.co.uk.

Selling

Regardless of whether your mortgage is with your bank or even if you don't have a mortgage, it is worth telling your bank what is going on. There will be a lot of extra expenses flowing out of your account as you move and they might offer you, temporarily, a larger overdraft facility in order to deal with the extra cash demands.

Sometimes a buyer might enquire where you have your mortgage. When mortgages are difficult to get it could be worth a buyer's while asking your building society for a mortgage on the property. Having checked out the value of the property before, a lender might be happy to give a loan on the same property to someone new.

Buying

If you need the money to buy or develop a property make your first appointment with your own bank or building society. They should give you a fairly accurate idea of what they think you are able to borrow.

Each bank and building society has its own criteria for lending money:

- how much it will lend, usually dependent on your income

- to whom, sometimes dependent on your relationship with them

- on what type of home, many won't lend on short leaseholds

These are rules which different branches of a society may bend slightly to suit differing local conditions, so always talk your specific circumstances through.

When there is low demand for funds, lenders often loosen their rules. When demand is high, they tighten them up and priority is given to people already investing with the society – however small their balance might be – or who already have a mortgage with that society. It is always worth opening one or two building society accounts with a modest amount of money – £50 will usually do – to secure your place in any queue.

The Building Societies Association / Council of Mortgage Lenders produce a leaflet, 'How to buy a home'. They also have a website – www.cml.org.uk – offering information about their publications and the mortgage code. If you are having difficulty obtaining a loan on a property it might be worth asking the current owner with whom they have their mortgage.

Remember:

The state of the market and the standard rates of interest and inflation change all the time so before clinching a deal check any new deals on offer.

The amount you will be lent will relate to the value put on the property by the building society or bank rather than the price you have agreed to pay.

If you are concerned about your treatment by a bank or building society you can contact the Building Societies Ombudsman or the Banking Ombudsman. During the year 2001–2 their services will be amalgamated and they will become the Financial Ombudsman. The Banking Ombudsman has a website which explains how to complain about a bank or building society: www.obo.org.uk.

(See also **Bridging Loans, Finances, Mortgages**.)

BASEMENTS

Born in a cellar . . . and living in a garret.
Samuel Foote, English actor and playwright, *The Author*

There are two sorts of basements: basement flats and basements in houses. The former have almost always been a good deal, the latter a boon to families in search of that extra inch of space.

Basement flats

Basement flats have always been less popular than their ground- and first- or even second-floor equivalents. They usually cost slightly less and appreciate comparatively more slowly in price but the percentage differentiation remains much the same.

Disadvantages are:

- less light

- less perceived security

- a greater tendency towards dampness

- nearness to the drains

- the possibility that the rubbish bins for the whole building are kept outside your front window

Advantages are:

- the possibility of your own front door

- the probability of at worst a tiny patio and at best your own garden

- less likelihood of disturbing your neighbours

Basements in houses
If there are two identical houses, one more attractively done up but the other with a basement, choose the one with the basement. Cosmetic decorations are easy, digging out a basement requires major investment. The advantages of having one even if it is just for storing bikes, bottles of wine and bags for the Hoover are enormous. And they can be usefully converted into utility rooms, exercise rooms, teenage dens, etc.

(See also **Damp**, **Extensions**, **Security**.)

BATHROOMS

Bath twice a day to be really clean, once a day to be passably clean, once a week to avoid being a public menace.
Anthony Burgess, *Inside Mr Enderby*

Cleanliness was formerly deemed to be next to godliness but nowadays keeping clean requires showers, his and her sinks and separate bathrooms for the children and the guests. Washing is a national pastime and bathrooms are no longer mere rooms where you wash yourself; they are havens where you can soak your worries away with an aromatherapy oiled bath or get your brain cells buzzing with a power shower after a long night out and before a demanding day of work.

Today all but the very smallest properties are expected to have at least a second loo if not a second bathroom.

Selling

Most important of all, however ancient your bathroom make sure it is glistening before anyone views your house. Dirty, smelly bathrooms are more off-putting than dirty kitchens for many people. If you do have only one bathroom you could suggest to potential buyers where another could go.

Buying

Don't be immediately put off if there is only one bathroom. Check that everything works properly; dripping faps, showers that sprinkle rather than swoosh and baths that take more than three minutes to run are irritating.

Work out how easily another bathroom, basin or loo could be installed. You need to check where the water supply and waste piping run in the building and remember that there should be two doors between a kitchen and a bathroom. Fitting an extra bathroom or refitting an old bathroom can be carried out fairly cheaply (£1,000 should easily cover a simple refurbish with a new bathroom suite) compared to other home improvements.

Remember:

The airing cupboard. Easily forgotten when you are totting up room sizes but important for many families. Is there one or space to make one?

BATS AND OTHER WILDLIFE

Either we've got bats or the mice have taken up hang-gliding.

Guy Bellamy, *The Nudists*

Bats are a protected species and, unless you are a keen naturalist with an interest in these creatures, it is a disaster when you find them in the barn you were planning to convert or roosting in the roof of the garage. Bat roosts cannot be destroyed and are difficult to move unless you build bats another roost nearby, which could be expensive. If you destroy a bat roost you are liable for prosecution under the Wildlife and Conservation Act.

Bats have enormous environmental appeal for some but unfortunately don't add value to your property or appeal to your sale. There is a bat conservation group attached to the RSPCA which is currently carrying out a ten-year study of bats in Britain. This group does give general advice to householders on how to live alongside a roost. More information about bats can be found on the internet site: www.bats.org.uk.

The main problem, say the RSPCA, is that bat roosts can smell if they are not in a well-ventilated building. Bat conservationists suggest you lay down old sheeting to collect the droppings during the season (bats hibernate in the winter) and put the droppings on your garden; they are a very good fertilizer. A good surveyor will probably be able to tell you if there are bats in a property.

It is worth remembering that lots of other wildlife is also protected including bees, badgers, field mice, red squirrels and the common toads. All can be a nuisance as well as a delight. For more information about protected species contact the Joint National Conservation Council or visit their website on www.jncc.gov.uk.

BLIGHT

If science has taught us anything it is that the environment is full of uncertainties. It makes no sense to test it to destruction. While we wait for the doctor's diagnosis, the patient might easily die.

Prince Charles, from a speech at the North Sea Summit, 1987

It used to be almost impossible to find out about the environmental nasties lurking in the area where you plan to buy a house. There are 400,000 disused industrial sites in Britain, 275,000 abandoned rubbish tips and 46,000 sites releasing pollution into the environment. You may be living in a house sitting astride a heap of junk but how would you know?

Now you can find out. Several Internet sites have

recently opened to help home owners establish just what sort of blight they might be sitting on, or buying into.

Ignorance is not bliss. Take the case of Dave Harrison from Hedon in Hull. He was astounded when he discovered one unhappy day that his home was subsiding because it had been built over a leaking gas tank left over from a gasworks which had closed more than eighty years ago. Insurance policies just don't necessarily cover that sort of environmental hazard and Mr Harrison was forced to demolish his bungalow at his own expense.

Nor could Mr Harrison blame his solicitor for carrying out a poor job when he bought the property. Solicitors' searches are unlikely to reveal this sort of contamination; they only cover local authority plans not hidden hazards like pollution and flooding.

The new websites attempt to reveal all. One is a government site called www.environment-agency.gov.uk. A box entitled 'what's in your back yard' offers information on pollution and flooding simply by entering your postcode.

Another site – www.homecheck.co.uk – has been set up by Sitescope, which is a company specializing in providing environmental information to lawyers, insurance companies and engineers. It draws its information from sources including the National Radiological Protection Board, the British Geological Survey and various specialist surveying companies. This site lists different types of hazard and rates them from 1 (low) to 7 (high). A test was made by a *Telegraph* journalist on the postcode SE10 0AX, the code of the much troubled Millennium Dome which is built on a site which has been home to a chemical works, steelworks,

power station and gasworks. It rated the Dome's risks as
follows:

- flood – 6

- subsidence – 4

- radon gas – 2

- coal-mining subsidence – 1

- waste disposal – 6

- contamination – 6

- pollution – 7

It also commented that ozone levels were 'low to medium'
and PM10s (the soot particles emitted by diesel engines
and implicated in lung cancer) were high to very high.

It is worth noting that the risk of contamination is much
higher if there is any history of industrial activity in an area.

Another website offering information about blighted
areas is www.homesight.co.uk which is run by a credit
agency called Equifax in association with Yellow Pages.
This has small-scale risk maps but you can order detailed
individual reports on your neighbourhood for £86.

An alternative way of finding out about contamination
risks is to contact Virgin One account (08456 000 001) who
publish a series of homebuyer's guides with maps and
postcodes of areas affected by flooding, subsidence and
radon gas.

(See also **Flight Paths, Flooding**.)

BOUNDARIES

My apple trees will never get across
And eat the cones under his pines, I tell him.
He only says, 'Good fences make good neighbours.'

Robert Frost, 'Mending Wall'

There is no room for wishy-washiness here. It is essential – whether you are buying or selling – to know exactly where the boundary of a property lies. A vague wave at a distant hedge is not enough.

We giggle and gasp at cases in newspapers where a feud of Wild West proportions has developed over a tiny strip of land, but even the most mild-mannered men and women are by nature territorial and brave is the person who claims one inch too many. Fights over the tiniest patch of land have cost tens of thousands of pounds. Beware.

As well as finding out exactly where the boundary to a property lies it is important to know who has responsibility for maintaining the wall, hedge or fence running along it. Hopefully the deeds or plans will show you this. Traditionally, a T mark on a boundary line drawn on an original site plan indicates that a particular wall belongs to the owner of the property inside which the T mark appears. Some deeds specify clearly your obligations as far as fencing is concerned – the type and its minimum or maximum height.

Remember:

If there is no specification of your obligation under general planning law, you may not erect a fence more than one metre high in front of a house or over two metres high at the rear. Walls dividing semi-detached or terraced properties with supports on both sides are generally regarded as belonging to both parties with repairs being a joint expense, though in many terraced properties each owner takes complete responsibility for one dividing wall – either the left wall all the way down the terrace or the right.

If your shared wall or boundary with your neighbour falls under the Party Walls, etc. Act 1996 you are required to give your neighbours two-months' notice of any intention to carry out works on the wall along with details of what those works will be. More information about this act is available from the Association of Building Engineers who have brought out an explanatory leaflet on the subject.

Selling

Ensure that your boundaries are clear and if possible well fenced. Be clear about who has the responsibility for maintaining each boundary wall. If there has been a dispute about a boundary wall or fence, make sure that it is completely over and you are not handing over a disgruntled neighbour and potential quarrel to a new buyer.

Buying

Ask to see the plans to the property so you can see just what you are buying and what rights you have over the land around you. You might find that the plans say one thing and the physical boundary – a hedge or wall – is in quite a different position. This will need to be clarified before you buy. Sometimes neighbours agree to an informal change in a boundary which is never formalized in the plans.

Deeds to the property are not always a help and can be imprecise about exactly where a boundary lies. Be careful and clear about where you believe the boundary lies. Overstep the mark and you could find yourself at the centre of a horrendous dispute.

If there has been a boundary dispute in recent years you may be well advised to look elsewhere for the home of your dreams. If you are determined to go ahead, chat to the neighbour concerned first to try to ensure that the dispute is not going to recur.

Remember:
If you decide to change a fence for a wall or to put up a higher fence, good neighbourliness requires you to notify the neighbour who will be affected.

Established boundaries are not always accurate and mistakes can be passed down and on.

(See also **Accessibility**, **Land Registry**, **Neighbours**, **Title Deeds**.)

BRIDGING LOANS

The human species, according to the best theory
I can form of it, is composed of two distinct races,
the men who borrow, and *the men who lend*.
Charles Lamb, 'The Two Races of Men'

Bridging loans are short-term loans which bridge the financial gap between the sale of your home and the purchase
of your new home – and everyone hates them.

There is usually some panic when you realize you might
need a bridging loan: the worry is that the 'few weeks
delay' you are anticipating could turn into a lifetime of
unmanageable debt. The panic is healthy. A bridging loan
is not something that should be undertaken lightly and the
very cautious would say it should never be undertaken at
all.

There are two types of bridging loan: A closed loan and
an open loan.

Closed loans

These are the safest sort of bridging loan and the easiest to
obtain. They apply to buyers who have exchanged on their
existing home but have not completed the sale by the time
they complete the purchase of their new home and so need
intermediate financing. A closed loan is made for a set
period of time. You can usually obtain a closed loan from
your mortgage lender or bank. The interest is high but
lower than that on an open loan.

Open loans

There is a three-star warning on an open loan. This is the loan you take on when you have bought but not sold at all. Banks and building societies are very cautious about handing these out and charge steep interest rates to deter all but the most determined. In a dipping market it can take two years to sell a property – or more in extreme cases – so be warned. Is that dream home really worth it?

(See also **Banks and Building Societies**, **Finances**, **Mortgages**.)

BROCHURES OR PROPERTY DETAILS

I have heard of a man who had a mind to sell his house,
and therefore carried a piece of brick in his pocket, which
he shewed as a pattern to encourage purchasers.

Jonathan Swift, 'The Drapier's Letters'

At their best brochures are glossy productions which show off a property like a prize bull in a ring – flanks shining, tail swishing and mouth smiling – but the owner never tells you how much the bull kicks and complains when in less salubrious surroundings.

For the seller it is important to show off the property's good points and to minimize but not to hide the bad points. The buyer has the task of trying to see past the rose-tinted view he is provided with, though laws now prevent the use of any purple prose which is not absolutely accurate. If the details say the house is sixteenth century, then it *is* sixteenth century. Beware of clever phrasing like 'believed to be' which can confuse, and watch out for much favoured euphemisms. 'Convenient' could mean backing on to the railway line, 100 yards from the M25, or yards from the centre of Bristol; 'easy to manage' could mean too small; 'exceptionally spacious' too big and expensive to heat; 'individual decor' means most people will hate it; 'ideal for modernizing' – the builders will need to be in for six months before you can even camp in the property.

Brochures vary enormously and the glossier they are the more expensive the property is likely to be.

Selling

One way to choose an agent is to look at the sort of brochures she or he uses to promote the property being sold. The brochure is the shopping ground for buyers and a first-rate house is often let down by a second-rate brochure. For smaller, less expensive properties the brochure is usually provided free as part of an estate agent's service but it is usually a charged extra on more expensive properties. The bigger and/or more expensive the property, the bigger and more expensive the brochure that describes it. Expect to pay anything from about £250 for a two-sided full-colour A4 glossy card brochure with one or two pictures to £5,000 plus for a very special brochure of sixteen pages or more with lots of pictures, maps and layout plans. You will be charged extra for professional photographs, anything from £350 to £700 plus.

It is always worth negotiating to see how much of the cost of producing a brochure the agent will bear but don't let them end up paying for the brochure and as a result charging you a higher agency fee.

If your property is attractive to people who do not live in the area and you need to cast your net wider it is probably worth investing in a glossy brochure.

Before photographs are taken of your property do everything you can to improve its celluloid image:

- Remove the dustbin from the front garden.

- Make sure hedges are trimmed and window boxes weeded.

- Consider painting the front door.

- Tidy up inside and ensure everything sparkles.

- Use fresh flowers to enhance and soften the image.

Buyers

Don't be fooled by pictures or an enticing description. The house, flat or cottage in the brochure in front of you might be the property you have always dreamed about at a bargain price, but then again it might not. There is nothing more depressing than arriving at your dream and finding the view they didn't show you was of the factory down the road, the pub next door or the train tracks at the bottom of the garden. Having got the details ask the agent what sort of road it is in, if it backs on to or is near a busy road or train station. Although proximity to busy roads is less of an issue in towns or cities, it spoils the ambience of a country cottage or house and makes a property ultimately less desirable: it will appreciate in value more slowly and sell on less easily.

(See also **Advertising**, **Estate Agents**, **Preparing Your Home For Sale**.)

BUILDERS

> How very little since things were made
> Things have altered in the building trade.
>
> Rudyard Kipling, 'A Truthful Song'

Builders are considered by many as the major obstacle in the process of making your home more beautiful. They always cost more, take longer and make more mess than was expected. For weeks and sometimes months you are reduced to eating dust sandwiches and fighting to find a tiny circle of calm in the whirlwind of chaos and noise that surrounds you.

The truth is that half of the time it isn't the builders' fault. Building work is horrendously dusty and messy and it is impossible to anticipate every problem. For instance, a builder may have quoted for putting in a new window but, having pulled out the old one, he or she discovers the frame is rotten. And at the same time you wonder whether you should put in a bigger window altogether. And so it goes on.

One conservationist who has made a career of buying and restoring old buildings calls the problem the 'wouldn't it be nice if' factor. This occurs as work progresses: 'Wouldn't it be nice if' . . . we put in a stone floor, granite worktop, tiled all the bathroom walls, etc. Other delays can be caused by late delivery of building materials as well as sickness, holidays, weather and all the other normal accidents of life.

But the other half of the truth is that there are cowboy builders out there – local papers thrive on stories of pensioners who wanted a few tiles replaced on their roof but ended up paying as much for this minor repair as their neighbour did for a new roof. There are also straightforward builders who are simply not very good at their trade: workmen who pay more attention to their tea break than to plastering the walls and others who set up trade with little experience and no qualifications and who shouldn't be trusted with a DIY kit.

If you need to carry out building work on a property before selling or after buying, do everything you can to ensure that things will go smoothly by:

- Getting estimates from at least three firms.

- Approaching companies who have been recommended to you. Ask neighbours, local estate agents and/or the architect or building surveyor working for you.

- Approaching the Federation of Master Builders (FMB) or the National Federation of Builders in England and Wales or the Building Employers Confederation (BEC) in Scotland for more names. All have websites.

The FMB have a National Register of Warranted Builders who are bound by a code of practice and offer a warranty that any defects arising within two years because of faulty workmanship or materials will be put right by that builder or another registered builder. The warranty also provides up to £10,000 towards any reasonable costs if your builder suddenly stops trading. The FMB has a 'Find a builder' service on its website – www.fmb.org.uk. The BEC has offices all over England and Wales (there is also a Scottish Building Employers Federation) and can supply the names of their members in your area. Members of the BEC participate in a guarantee scheme which includes a six-month defects liability period and a two-year guarantee period covering structural defects and some cover if the builder goes bankrupt.

When choosing a builder don't just chose the cheapest but find out when he can start; how long he thinks the job will take; what his workmanship is like. Check work he has done for previous clients; their standards may not come up to yours.

Be extremely clear about all the work you want done, down to how many plug sockets you want fitted along each wall and how you want the walls finished. Write down a clear list and add to it during your discussions. Try hard to keep to standard sizes both in order to keep costs down and to ensure you are not held up by the late arrival of a bespoke piece of material.

Remember to consider: heating and insulation, roofing, electricity, plumbing, flooring, telephones, any extension to your burglar alarm system, cupboards and shelves, final decoration. Give every builder you ask to quote a copy of the same list.

Agree to a specific timetable for the work with payment penalty clauses for stepping too far outside its limits without very good reason. Remember to make allowances for the late delivery of materials, their errors, your errors and unexpected problems and sickness. One builder I encountered told me that his estimate would probably be higher than his competitors but he could guarantee that work would start when I wanted it to and would be finished within a set period of time and with the minimum of dust. Extraordinarily, despite hitting a number of problems along the way, he lived up to his word.

Ensure that the builder has a good relationship with you and with the architect and/or building surveyor working for you. It's always easier working out a problem with somebody you have some sort of rapport with.

Selling

Don't employ a builder unless you have to. Keep any building work to a minimum. It is just repair time. It is worth patching up unsightly cracks in the plaster, fixing the guttering, replastering the damp patch caused by a leaking downpipe and dealing with any rotten windows but don't start doing anything dramatic. Nothing is more depressing for a buyer than to hear that you have just retiled or refloored the kitchen for their benefit. Renowned as you undoubtedly are for your good taste, they might hate it. Keep any redecoration simple; very few people object to white paint.

Buying

Your choice of builder is crucial to your sanity over the next months – sometimes years. Check him or her out thoroughly and work out clearly what work you want done in as much detail as possible. If you know that building works are going to have to be done immediately take the builder round before you have completed the deal to explain what you will want done so that you know how much these essential building works will cost and if your plans are feasible.

(See also **Architects, Conservation Areas, Conservatories, Extensions, Listed Buildings, Permitted Development Rights, Planning Permission, Surveyors.**)

BUNGALOWS

If the property world possesses an equivalent to the flared trouser it is surely the bungalow. Either it instils in you feelings of warm homeliness, or fills you with contempt.
There is very little in between.
Lewis Bessemer, *Daily Telegraph*, 2000

Bungalows are generally associated with seaside retirement towns like Worthing, Lytham St Anne's and large patches of Dorset, Devon and Cornwall. But outside the high-money-earning acres of city commuter land and well before you hit the coast you can find them in pockets almost everywhere in England, Scotland and Wales.

Although unfashionable – a home buyers' survey by one hagent recently suggested that only 18 per cent of buyers favoured one-storey living and they avoided using the 'b' word – bungalows did have a heyday and are still the ultimate for many buyers.

Bungalows were originally built for Britons returning from India; bungalow means 'of Bengal'. Until the end of the 1970s they were considered quite the thing but lost favour as Britain's colonial past passed from pleasant memory into history. They ceased to remind people of the glamorous days of another age and instead marked in brick, stone, wood and cement the passing of life – the purchase of a bungalow was seen as a public declaration of your age. You had accepted you were past it – past climbing upstairs to bed.

Like black lace-up shoes for school children, bungalows are 'sensible' for older people and for the less able because there are no stairs to climb and they are easy to run with less risk of accidents. But, overall, bungalows are no cheaper to maintain than an ordinary house; for one thing they have bigger roofs for their volume.

Beyond the lack of stairs, there are advantages to buying a bungalow:

- They are often built on bigger plots of land.

- They sometimes afford more privacy and can easily hide behind a hedge.

- They allow for more flexibility of space; you can have a dining room or study instead of a second or third bedroom.

- Because they are considered unfashionable and appeal primarily to those who are downsizing, they tend not to escalate in price at quite the same rate as other properties in the same area, though as with all properties the most attractive in a good position will always rise with the top of the local market.

Developers today tend to describe any bungalows they build as 'cottages' or 'low-rise barn conversions'.

Selling
Highlight the location, views and garden not the fact that it is a bungalow. Use all the tricks to emphasize what an attractive home you have. Make sure your windows are sparkling as one of the big advantages of many bungalows is the light and views they have.

Buying
Don't be put off. A lot can be made of a bungalow; that barren garden and grey image which taints so many bungalows can be easily remedied with some good planting and whitewash. Surprisingly perhaps they can be the ideal home for a young family because you can get more for your money and very often you get a bigger garden, ideal for the climbing frame and slide. One-level living also means no stair gates and no need for a separate playroom or for toys all over the house as the children's bedrooms are on the same level.

C

CASH BUYERS

Nothing links man to man . . . like the frequent
passage from hand to hand of cash.

Walter Sickert, 'The Language of Art' in *New Age*, 1910

A cash buyer is someone who does not need to arrange a
mortgage and has sold their own property or just happens
to have sufficient cash to buy a property outright. If you
are a buyer this is the best position to be in. If you are a
seller this is the buyer you are waiting for: someone who
has the money to pay up and move in straightaway. If you
are a competing buyer, without cash, this is the buyer you
dread.

Except in a boom market, most buyers with cash
will expect to pay under the asking price and to get a
slightly better deal because they are in a position to move
quickly. As a seller, if you are not in a hurry or haven't
found the house of your dreams you don't need to grab
at this particular financial plum. Before accepting consider your needs. You might decide that the enthusiastic
buyer who has a solicitor and mortgage lined up and
is willing to pay a fraction more is the right buyer for
you.

(See also **Chains**, **Estate Agents**, **First-time Buyers**, **Home Hunting**, **Negotiating**, **Queue Jumping Without Gazumping**.)

CENTRAL HEATING

How can you expect a man
who's warm to understand one who's cold?
Alexander Solzhenitsyn, *One Day in the Life of Ivan Denisovich*

The great majority of houses today are centrally heated although properties that have not been renovated for a long time, small or remote second homes and country cottages are often not and can be chilly.

Selling

As central heating is so common today, not having it will reduce the price you get for your property, but it is unlikely to be worth putting in just for a sale. If you do have central heating check that it works properly and have it serviced; a service record always impresses a buyer. If you don't have central heating, make sure that rooms smell fresh and are warm and dry. There is nothing more unwelcoming or unenticing than a cold house that feels somehow damp and musty, but a log fire or a well-stoked Aga can make all the difference.

Buying

Check that any central heating system has been well maintained and is in good working order. The service record should give you a good indication of this.

If there is no central heating calculate the cost of installing it, particularly if you are planning to make the property your primary home. Contact the Heating and Ventilating Contractors Association who will give you information on residential heating. If you are buying a property without central heating this should be taken into account in the asking price.

Lack of central heating is often, though not always, an indication that significant work has not been done on the property for some time. This might mean that there are other major renovation works to be done.

(See also **Services**.)

CHAINS

Like a hick'ry cog in the old mill wheel
He did his part as his turn came 'round'

Anon

For most of us a buying and selling chain is part of the process of acquiring or selling a property. The shorter the chain the fewer chances of a chain reaction and the better it is for you; the longer the chain the greater the risks.

Many people try to avoid the chain situation by selling first and renting, thus putting themselves in the attractive position of being cash buyers. But this is not always possible or always sensible. If house prices are going steadily upwards and you sell before you buy, prices will continue to rise while you look for your new home; this might cost you thousands. The ideal in most markets is to sell and buy at the same time, completing on the same day.

If you are relying on your buyer's buyer to sell the whole situation can become fairly fraught. Everything goes at the rate of the slowest link in the chain. This can be very frustrating, particularly if the person ahead of you in the chain has another buyer in the wings. The chain does occasionally break, setting you back to square one. If you are buying you have to decide whether to continue the sale of your own house or move into rented accommodation.

Selling

Cash buyers or first-time buyers are best, or someone who is prepared to stick their neck out and get a bridging loan to keep the pace of the sale going.

If you do get involved in a chain then it is worth checking if the agent you are selling through takes part in a chain-linking scheme. This is useful when a chain breaks. Under these schemes – rarely used except during a boom market – the agent will buy your house at a discounted price based on an agreed valuation so that you can move and the chain is unbroken. The agent will then sell the house and recoup his expenses. One of the better-known schemes is called Chainmaker. Under this, if the house is eventually sold for more than the agreed valuation the difference goes to the original seller.

If no such scheme is offered and the chain breaks you have three options:

- To delay your own move and hope the person you are buying from doesn't decide to sell to someone else.

- To move and take out a bridging loan (very risky if you are in a slow market and your house has been difficult to sell in the first place).

- To start again, holding on to the house you have found for as long as you can but being prepared to look at other properties.

Buying

If you are relying on the purchaser of your property to exchange so that you can purchase your future home, be aware that you are the least desirable of buyers. If someone else comes along who has sold and become a cash buyer or who has already exchanged then they may well be seen as a preferable option.

If you are in a chain keep tabs on all parts of it; try and find out where there are any weak links.

If the chain breaks and the seller decides not to move or to sell to someone else you have two options. You can either continue with your own sale and be prepared to rent for a short while. This will put you in a very strong buying position (a good option in a normal market). Alternatively, you can stay put, tell your buyers, and start looking for other homes (a better option in a boom market if your house is very easy to sell).

(See also **Cash Buyers, Home Hunting, Negotiating, Queue Jumping Without Gazumping**.)

CHANGE OF ADDRESS NOTIFICATION

> As an address it was perfectly genuine,
> only it didn't happen to be mine.
> Storer Clouston, *The Lunatic at Large*

Letting people know where you are is essential to the smooth running of your life. You should get change of address cards printed up after you have exchanged on your property and as soon as you manage to obtain your new telephone number. The card should include the names of all members of your family, your old address, your new address and phone number and the date when you will move.

For example:

John, Jane, Jenny and Michael Evans
are moving
from 10 Station Row, Reading RWX 6JQ *to*
Rose Cottage, Henley on Thames, HX6 5JH

Telephone: 0956 459 235
on 18th July, 2001

Everyone needs to know you're on the move; the friends and family in your address book are the easy ones. You also need to notify: bank, building society, credit card companies, insurance broker and insurance companies, car registration and driving licence authorities (there are sections on your vehicle registration and licence documents for this), any hospital or clinic you attend, doctor, employer, colleagues at work, children's school, clubs or societies you belong to, utility companies, the council, publishers of any magazines you subscribe to, charities you support.

It is wise to get the Post Office to redirect mail from your previous address for six months at least. It is almost impossible to remember everyone who needs to know about the move and it takes time for some organizations to update their systems.

Selling

Make it as easy as possible for the new owner: leave some change of address cards to give to any callers and two or three stamped A4 envelopes with your name and new address on them. It sometimes takes time for the Post Office's redirection system to get into gear. The new owner can slip any mail in the envelopes and post them on.

Keep some change of address cards so that when you do receive mail through the Post Office redirection system or from the new owners of the property, you can send

cards (sometimes for the second time) to your corres-
pondents.

Buying

Be kind. This is a do-as-you-would-be-done-by occasion.
Keep a note by the telephone and in the hallway of the
address and phone number of the former owner and send
mail on to them, unless it really does look like junk mail.

This kindness may have its reward: if you have bought
a property with a quirk – most properties have them in
some form – then you will feel more comfortable about
calling up the former owner and asking them how they
dealt with it (rooks nesting on the chimney, badgers in the
garden, a tricky old-fashioned lock on the hall cupboard).

If you hate the name of the house you have bought it is
usually quite simple to change it – from The Ice House
to Sunny View if you like. There is no legal requirement to
advise anyone of a change of name though it is recommended that you send a notification of the change to the
council so the correct address goes on the electoral register
and another to the Post Office so that they can deliver your
mail.

(See also **Telephones**, **Buying Checklists**, **Selling
Checklists**.)

CHILDREN

The place is very well and quiet and
the children only scream in a low voice.
Lord Byron, letter to Lady Melbourne, 1812

The trouble with children (love them as we all do) is that they are too honest, too noisy and too messy; not useful qualities when you are trying to buy or sell a property. Although not always possible, it is better both to view and to show property when they are not about.

But it is more than this. Many children find the idea of a move unsettling; you propose to take them away from the world they know and their friends at school. Their horizons are small. They can't believe that the house with peeling wallpaper in the living room and ghastly green paint in the bedrooms will one day be a lovely home. So take time to explain to your children why the family is moving.

Explain what they will gain from the move: a bigger house might mean they will finally get their own room, a move to the country could mean the longed-for dog, cat or rabbit becomes a reality. Although they might be leaving some friends, they could be nearer other friends or family.

Ensure they spend a day at their new school before they leave their old one. Most schools make a fuss of children in this situation and the curiosity of their peers and the novelty factor of a different environment can be interesting and appealing, however much they like their old environment.

Include the children's names on change of address cards and send them to their friends as well as yours.

Make a firm date for good friends of theirs to visit your new home within one or two weeks of the move. Such friendships might fall away after a few months or remain in their lives for many years, but it is important for children to see that they are not saying goodbye to everything they know and friendships can survive over a distance of many miles.

If you know people in the area you are moving to, make an effort to get together before you move, perhaps several times, so that your children see that there are friends living near their new home.

Selling

Children's noise and clutter can be detrimental to a potential sale. Remove at least half their toys and put them in the cellar, the garage or the garden shed. There really is only one Mary Poppins and no one has yet invented a box or cupboard that can take the endless variety of children's toys that are now considered necessary to life. Toys not only get in the way, the clutter tends to make a room look smaller and less inviting than it should.

Noise is another factor to consider. Small children's squeals of delight and amusement are music to the parental ear but noise also makes a house seem smaller. Most people want to emphasize the space they are selling and it is space most people are looking for.

If they are not at school, granny's, a neighbour's or a friend's (the preferred options), this is the time to get a video out in an attempt to contain both them and the noise they make.

Buying

If possible don't take children with you. Apart from being a distraction (touching things they are not meant to) when you are trying to imagine the next ten years in the property, they can be too honest about the taste of the owners. Everything from 'Euch, I think this room is a horrible colour' to 'My mum says exercise bikes are for people who have nothing better to do' or 'We're not going to live here!' come from their cherubic lips. Chuckle as both you and the owner might, such behaviour may not foster the good relationship you will need to help you work your way smoothly through a purchase.

However, your children's needs are almost paramount when deciding on a new home. You will already have taken into consideration the size of the house and the garden, but remember their need for friends nearby – a neighbour within a hundred yards with a family of similar ages is a positive boon, for most families. Proximity to schools, parks, clubs like brownies and scouts, ballet classes and swimming pools can also make or break the success of the move for them.

(See also **Accessibility**, **Preparing Your Home for Sale**, **Schools**, **Selling Checklists**.)

COMMISSION

I'm tired of Love: I'm still more tired of Rhyme.
But Money gives me pleasure all the time.

Hilaire Belloc, 'Fatigued'

Commission is what you pay to an estate agent for selling your property or a relocation agent for finding you a property to buy.

Commission is usually based on a percentage of the sale price of a property and varies enormously from agent to agent and from area to area. It can also fluctuate with the market and the type of property you are selling or buying. If there is a shortage of properties you can usually arrange a better (smaller) commission deal. Although fees always appear to be set at a certain rate try to negotiate a better deal; most agents are like Moroccan carpet traders – always ready to haggle.

Solicitors also sometimes charge a percentage fee for carrying out the conveyancing

Whether buying or selling most agents and solicitors will expect fees to be settled on the day of completion.

Selling

Commission charged by an estate agent selling your house can range from 1 per cent to 4 per cent. It is very rarely outside this band and is most likely to be 1.5–3 per cent. The rate is dependent on where you live, the state of the market and the desirability of your property. If the market is booming and your house is desirable you will probably get a good rate as the agent knows they will have no problem selling the property quickly. However, whatever the state of the market you must negotiate the commission rate.

To get the best deal don't demand that the house is put at a higher price than the agent genuinely believes they can sell it for; they will want to ensure they are recompensed for the time and energy put into selling your property. Don't ask for too many extras for free. The fee is the most important thing to keep to a minimum.

Remember:
It is standard practice for an agent to charge a lower percentage commission if they are given sole agency.

Buying
An increasing number of busy buyers are using relocation agents or buying services to find their ideal home for them. These agents also charge a variable commission. It is possible that they will be prepared to negotiate a deal but it is less likely.

(See also **Architects, Estate Agents, Relocation Agents**.)

COMMON PARTS

Suppose everybody cared enough, everybody shared
enough, wouldn't everybody have enough? There is enough in
the world for everyone's need but not for everyone's greed.

Frank Buchman, American evangelist, *Remaking the World*

This is a situation encountered by flat dwellers and occasionally those living on an estate who share a garage block or garden. If any part of a property is shared it is essential to know your personal rights over it and your responsibility towards maintaining it.

I know one flat dweller who was annoyed when a neighbour decided to decorate their shared hallway with pictures and a table of potted plants – the 'improvements' weren't to her taste and she wanted the hall kept clear. The pictures and the plants were removed but it created some tension.

Responsibility for shared parts should be set out in your lease. If not try to ensure there is some sort of written agreement, or ask your solicitor to request a written agreement about your rights and responsibilities and those of others involved.

Selling
Be clear about your rights and responsibilities.

Buying

If you are going to share any part of a building it is important to quiz the seller about the neighbours and how well the joint parts of the property are maintained. You don't want to find out too late that the last owner always took it upon herself to polish the letterbox, tidy up the bin enclosure and clean the stairs and hallway every week.

(See also **Accessibility**, **Neighbours**.)

COMPLETION

For a man's house is his castle.

Sir Edward Coke, *The Third Part of the Institutes of the Laws of England*

The moment you have been waiting for: the wrangling is over, the moving van ordered, the best china packed and it is time to complete the purchase and move. You just have to get through this one day of peak stress.

On exchange you agree a day when the sale will be completed. You are then legally bound to complete and move on that day. You *must* do so or risk facing large claims for compensation by other parties involved.

When deciding on which day to complete think about what will fit in with your family timetable best and when you can get most help from family and friends. Most of us have a handful of people who turn up and help at times of stress and crisis – this is one of those times. Even the friend who just keeps you calm by making coffee is valuable. However organised and able you are no one can legislate for traumas like a lost cat, not being able to get the double bed out of the bedroom door because you built bookcases along one wall or your five-year-old son being sick.

It is also probably less than wise to move on a Friday, although according to many moving firms this is a much favoured day because we then have the weekend to sort everything out. But if things aren't right in your new home – the electricity and phones have been cut off rather than transferred into your name – then it may be three days before anyone can come to your rescue. Despite our desire to shop twenty-four hours a day, seven days a week, most people still like their weekends off and feel justified in charging you considerably more if you call them out on a Saturday or Sunday.

Remember:
There are serious legal penalties for not completing a sale once you have exchanged contracts. It does happen and if you know that for some reason there will be a delay on the completion date don't panic. Warn the other side so that everything can be sorted out as smoothly as possible.

It is a condition of all mortgages that the loan is repaid on completion of the sale of the property that is mortgaged.

Selling
You get the money but you no longer have the house. Even if you cannot move immediately into your next property you are legally bound to move out and hand over the keys.

You cannot get too much help or be too organized for completion day. By now:

- Everything should have gone or be packed and ready to go.

- All gas, electricity and other services should have been terminated or meters read and switched to the names of the new owners.

- Everything that isn't packed ready for the removal men should have been deposited with friends or family (including the cat and the children).

- You should have: an overnight bag in which to pack your toothbrush, night clothes, alarm clock and the charger for your mobile phone; frugal supplies for breakfast (hang on to the kettle); wads of cash for takeaway meals, tips, etc.; your mobile phone.

- You should have collected in all the keys from your cleaner, neighbour, relatives, etc. Complete sets – front and back door keys, garage keys – should be labelled and, once you have closed the door for the last time, deposited somewhere the new owner will be able to pick them up (usually the estate agent who sold the property for you or a solicitor).

The contract usually specifies at what time completion will take place and you should aim to be out of the house or flat by then. When your solicitor tells you that completion has taken place – the rest of the agreed money has been transferred to them or to your bank account – inform the key holders; who will tell the new owners that they can pick up the keys. Everything must be out of the house; if you forget something it is up to the new owners to decide what to do with it.

Remember:
Be careful not to take something you agreed to leave behind – the cooker or the curtains in the living room.

If you fail to complete on the day a 'notice to complete' will be served by the buyer's solicitor; this will legally require you to complete within a specified time. Legal proceedings can be instigated against you and the buyer may claim justified expenses – for example, storage of furniture and hotel bills – in the interim.

If the buyers fail to pay the money due on completion you should not under any circumstances let them move in. A notice to complete may be served by your solicitor to enforce the contract. Ultimately the buyers could lose their deposit.

Buying

Your main task is to ensure that the money is due in place, usually with your solicitor, ready for completion to take place on the appointed day. This money may be your own savings, a new mortgage, a bank loan, or the proceeds of the sale of another property.

Remember:
Before completion the solicitor will expect you to provide enough money to cover his or her fees and disbursements

(charges paid on your behalf like Stamp Duty and Land Registry fees). He will expect a cheque several days in advance of completion so that it can be cleared, or a banker's draft (a cheque signed by an authorized bank employee which cannot be stopped).

The completion payment is usually made by telegraphic transfer from one bank to another; you will be charged about £20 for this transaction.

If you find when entering a property that things have been taken away that were included in the sale price you can make a claim for their return, or the seller can be sued for compensation.

There are serious penalties if you fail to complete (see under selling above).

(See also **Conveyancing**, **Removal Firms**, **Services**, **Solicitors and Licensed Conveyancers**, **Telephones**, **Buying Checklists**, **Selling Checklists**.)

CONSERVATION AREAS

Heredity is just environment stored.

Luther Burbank, American horticulturalist,
Dictionary of Scientific Quotations

In order to protect the character of some of Britain's villages, towns, streets and squares, certain areas have been designated conservation areas. This means that no building development and no demolition of property is allowed.

Selling

For many this is a good selling point as it means that you live in an area of special architectural interest and there is no threat of development in the immediate surroundings. It will certainly attract more people to view your property.

Buying

The good news is that the environment around the property you are buying is protected and will not change. Many of Britain's most attractive villages, and streets are designated conservation areas. You may also be able to obtain grants for any structural repairs through the local authority or – for outstanding buildings – through English Heritage. A list of their grants and services can be seen on their website: www.english-heritage.org.uk.

The bad news – if you can call it that – is that you will not be allowed to build any significant extension on to your property and you will have to get listed building consent for any alteration or extension you want to carry out. You only have a chance of getting planning permission for any change to the property if it does not affect the character of the building or the environment around it.

Remember:

Even the trees in your garden are protected under a conservation area order.

(See also **Listed Buildings, Planning Permission**.)

CONSERVATORIES

Light (God's eldest daughter) is a principal beauty in building.

Thomas Fuller, English preacher and historian,
The Holy State and the Profane State, 'Of Building', 1642

Once a place for potted palms, vines and genteel cups of tea in the sun and out of the wind, the conservatory has become the essential extension to our houses and our domestic lives. Conservatories are now dining rooms, playrooms, living rooms and offices, the means by which we draw light and sunshine into our homes.

The trouble with too many conservatories is that they are freezing in winter and unbearably hot in summer when the ideal would be the other way round. We forget that placing a conservatory on the sunny south side of the house invites a double dose of heat and light where we least need it. North-facing conservatories allow light into an otherwise dark area and provide warmth without excessive heat.

Conservatories come in all shapes and sizes and quality levels. The best are made of steel or hardwood and today use double-glazed low-emissivity glass like Pilkington K. This means that even if it does get seriously hot outside this will not be reflected into the house and the conservatory will remain sunny but cool.

Selling

This is what everyone is looking for. A conservatory is the added extra that is almost a must, so make the most of it. Ensure that it is not full of unused toys or just a place to keep the freezer. Show it off to its best advantage.

If you don't have one, then show viewers where you thought of putting one.

Buying

If a property doesn't have a conservatory extension and this is your heart's desire remember to add at least £10,000 and up to and beyond £50,000 to have one professionally installed that will add real value and living space to your property. Remember a conservatory does need foundations and walls. There is a lot of building work involved in putting up a conservatory and it is a real extension to the house. You may need planning permission, depending on the size of conservatory you want to build.

There are plenty of reputable companies which specialize in conservatories; many advertise in magazines. Get some brochures and ask three or four to quote for the job. Ask to go and see conservatories they have already built. You can then talk to previous customers about the time and trouble involved and about anything they wish they had done differently. You may well find that prices from different firms vary enormously. Examine the quality of the materials used and the craftsmanship.

Unless you have a lot of space or want something rather special it should not be necessary to call in an architect to design the conservatory for you but you may need a surveyor.

Remember:
If you intend to make the conservatory an extension to a room and knock down a section of exterior wall you will add to the expense as steel beams will probably have to be put in to support the structure above.

The work and upheaval involved is on a par with any other extension work undertaken.

(See also **Builders, Extensions, Fashion in Property, Planning Permission**.)

CONTRACT RACES

Know ye not that they which run in a race run all,
but one receiveth the prize.
I Corinthians 9.24

If you can avoid it don't get into a contract race unless you really truly want the property and your finances are already in order; it may be expensive and have an unhappy ending.

Contract races are when two or more potential buyers are told that the buyer who reaches exchange of contract first can have the property. They are usually entered into for one of two reasons:

- They are considered by some as the fairest option when one or more buyers want the same property.

- The seller needs to move quickly. Although an offer has been accepted the seller instructs his or her solicitor to send out a further contract or contracts when other offers are made in order to put pressure on the first buyer or to see if someone else can complete in a shorter time.

Contract races are most likely when there is a shortage of properties for sale and prices are rising. By law solicitors or conveyancers are required to tell the legal representatives of all would-be buyers when there is a contract race.

Selling
This can mean a speedier sale if you are under pressure to complete on the house you are buying, but you will not endear yourself to the purchaser.

Some banks and building societies have been known to encourage contract races on repossessed houses in order to realize the capital more quickly.

Buying
Unless this is the house of your dreams, you have financing ready and your solicitor is prepared to push hard so that you have a good chance of success, don't even think about entering a contract race.

A contract race is a misery for all but the winner – and even if you get there first the seller isn't obliged to sell to you; they might opt to sell to the buyer who has a passion for Persian cats which they also adore. Meanwhile you could run up a lot of survey fees, search costs and legal bills.

If you do decide to go ahead, talk to your solicitor. Be prepared to pay him a higher fee for making this property purchase a priority. If the house is being sold for a good price and you desperately want it the extra charge is worthwhile. You may still lose, but at least you will have tried.

(See also **Estate Agents**, **Exchange of Contracts**, **Queue Jumping Without Gazumping**, **Sealed Bids**, **Solicitors and Licensed Conveyancers**, **Surveys**.)

CONVERSIONS

Plus ca change, plus c'est la même chose.
(The more things change, the more they are the same.)
Alphonse Karr, French novelist and journalist, *Les Guêpes*, 1849

This is when a house, barn or other building isn't what it once was but has undergone a metamorphosis into a new existence.

Conversions have a charm all of their own. Converted farm buildings with attractive names like The Old Dairy, The Orangery or Tithe Barn are popular with buyers looking for something different and a home with character. But the quality of the conversion can make all the difference to the quality of life you have in such a home. This applies to grand old houses that have been transformed into flats, or city office blocks converted into fashionable open-plan loft apartments.

Selling

If you are selling a converted flat or loft apartment make sure that you know who is responsible for the common parts of the building. When selling any conversion make sure that you have all the guarantees for the building work, central-heating system, etc. to hand. Buyers will also be interested in the history of the property, even if it was formerly a furniture polish factory.

Buying

You can usually get at least some character and often a lot by buying a conversion – whether it is a flat or a house. If buying either make sure that you get as many guarantees as possible of the building and other work, particularly if it is a new conversion. If the work has been carried out by an approved builder there should be guarantees attached. Make sure you know whom you should approach if things go wrong.

If the builder has not provided or refuses to give guarantees be sure to get the property thoroughly surveyed or you will have no redress if you discover damp walls, damaged drain pipes or any of the other million problems that occur in a building.

Flats

Ensure you know who is responsible for the common parts of the property. If the responsibility falls jointly on the flat owners then make sure it is being observed. Many Victorian houses converted into flats lose their attractiveness simply because the outside and common parts of the building are badly kept. This can ultimately effect the value as well as leading to tensions between the residents.

Some conversions create rooms that are very awkward in shape. This can be quirkily attractive but it can also make a flat less convenient to live in by limiting the size and type of furniture you can use.

Houses

You can get some very unusual and delightful conversions, particularly of old barns. But watch out – barns are big spaces. You may exchange a four-bedroom barn conversion for a three-bedroom house to acquire one extra room but twice the heating bill. Curtaining, carpeting and furnishing these big spaces can also cost a fortune; your standard-sized couch can look surprisingly lonely in a big space.

(See also **Accessibility**, **Builders**, **Common Parts**, **Leasehold Properties**.)

CONVEYANCING

No brilliance is needed in the law. Nothing
but common sense, and relatively clean finger nails.

John Mortimer, *A Voyage Round My Father*

Conveyancing is the legal term for the tangle of legal and
administrative procedures involved in buying and selling
property, and it is usual to get a solicitor or licensed
conveyancer to work through this paper mountain for you.
But it is worth knowing the basics: at least you can then
listen intelligently.

The solicitor's ultimate objective in conveyancing is a
good clean sale. Specifically, the solicitor aims to ensure
that:

- The property you are buying or selling is everything
  that it purports to be.

- It belongs to whoever you say it belongs to and no one
  else.

- It is not under threat of any local authority horror like a
  compulsory purchase order for a village bypass

Although your solicitor will hopefully have the nose
of Sherlock Homes, the patience of Job and the wisdom of
Solomon they are not clairvoyants and it is always worth
talking to them about any niggling worries you have. Tell
them if you are concerned that a boundary is unclearly

marked or that the side extension was built without planning permission.

In order to speed things along many solicitors or licensed conveyancers now use something called the TransAction Protocol, a scheme devised by the Law Society. The seller's solicitor decides whether to use this. If they do, they send the buyer's solicitor a package of information at the outset including: the draft contract; copies of earlier title deeds if unregistered or official copies of the entries if registered; the property information form which is a special form of preliminary enquiry; a fixtures, fittings and contents form listing what is and what is not being sold as part and parcel of the deal.

The Building Societies Association/Council of Mortgage Lenders produces a leaflet about conveyancing. Information is also available on their website: www.cml.org.uk.

Selling

Tell your solicitor as much as you possibly can about the sale and be clear about any agreements you have made informally with the buyer which will need to be formalized: you have decided not to sell the orchard but you have agreed to include the summer house in the sale; the buyer can not move in until after the New Year.

Make sure your solicitor is fully informed of any personal problems: your mother-in-law is refusing to move out of her granny flat; you and your husband are splitting up; you need to sell by a certain date.

To carry out the conveyancing:

1. Your solicitor will: ask for the title deeds to the property you are selling (if mortgaged these will be with the lender) and details of what is and is not included in the sale. You should also hand over any relevant documents: guarantees for any work carried out, copies of planning permission for any extension, etc.

2. Copies of the deeds with the TransAction package, if being used, will be sent to the buyer's solicitor with a draft of the contract regarding the sale.

3. The buyer's solicitor will send back a list of any queries which will need to be answered and returned.

4. If the buyer is satisfied an engrossed contract (containing all the new information necessary) and an agreement on the completion date will be sent to your solicitor who will arrange for you to sign it at the same time as the buyer, at which time the buyer will hand over a percentage of the agreed purchase price (usually 10 per cent). You have now exchanged and the contract is legally binding.

5. Your solicitor will write to the building society to discover how much money is needed from the sale in order for him to redeem the mortgage on your current property.

6. A draft transfer document for the sale will now be drawn up which you must sign.

7. You will now be told how much money is needed to

complete the sale (paying off the remaining mortgage if applicable, paying the estate agent and other accounts).

8. Completion. The contract is finalized and the property now passes to the buyer. Your solicitor will arrange to receive the outstanding purchase money and hand the keys over.

9. Your solicitor settles any accounts and fees outstanding including the mortgage account, and the estate agent's bill and finally hands you the rest of the money.

Buying

Make sure you know the following before you buy or if you are concerned about any of these issues put them forward to your solicitor so that he can obtain the answers for you and the conveyancing can move swiftly ahead:

- the precise boundaries of the property

- any shared rights of access or easements

- any structural additions or alterations carried out by the last owners

- any guarantees in place for treatment of damp or woodworm, a new roof, boiler, etc.

- any confusion over ownership

- any sitting tenants – even the seller's granny

To carry out the conveyancing for you your solicitor will:

1. Make contact with the seller's solicitor and await the draft contract. etc.

2. Having received the draft contract, etc. your solicitor will make a number of different enquiries to ensure that the seller really owns the property and that you are buying all you believe you are buying.

3. Send in local and other search forms and fees to the relevant authorities. This is to ensure there are no plans to build a road through your property. Be warned: these searches are against the house; plans for nearby land are not included and if the property is adjacent to a patch of derelict land it is worth asking your solicitor to find out about plans for that also. It is up to you to ask; your solicitor has no reason to visit the property and so such questions will not occur to him.

4. Check property plans against the property itself, send any preliminary enquiries to the seller and deal with any requirements by your mortgage lender (if you have one).

5. Discuss completion date and the amount of the deposit.

6. Check the survey and searches and make sure your mortgage offer has no difficult conditions attached.

7. Having received answers to his queries, he will agree the terms of the contract down to the last detail before it is signed and sent with the deposit to the seller. The contract to the seller and the contract to the buyer must be identical.

8. Exchange and receive contract signed by the seller.

9. Prepare and send the transfer, carry out final Land Registry searches checking seller's title to the property.

10. Receive back the transfer signed by the seller, check amendments, have you (the buyer) signed the transfer? This signature must be witnessed. Send the signed transfer back to the seller.

11. Check searches and make arrangement for finances on completion.

12. On completion receive the title deeds and all relevant documents and guarantees and the property transfer. Hand over a bank draft for the balance of the money.

13. After moving, send the transfer and necessary Stamp Duty to the Inland Revenue.

14. Complete and send off Land Registry application. This will eventually be sent to you or your lender with a land certificate.

DIY Conveyancing

You can do it yourself, but you need:

- the mind of a detective to uncover potential problems attached to the property

- time to be on call during the day and to travel around

- a grasp of legal jargon and the stages of property purchase

- to love filling in forms

- the facilities to type and fax information

If you still decide to go ahead, get a copy of the TransAction Protocol from the Law Society and a book on the subject, for example the *Which? Guide to Conveyancing*.

Remember:
It is considered inadvisable to even attempt DIY conveyancing unless the property is not a vacant, freehold house.

If you are buying and getting a mortgage the saving is not going to be massive; you will still have to pay the lender's solicitor's charges which would usually be included in the work your solicitor would have done for you.

Most mortgage companies are against buyers not qualified as solicitors carrying out their own conveyancing. Some solicitors refuse to deal with individuals rather than other solicitiors as it delays the process so much.

If you are unfamiliar with the system it will probably take you longer to carry out the conveyancing than it would a solicitor. This could discourage the owner of the property you are buying and you might lose out to another buyer.

(See also **Banks and Building Societies, Completion, Exchange of Contracts, Finances, Solicitors and Licensed Conveyancers**.)

COUNCIL TAX

There is one difference between a tax collector
and a taxidermist – the taxidermist leaves the hide.

Mortimer Caplin, in *Time* magazine, 1963

Local authorities charge a Council Tax on all property. The tax you are charged depends on the tax band your property is in and the tax charged for that band in your area. The Council Tax band of the property you are interested in and the rate that is payable are often provided in details of the property. If they are not, enquire from the agent or the owner how much they pay in Council Tax.

Amounts charged vary widely from council to council and you could find yourself paying substantially more or less than owners of similar property in the next street simply because their property comes under a different council.

Remember:
If you cannot immediately move into a property because you are having work done to extend, restore or decorate it then you may be liable for a Council Tax refund. If work makes the property totally uninhabitable no Council Tax may be payable.

COVENANTS

Never break a covenant, whether you make it with a
false man or a just man of good conscience. The covenant
holds for both, the false and the just.

Zoroastrian Scriptures, *The Yashts*

Some properties are subject to restrictive covenants. These
have either been put in place by an eccentric builder, are
intended to protect the interests of other properties in the
area, or are historic.

Historic covenants can be somewhat quaint – perhaps
preventing you from keeping a sheep or pig in the garden
or hanging your washing out on a Sunday. More common
are restrictive covenants preventing you from extending
the property, building in the grounds or running a business
from the house.

Although some covenants may seem merely relics of the
past – when keeping a pig was a common habit of most
families and running a business meant tradesmen coming
back and forth to your door daily – it is not safe to ignore
them. Whatever the original intention and however out-
dated the restriction, covenants are legally indefinitely
binding.

Selling

Be open about any restrictive covenant you know of.
Buyers will not be amused if they find out from their
solicitor at a later date that they cannot run a business

from the property and they carry out some consultancy work – albeit on the telephone – from home on one or two days a week. They might pull out of the sale.

Remember:
A failed sale – for whatever reason – almost always hinders the ultimate sale of the property.

Buying

Any restrictive covenant should come to light when your solicitor receives the draft contract from the owner's solicitor. However, if a covenant is mentioned by the owner when you are viewing the property or is in the estate agent's details, pass this information on to your solicitor anyway.

CUPBOARDS

What you see is what you get.

Flip Wilson, from *The Book of Quotes*

It is almost impossible to find a house with too many cupboards; we need more and more space to keep more and more things – from sets of china to summer clothes, skiing equipment and DIY stores.

Selling

Emphasize every square inch of cupboard space. Today most families expect fitted cupboards in some if not all bedrooms and see a walk-in clothes cupboard or walk-in larder as real luxuries. Attic and cellar space are greedily sought after extras.

Buying

We all need cupboards. The most beautiful house without any good cupboards is going to be a major mess in the hands of most owners. Don't be fooled. The current owners have probably hidden their detritus in the garage or don't live in the house any more. If there isn't enough storage space, take into consideration the cost of installing fitted cupboards; wood and good carpentry aren't cheap and a fitted wardrobe is unlikely to cost you less than £300, and possibly twice or three times as much.

Remember:

A room can look big enough for a double bed or two singles but may not then accommodate a cupboard. If there is insufficient space in a room, look at the possibility of putting cupboards in the bathroom or hall. Don't forget the need for cupboards for boring things like the Hoover and ironing board, your spare bed linen and towels, coats, tools, etc.

(See also **Buying Checklists**.)

D

DAMP

Muddle makes more muddle.

Mrs Beaton, *Mrs Beaton's Cookery Book*

The great fear is rising damp. This happens when a damp-proof course breaks down and brick walls – which are porous – suck up water from the ground. The result of rising damp is wet walls, causing damp and discoloured wallpaper on the lower half of your walls, flaking paintwork and sometimes a smell of drying mouldy paper.

Not all damp is the rising variety. There is also penetrative damp caused by a leaking roof, gutter or window and damp caused by incorrect ground levels when the damp course is below the level of the ground outside. Most penetrative damp will disappear once the cause has been fixed.

When you are having a property surveyed it is worth remembering that many companies test for damp by using a meter that records dampness but does not indicate why a property is damp. If you believe that a property you are living in, buying or selling is suffering from damp but you are not sure of the cause, before you carry out any drastic remedial action contact the British Wood Preserving and

Damp-Proofing Association who will be able to give you the names of experienced damp consultants in your area. They publish free leaflets about damp proofing and also have a website: www.bwpda.co.uk.

Selling

Most people are very sensitive about damp; you might have got used to the damp patch in the kitchen and have put off doing something about it but it might deter a potential buyer from making an offer or encourage her to make a lower offer than she would otherwise have done. It will be detected by a surveyor and is one of the classic levers that buyers use to negotiate a reduction of the agreed price.

If you suspect any damp problems, get them sorted out before selling. Call in a professional and get more than one estimate; it may not be as bad as you think and it might save the sale of your house.

Buying

You can often but not always detect damp in a property; on a sunny day when the windows are flung open you might never know it is there. It is essential to get property checked out by a surveyor, or you may find yourself stuck with this problem without any recourse to compensation. Your surveyor should be able to pick up just what the cause of any damp is and the good news is that any problem like this can be used to negotiate the price of the property downwards.

Remember:
Damp can indicate that building work has been less than well done or that the property has not been particularly well maintained and it might be the first of a string of problems.

DEBT, DIVORCE AND DEATH (THE 3 Ds)

I am a marvellous housekeeper.
Every time I leave a man, I keep his house.
Zsa Zsa Gabor, in *Was It Good For You Too?*

Most agents will tell you that a high proportion of property comes on to their books for these three reasons. In a boom market it is probably around 25 per cent of an average agent's sales portfolio, in a slow market it can be as much as 70 per cent. Few of us move for the fun of it, although I have a friend who moves every two years because she wants to make her way up the property ladder; we are usually driven by the need for more space, less space or a different environment – or debt, divorce or death.

Selling

Debt
If your house has been repossessed, it is hard not to leave without furiously pulling out every last light bulb (and the

new boiler, the brass door handles and the fireplace you installed in the living room). But try to resist; the worse the property looks, the poorer the price the agent will be able to achieve for it, the less you will receive and the more you will remain in debt.

If you are selling because of your personal debts don't tell every punter your embittered tale. You will only put them off and reduce the likelihood of a good sale. Prospective buyers might be uncomfortable with the thought of evicting you from your beloved home, concerned that you will be wide open to gazumping offers and worried that you *will* remove the new boiler, brass door handles and the fireplace you installed in the living room.

Divorce

Ensure that you and your (soon to be ex-) partner are in agreement that you are going to sell and have agreed on which agent will sell your property for you.

The minute you even mention the word divorce prospective buyers see the walls of a house weep and the atmosphere change. If you find it difficult not to tell people why you are selling, don't offer to show anyone around the property yourself. There are few things more off-putting than divorce tales. I remember viewing a wonderful house in Clapham and complimented the owner on her Rolls-Royce of a kitchen, at which point she told me that she and her former husband had both enjoyed cooking and the kitchen had been completed one month before he left her and moved in with his new 'lady'. I had been married for less than two years and as she continued to point out the kitchen's wonders I knew I would choke on every mouthful I ate there if we bought the house.

Death

It is often nice for buyers to know that someone loved a house and lived in it for a long time but avoid discussion of a previous occupant's sickness and where they died. It can spook people. Give the property a good clean and polish and some fresh flowers. People associate musty smells with death and there is nothing like the healthy smell of lemon and beeswax polish to remove them.

Buying

Debt

Tread cautiously if the person selling the property is in debt; they may borrow some more money or change their mind. Don't be put off by a house where everything including the kitchen sink has been ripped out; look at the structure and position of the property. These are the essentials, the fixtures and fittings are extras. Don't get depressed by the thought that you are depriving someone of their home; by buying you are helping them out of debt.

Divorce

If you discover a house is being sold by a couple splitting up then ensure through the agent that both parties are in full agreement about the sale. If you know about the divorce before viewing the house, insist the agent shows you around, not the vendor.

Death
Make sure there is no disagreement about the sale between
those inheriting the property.

(See also **Repossession**.)

DEPOSITS

> The importance of money essentially flows from
> its being a link between the present and the future.
>
> John Maynard Keynes, *The General Theory of Employment*

When the deposit changes hands at exchange of contracts
the deal for the purchase and sale of a property is technically secure.

   Most deposits are about 10 per cent of the purchase
price of the property but can be less; and you can even
purchase a property without a deposit if you exchange and
complete on the same day. The deposit is handed over by
the buyer to the seller's solicitors. It is non refundable and
is held as security for the completion of the contract. The
deposit is deducted at completion from the total amount of
the agreed sale.

Selling
If you need the deposit from the person purchasing your
property in order to put the deposit down on your next
property it is quite common for a special condition to be

written into the draft contract whereby your solicitor passes the money forward to you. This money can then be used as the deposit on your next property and a whole chain of property purchases can work in this way.

Buying

If you don't have sufficient money for a deposit you will need a bridging loan which is paid off when you receive the proceeds of the sale of your existing home or when the mortgage loan comes through on completion of the purchase. Avoid this if you can; bridging loans are expensive and there is always the risk that completion won't take place when planned.

(See also **Bridging Loans**, **Conveyancing**, **Exchange of Contract**, **Finances**, **Solicitors**.)

DO-IT-YOURSELF BUYING
AND SELLING

A penny saved is a penny earned.

Seventeenth-century proverb

There is a tremendous temptation to do it yourself when it comes to selling property. There are three basic reasons:

- A distrust of estate agents as a breed; they are now seen by many people as a lower form of life than even second-hand car dealers.

- A desire to save every penny possible and make every pound we can out of our major asset.

- A firm belief that we alone understand the charms and intricacies of the much-loved home we are about to sell.

But don't be fooled; it is not easy. You need large amounts of time and patience, a cool head and a clear idea of property values.

Selling

Be realistic – ask yourself the following questions: have you got the time? Are you sufficiently dispassionate about the property to know its faults and be its agent rather than its loving owner? Are you good at negotiation? Have you the resources and skills necessary to draw up and have printed or photocopied the details of your property?

If the answer to all the above is yes:

1. Prepare your house for sale.

2. Decide on an asking price. Make sure you have a good idea of what houses like yours are selling for and use the common technique of fixing the price just under the next key figure; £149,000 is a lot more attractive than £150,000.

3. Decide what is to be included and excluded from the sale price. Have an idea of what price you will ask if the buyer wants the living-room curtains you were planning to take with you. You are, however, not obliged to sell anything with the property. Remember

that fixtures – door knobs, light fittings, etc. – are considered to be included unless you specifically exclude them.

4. Draw up particulars to give to potential buyers. Measure your rooms carefully and usually to their widest points (but point this out or you could be accused of misrepresentation). You will also need to take and have printed several good-quality photographs of the house. These should emphasize the best features of your home: a spectacular view, a pretty garden, a charming Georgian front, good fireplaces and bookcases in the living room, a gracious staircase.

5. Find your buyer. There are several ways to go about this:

   • Through advertisements.

   • Through the Internet. There are now a number of property sites and several specialize in advertising properties that are privately for sale. Make sure you know how long your advert will remain on the site.

   • Through a property shop. These usually charge you a set fee for putting your details in their window and some offer to match you with people looking for your sort of house. Except in Scotland – where they are the norm – property shops are becoming less popular as more and more Internet property sites set up.

- Networking through friends. Make it known among the widest circle of your friends and contacts possible – work, clubs, family, neighbours, church – that you are planning to sell.

- You could also put a 'For Sale' sign outside your home. Signs are legally limited to two square metres in area.

Now comes the selling. Be prepared to:

6. Arrange appointments to view. Keep a diary, take names and phone numbers.

7. Show all viewers around with the same enthusiasm and interest. Make a list of the key points of your property; remember what attracted *you* to the house. Ask friends what they think are the major assets of your house and your area – the closeness of a gym, railway line, school or park can sometimes be the clinching factor. Remember that the chatty enthusiasts often are never heard of again and the rather sullen and serious viewer could be the one who wants to buy; you never can tell.

8. Calmly evaluate the merits of any offer. Remember to ask what financial position the potential purchaser is in (cash buyer, first-time buyer, part of a chain); there is a lot of difference between a cash buyer and someone who has just put their own property on the market.

9. Dispassionately negotiate the final asking price.

10. Be prepared to give up, try again or finally end up calling in the agent you were trying to avoid.

Remember:
Be careful – there are criminals who pose as potential buyers in order to find out whether there is anything to steal from the property. One way of ensuring your prospective buyer is genuine is to ask for a phone number in order to confirm the appointment or in case you have to cancel at the last minute.

Buying

There are always a number of houses being sold privately and it may be interesting to search out what is on offer without relying on an agent to tell you.

The motivation behind DIY purchase is the possibility of a better bargain; the agent has been cut out so their 2 per cent profit often ultimately gets split between the seller and purchaser. The biggest disadvantage is that the house could be overpriced. People are often very fond of their homes and tend to forget that the drawbacks – like the major road 75 metres from the foot of their garden – also affects its price. You should bear in mind that direct negotiation with the owner of a property needs to be conducted sensitively if you are to reach a successful conclusion.

There are several ways of finding out about private sales:

- Search the small ads of local and national newspapers and the notice boards at churches, schools, clubs, etc.

- Put your own 'Wanted' ad in any of the above saying what you want, where and what you can pay.

- Type out a 'we are searching for a house like yours' letter and drop it through the letter boxes of houses in the road or area that you are interested in. Make it clear you are a private buyer and so no commission is payable.

- Search on the Internet; there are a large number of Internet sites now advertising properties privately for sale.

- Private networking. Tell everyone you know that you are looking for a new home, what you are looking for and at what price. I can vouch for the effectiveness of this method. A second cousin, knowing of my hankering for a granite cottage in Cornwall, found my dream property. She lives locally and knew the owner who had gone into a home. She contacted the owner's nephew who was dealing with his affairs and when the decision was made to sell the property he called her before calling in any agents.

(See also **Advertising, Brochures or Property Details, Internet Buying and Selling, Preparing Your Home for Sale, Private Treaty**.)

DRY ROT

Don't clap too hard – it's a very old building.
John Osborne, *The Entertainer*

Dry rot is the horror that no one ever wants to see on a surveyor's report; it is hard to detect how far it has invaded until work on resolving the problem has begun and it is expensive to put right.

So what exactly is it? Dry rot is caused by a fungus called *Serpula lacrynens* which takes hold when an open, potentially damp, area – a chimney breast or the space under the floor – is insufficiently ventilated. It looks like a white pancake. There is a rather unpleasant musty smell in a house with dry rot and it is recognizable by the distinctive cracking it causes in woodwork.

To treat dry rot is expensive: all the affected wood – possibly up to and including floorboards, joists and window frames – must be replaced as well as any adjacent timber and the rest of the woodwork. It costs thousands rather than hundreds of pounds. Treatment must be carried out by a qualified professional; a list of specialists is available from the British Wood Preserving and Damp-Proofing Association. As always, get (free) estimates from more than one company.

Get a guarantee for any work done. The guarantee usually lasts for twenty years and means that if the treatment isn't successful then you can call the company back to redress the situation. It is best to use a company who is a member of the Guarantee Protection Trust; they under-take to back up the guarantee in the event of the company you used going out of business. It might add very slightly to the cost but it is well worth it.

Selling

If detected – which it will be by a surveyor – many buyers will run a mile. If they don't they will expect a very substantial discount on the purchase price. If you want a smooth sale sort dry rot out yourself beforehand – there is always the chance that it might not be as bad as you suspect. Otherwise you have to accept, even in a boom market, that your property might be a lot harder to sell and could end up under the auctioneer's hammer.

Remember:
It is impossible to know how extensive dry rot is until it is treated; it may not be nearly as bad as you think.

Buying

The usual advice is to run a mile. But if this is your ideal property then be aware that you will have to deal with this problem before you do anything else. So, ask to send in your own specialist to determine the extent of the problem and to give you an estimate of what it will cost to put right. Then, negotiate a reduction in the price. If you do buy the property, do not put off dealing with dry rot; it damages the structure of the building and just gets worse and more expensive to deal with.

Remember:
The cure for dry rot is drastic and will mean parts of the building being ripped apart, so you might want to consider finding somewhere else to stay until the work is done. It is also expensive.

(See also **Builders, Insurance, Surveys, Valuation**.)

E

EMPTY HOUSES

*It is contrary to reason to say that there is a vacuum
or space in which there is absolutely nothing.*

Rene Descartes, *Principa Philosophiae*

According to the Department of the Environment there are
772,300 empty houses in Britain of which 637,000 belong to
the private sector (see www.emptyhomes.com).

Selling

Unfortunately for the seller empty means empty of life and
heart. If possible it is best not to leave your house without
any furniture in it.

If you have moved out:

- Leave a few pieces of furniture behind – perhaps a sofa,
  lamp and table to help give viewers a sense of the
  dimensions of the room and that it was once lived in.
  Rooms should be clean; don't leave piles of rubbish and
  odd boxes about.

- For security purposes don't take down the curtains.

- Leave the heating on. As well as ensuring that pipes don't freeze it keeps that damp chill away which can put off potential buyers.

- Notify your local authority that the property is vacant. A Council Tax refund is payable on any property empty for a certain amount of time.

- Be very careful about keys. Ensure that the agent personally shows anyone around and does not hand out keys to potential purchasers. The last thing you want is someone copying your keys, moving in and squatting in your home.

Buying

An empty house is not particularly enticing but it does have one major advantage: you have definitely reached the end of a chain. There need be no delay to your moving in as the owner is not reliant on anyone else in order to complete the sale. The owner is often keener to sell so you might also get the property for a better price.

Homes that have been empty for even a short time deteriorate quite rapidly; a storm resulting in a blocked gutter and a few tiles off the roof can have serious consequences if repairs are not put in hand immediately. Frozen pipes are another common hazard. Note any problems and point them out to the agent – these are bargaining points. Make sure the owner knows what has happened so that they have the opportunity to put it right before matters become worse.

(See also **Estate Agents**, **Security**, **Services**.)

ESTATE AGENTS

One does not sell the earth upon which the people walk.

Crazy Horse, Oglala Sioux leader, from *Bury My Heart at Wounded Knee*

No high street is complete without a sprinkling of estate agents. Window-shopping for flats and houses is a national pastime. For most it's a quick check on the rise and fall of property prices, but for others it's the first step towards buying or moving. But how do you know which agents are good and which are not?

Some agents try to convince you that they can sell anything, even a damp viewless basement flat; at the same time they promise they will find you all your heart desires. Others tut-tut about the timing of your proposed sale and tut-tut again about the chances of finding you the perfect home. Luckily, most agents fall somewhere between these two extremes and are like the rest of us – trying their best within the parameters that they have been set, usually by us.

In order to improve their public image the Ombudsman for Corporate Estate Agents Scheme was launched in 1990. As of 1 May 2000, 2,519 offices from ten corporate estate agencies and 887 offices from independent firms were signed up to this scheme, which binds them to a code of practice. Basically, this code promises that information given in sales particulars will not be misleading and there will be no compulsory tie-in of financial services. It also stipulates that all offers must be in writing. Further information about the code of practice is available on the website: www.oea.co.uk. The ombudsman received 3,889 complaints about agents in 1999, most of which related to maladministration. If the ombudsman finds against an agency he may make an award of up to £25,000 against it, although awards are more commonly for hundreds rather than thousands of pounds.

Members of the Royal Institute of Chartered Surveyors, the Incorporated Society of Valuers and Auctioneers, and the National Association of Estate Agents (NAEA) have also agreed to a code of practice. The NAEA has a website – www.naea.co.uk – which gives advice on buying and selling homes, auctions, finding an agent and complaints.

When choosing an agent whether **buying or selling**:

- Focus on agents who are the prime dealers in the type and price of property you have or want. Do this by looking in the newspapers, agents' windows, magazines and just cruising the area. Go into the offices. Make name and face contact with one of their sales people.

- Check the agent's qualifications. The qualifications to look for are FRICS or ARICS (Fellow or Associate of the Royal Institute of Chartered Surveyors) and FSVA or ASVA (Fellow or Associate of the Incorporated Society of Valuers and Auctioneers). Other qualifications are ANAEA or FNAEA (Associate or Fellow of the National Association of Estate Agents) which are only available to experienced agents.

- Ask friends, neighbours and colleagues who have moved into the area recently who they bought or sold through and what their experience was like.

- Make sure you have a positive rapport with the agent you are dealing with and trust their judgment.

Remember:

There are lots of sharks out there and a number of agents who are not professionally qualified and don't know what they are doing. Hugh Dunsmore Hardy, Chief Executive of the National Association of Estate Agents says: 'We urge the public to be more discerning about which agent they select. As in any business, some agents fail miserably the code of best practice. Any Tom, Dick or Harry can set up as an estate agent without any pre-qualifications, training or even understanding of the legislation which governs them.'

The Estate Agency Act (1979) sets out the key principles estate agents must adhere to. It recommends that buyers and sellers are treated honestly, fairly and promptly.

Estate agents don't always have an easy time. Actor Oliver Reed is reputed to have once thrown a frozen goose, a bottle of gin and an African spear at an agent buying his house for a client.

Selling

Make a selection of agents who fit the criteria above – and ask three to come round and value your property. When the valuers arrive ask them what their qualifications are, test them on their knowledge of the area and notice how thoroughly they inspect the house, inside and out.

Once you receive the valuations, look at the agent's fee and the package of services included within it. Remember that the fee is negotiable and that VAT is charged. Fees vary dramatically from area to area and from agent to agent. They can range from 1 per cent to 4 per cent but are more generally 1.25–3 per cent. The highest fees tend to be charged in the South East; lower fees are asked the further north, south and west you go. Now look carefully at the box of delights that you are being offered as part of the sales package. These are the marketing tools that could lead to a successful sale and what is free and what is not is almost always negotiable. If the following are not clear in the initial letter call up and ask about:

- Advertising – local and/or national. Note where, when and how big the advertisement will be and how many times it will appear.

- Details. Check the quality and whether they include a floor plan.

- Photographs: will they be professionally taken?

- Viewing: will they undertake to show people around the property?

- Display of details in the shop front window: where in the shop window and for how long?

- Network sales: how many offices will market your property? How extensive is their mailing list and how often do they send out details?

- Free promotion in their own magazine or newspaper if they have one.

- Access to the Internet via their website: how many hits do they get per property?

- Publicity: do they have good relations with the local and national press? Could they get publicity for your property?

The more expensive the property the more likely it is that the agent will negotiate a separate marketing sum to cover many of these items.

Wherever you are on the property ladder, the offer made by the agent whose services you are thinking of employing is an opening gambit. It is up to you to negotiate a better deal. Don't just sign up with the agent you didn't like because he is charging half a percent less and giving you a free brochure, first ask the agent you felt you had the best rapport with and whose reputation you respect most if he can match that deal. It won't always work but in a surprising number of cases it will.

Having verbally agreed the deal ask the agency to confirm their fees and what will be included in them in writing and establish when they will expect their commission to be paid. Don't forget that VAT is charged on the fee. The agreement you will then be asked to sign is a minefield. Beware of and avoid at all costs:

- Committing yourself to a long sole agency contract. You want a contract that can be terminated quickly if you are not getting the right service.

- Unwittingly agreeing to allow the agent to earn a fee on the sale for a certain time after the agreement is terminated, regardless of who sells the house.

- Undertaking to pay commission to an agent for introducing a buyer 'ready, able and willing to buy'. If anything goes wrong (suddenly you are not moving to Southampton) you might still have to pay the agent's fee.

- Sole selling rights. Establish what will happen if you sell the house yourself through your own network of friends and colleagues. Some agents ask for sole selling rights (not to be confused with sole agency) entitling them to a commission even if they don't introduce the buyer.

Don't be surprised at some agents' enthusiasm. If your house is attractive they want to have it on their books and there is no telling the lengths they will go to. A favourite story from estate agents Knight Frank concerns one of their agents who, in an effort to build a rapport with an elderly house vendor, spent several minutes stroking and talking to the owner's small, fluffy dog. It didn't work; the dog was stuffed. A partner in the same firm's Hungerford office went further: he agreed to have a hernia operation under local anaesthetic and won an instruction from the surgeon while the operation was going on.

Buying
Having sorted out the agents who fit the four criteria above, visit their offices. Choose two or three that you feel are key players in the area where you want to buy.

During your visit a good agent will:

- Make a careful note of what you are looking for and of your telephone number and then give you a clear picture of the state of the market.

- Show you details of properties that might interest you and fix up appointments, or listen carefully when you tell them why those properties are wrong.

Subsequently, a good agent will call you when the right properties come up and not pressure you into viewing unsuitable properties, try to set up a couple of viewings at a time so that if you are not living in the area you waste less time.

Although you should concentrate on the best agents it is still worth putting yourself on the books of all agents in the area.

(See also **Advertising, Brochures or Property Details, Home Hunting, Private Treaty, Preparing Your Home for Sale, Relocation Agents, Valuation**.)

EXCHANGE OF CONTRACTS

I would like to quote what a judge said not long ago –
that all his experience both as Counsel and Judge had been
spent in sorting out the difficulties of people who, upon the
recommendation of people they did not know, signed
documents which they did not read, to buy goods they did
not need, with money they had not got.

Gilbert Harding, *Gilbert Harding and His Friends*

This is when the deal is done. Although not all the money is passed over – just a percentage – it is when both sides sign a contract agreeing what is being bought and sold: the buyer's solicitor/conveyancer sends a signed contract to the seller's solicitor/conveyancer who sends an identical signed contract back.

The signing usually takes place some time before the actual exchange, so read the details of the contract carefully. The exchange normally takes place over the phone and is handled by the solicitors or conveyancers employed by each party. A procedure laid down by the Law Society is used.

Exchange is the moment when: both sides agree what is included in the sale of the property; both sides agree what is being paid for the property; a date for completion is agreed; the buyer pays over a deposit – usually 10 per cent of the purchase price of the property.

Three major problems can delay exchange and/or cause a sale to collapse before exchange:

- Arguments over exactly what fixtures and fittings are included in the sale and what is being sold for extra cash. Agents tell many tales of sales breaking down at the last minute because someone refuses to leave something basic like a fridge behind unless the new owner pays £150 for it.

- Arguments over completion date. Patience and understanding is required by all parties. You may not want to take out a bridging loan or move in with your mum for two weeks but sometimes it is the only answer if the rest of the carefully assembled chain is to stay in one piece.

- Gazumping/gazundering. These are two very nasty habits. Gazumping happens in a rising market; it is when a vendor sells to someone else who has offered more money. Gazundering happens in a falling market and is when a buyer suddenly offers the vendor several thousand pounds less just before exchange.

Following exchange and before completion it is important to remain in contact with your solicitor as a number of things happen:

- The vendor's solicitor sends the buyer's solicitor a draft transfer for a registered property or conveyance for an unregistered property. This passes the title of the property into the buyer's name.

- The buyer's solicitor will write to the mortgage lender to ensure that funds are available on the day of completion or ask the buyer to arrange transfer of the money required to fund completion.

- The final 'engrossed' version of the sale transfer will then be prepared for signature and signed by both vendor and buyer.

- The buyer's solicitor will conduct a bankruptcy search in case the vendor has been declared a bankrupt as a bankrupt cannot legally sell a property. The buyer's solicitor will also make a Land Registry priority search so that no one else can register the title before the sale is completed.

Remember:
Before exchange both sides should carefully check the terms of the contract and the date of completion.

Selling
Before exchange check that arrangements are in place for your forward move and you have organized or already completed any works you told the buyer would be done before the sale was completed.

Buying
Before exchange double-check the surveyors report; the availability of your finances for the deposit and purchase; that building insurance for the new property is in place; that you are completely happy with all aspects of the contract.

After exchange and before completion check that the vendor has done all the work on the property that was agreed and book the removal van.

(See also **Bridging Loans, Completion, Conveyancing, Deposits, Removal Firms, Solicitors and Licensed Conveyancers.**)

EXTENSIONS

For which of you intending to build a tower
sitteth not down first and counteth the cost, whether he
have sufficient to finish it.

St Luke 14.28

It is rare to find a property that suits all your needs; it is even rarer to find a property that will suit your needs throughout your adult life. But you may decide at times that rather than move you would like to build on or change the layout of your home. However, 'having the builders in' for a major extension can sometimes be more stressful than a move as you cope with layers of dust and dirt, and sometimes weeks without use of a kitchen, bathrooms or heating.

In some parts of the country, like Devon, moving from a four-bedroom house to a six-bedroom house will cost you £25,000 and converting the attic into two new bedrooms will cost a similar amount. In other areas the cost of buying a larger property may be much higher; for instance in London an attic conversion might cost £40,000–£50,000 but moving within the same area to a bigger house could cost at least twice that – plus the Stamp Duty and all the other costs involved in moving. It is also true that demand for perfect family homes in the country is greater than supply. As a buyer today you might find the perfect plot but know the house is too small. It is becoming increasingly common to buy the wrong property in the right place and extend.

According to research by one major estate agent most extensions are to provide a playroom, an office or workroom, a larger family room/eat-in kitchen or a granny annexe. The best options in terms of investment are kitchen/family rooms which add to the market value of a house. Another good value extension is a granny annexe. However small, buyers at a later date perceive they are getting two properties for the price of one. An annexe has the added advantage that it could be let to provide extra income.

Selling

Make sure that you have the correct letters of authority and guarantees for any building work you have had carried out. Ensure that the agent points out to possible buyers any potential for extension – a large loft or basement, barn or stable blocks. It can sometimes add to the value of your property if you have obtained outline planning permission for conversion of an empty space. In order to do this you have to apply to the local planning department. A single planning application usually costs less than £100.

Buying

Whatever you are buying ensure that there are guarantees for any building work that has been carried out, the work complies with building regulations and planning consent, if necessary, was obtained.

Building your own extension

So you have found the perfect plot but not the perfect house. Before steaming ahead and assuming that you will be able to carry out the extension that would make your home perfect or pull down the eyesore currently gracing your bit of heaven and put up something more pleasing you should:

1. Consult the local planning authority who will tell you if you need planning permission for the work you want to do and the limitations constraining your plans (usually to do with height and volume). Remember that if the property you are buying is listed or is in a conservation area it will be subject to more restrictive planning laws. The Department of the Environment and the Welsh Office publish a free booklet 'Planning Permission: a Guide for Householders' which is available at council offices. Information is also available on their website: www.detr.gov.uk. Don't forget to check if you are eligible for any house improvement grants.

   You may be able to extend your house minimally without needing to apply for planning permission (see **Permitted Development Rights**).

2. Appoint an architect, surveyor and/or builder. All will quote for the work and tell you whether your vision is realizable. A building surveyor or architect can either quote you separately for their work or quote for overseeing the whole job from start to finish.

3. Once you have the plans then approach several reput-

able building firms – if your architect or surveyor is not doing this for you – get estimates and choose one. Remember all building work must meet building standards and regulations which are monitored by the local authority's planning department. Building Regulations are concerned with the quality of the materials and work, health and safety, services and fire precautions. They apply to new building and extensions.

4. Sort out how you are going to finance the project. You may have the cash available or need to get a second mortgage or short-term loan. When calculating the budget include:

- Construction costs including materials, architects' and surveyors' fees and VAT.

- New fittings: curtains, carpets, cupboards, shelves, tiles, sinks, etc.

- Temporary accommodation (if necessary) while the work is being carried out.

- Add 25 per cent to the maximum amount. However final the estimate seems, extras inevitably appear. Having put a side extension on the kitchen it suddenly seems irrational not to finish the job and put in a new kitchen; and you want more cupboards, extra windows. Moreoever, your builders are at the mercy of the building controls officer who will make regular visits to the site to see that the work not only meets all legal requirements and regulations but also comes up to the standards set by your local authority. The

building controls officer may demand extra foundations under an extension wall, a heavier beam, more
drainage – all extra work not envisaged by the
builder, architect or surveyor.

5. Plan when and how long the building work will take.
   Tie the builder/architect/surveyor down to a contract
   which includes full details of price, cancellations rights
   and some sort of guarantee as to when the work will
   start and finish. Ensure that failure to meet deadlines
   carries financial penalties for your contractors.

6. Sort out where you are going to live while the work is
   being carried out. Sometimes you can camp in another
   part of the house but sometimes you can't, particularly if
   you have a young family. Most builders will move along
   a lot faster without you in the house but if you move out
   visit daily to check progress and clear up any problems.

7. If you do move out of the property – or don't move in
   immediately – remember to notify your local authority
   that the property is vacant. A Council Tax refund is
   payable on any property uninhabitable for a certain
   amount of time. Also inform your insurance company
   as you may find you need to pay less insurance or to
   have a different type of insurance cover.

Remember:
Don't go ahead with any building work without the
necessary planning permission, listed building consent
(when necessary) and building regulations approval.

Keep your new neighbours informed of what is happening and what you are planning to do. They will be inconvenienced by the comings and goings of your builders and they will want to be assured that any change to your property doesn't impinge on their privacy or light. A good neighbour is worth a fortune and it is better to keep them informed.

Value
If you are interested in improving the value of your property as well as your quality of life:

- Don't turn two large bedrooms into three small ones.

- Don't overdevelop a plot; the proportion of land to size of property is important.

- Don't build an extension which is more than 30 per cent of the current volume of a house unless you can do it without spoiling the balance of the property.

- Don't try too hard to build an extension that matches the existing structure, and fail. It is better to build on in a complementary style.

- Utilize garage, attic and cellar space.

- Make maximum use of natural light.

- Make sure the extension maintains the balance of the house.

- Ensure that building materials match or complement the existing building.

- Get planning permission for any work done.

(See also **Architects, Builders, Permitted Development Rights, Planning Permission, Surveyors.**)

F

FARMS

I grant indeed that fields and flocks have charms,
For him that gazes or for him that farms.

George Crabbe, 'The Village'

Many of us have an idealized picture of the country life we would one day like to lead. And for those of us with fond memories of the Little Red Hen, Peter Rabbit and Pigling Bland this picture includes a smallholding with a clutch of hens pecking in the yard, a goat nibbling at the grass and a pot-bellied pig grunting in a friendly Babe-ish way.

Selling

If you have a smallholding, don't ignore the possibilities of trying to sell through a residential rather than a commercial agent or of dividing the farm into lots and selling some of these through a residential agent. Ask – many major agents have both residential and farm divisions.

Buying

With a shortage of substantial country houses, farms which are now not as commercially viable as they once were are being bought by families looking for a good-sized house with land around. The land around the house provides a protective belt of privacy and can often be let out to another farmer in the area. If you can't find the house you want through an estate agent skim through the pages of *Farmer's Weekly*.

Living next door to a farm

Be warned; commercial farms these days are big businesses. Farmyards aren't filled with Harry the red tractor and bales of straw; they contain combine harvesters and drums of pesticide. And farms are smelly places; no one has yet come up with a chemical that can control the pungently acrid smell of sileage. Barns are no longer pretty orange brick constructions (they've been converted into houses) but massive metal monstrosities that can dominate the skyline. The farmer's day starts early and can go on late into the evening and even the prettiest of farms has drawbacks. We have friends who bought a beautiful barn conversion in Hampshire but a hundred yards from them behind an old brick wall is the farmyard with its resident cockerel that wakes them every morning – before dawn.

(See also **Adjacent Land and Property**, **Land**, **Paddocks and Ponies**.)

FASHION IN PROPERTY

Fashion is more usually a gentle progression of revisited ideas.
Bruce Oldfield, British fashion designer, *Independent*, 1989

Like clothes, food and music, property goes through different fashions although trends in property are relatively slow and mainly reflect evolutions in lifestyle.

Twenty years ago – a short time in property terms – a buyers wish list would have included: a breakfast bar in the kitchen, a separate dining room, a cloakroom or second bathroom in a four-bedroom property and a master bedroom with dressing room and en suite bathroom. Today's demands are different. We no longer want breakfast bars, dining rooms or small bedrooms; instead we want: a large family room/eat-in kitchen, a minimum ratio of two bathrooms to every three bedrooms, large bedrooms, a separate study/computer room or playroom, a conservatory extension, walk-in cupboards and outside space even if it's just a Juliet balcony on a flat.

The trend towards the family room/kitchen which has been at the top of the property priority list for house buyers for several years has created demands for other types of private space. We don't like sharing bathrooms; families want at least one for the parents, one for the children and one for guests. More and more people own computers and work from home, even if it is only for one or two days a week, and so there is a requirement for separate studies. There has also been a demand for playrooms in order to keep children's toys in one place and out of the way.

One of the most interesting changes is the demand for bigger bedrooms. In the 1970s the fashion was for large open-plan living areas with smaller bedrooms simply for sleeping in. But what families have now realized is that with more open-plan living downstairs, bedrooms upstairs need to be retreats – sanctuaries for adults and children. Developers are always keen to stay ahead of the trends; they used to try and fit in as many bedrooms as possible but today they put in fewer but bigger bedrooms and almost always add on a study or computer room. Trying to predict the future is always dangerous but there is certainly a move towards much greater security consciousness and completely self-contained annexes which can be used for teenagers, granny or nanny; or let in order to provide extra income.

(See also **Extensions**.)

FINANCES

*Money is good for bribing yourself through
the inconveniences of life.*
Gottfried Reinhardt, *Looks Like We're Still in Business*

This is the ghastly bit – working out just what the move is going to cost.

Find out how much your current property is worth and subtract the amount you will have to pay back to any lending institution. Estate agents will usually give you a free valuation on the basis that you will return to them when you finally decide to sell. Add on any other capital you have that you intend to spend on the new house. Find out how big a mortgage you can get over how many years; work out the amount you are comfortable borrowing considering your other personal outgoings.

Although banks and building societies today are much more generous about the time they give you to pay off a mortgage they still limit the amount they are prepared to lend on the basis of your income. Shop around, decide who you are getting a mortgage with and establish firmly what they are prepared to lend you. That settled, start adding up the actual cost of the move.

Remember:
If you have trouble getting credit find out why and how to change the situation by contacting the Office of the Data Protection Commissioner by phone or via their website: www.dataprotection.gov.uk. They produce a free leaflet with clear guidance to credit referencing and how to correct a bad credit reference.

Selling
You are looking at the nice round figure that your house is being marketed for, but of course you won't be quite as rich as that. You have to subtract the following costs:

- Estate agent's fees (1–4 per cent of the purchase price of the property plus VAT).

- Legal fees (either 0.5 per cent of the price of the house plus VAT or a flat fee).

- Advertising and other marketing costs. These may or may not be included in the estate agent's fee and must always be taken into account if you decide on a DIY sale.

- Mortgage redemption charges which can be three months' interest and sometimes more if you are repaying within a short period – usually considered to be less than five years.

- Moving costs possibly including storage.

Buying

Buying a property is not cheap and costs a lot more than the purchase price. Add on to the cost of the property the following:

- Legal fees (either 0.5 per cent of the price of the house plus VAT or a flat fee). You will get a better overall deal if the solicitors are involved in both the sale of your current property and the purchase of another one.

- Stamp Duty. See separate entry.

- Land Registry fee. See separate entry.

- Local authority searches (if these are not included in the legal fee).

- Other search fees and disbursements. These differ depending on the property you are buying.

- Lender's legal fee. Your solicitor will almost always also act for the lender but check this out or you could be in for two sets of fees.

- Lender's surveyor's fee which is based on the price of a house.

- Mortgage arrangement fee (payable on most fixed-rate mortgages).

- Structural survey. See separate entry.

Refer to the checklists on pages 379–96 where you can add up these costs and look at additional costs connected with moving – from new locks on the doors to reconnection of your washing machine by a plumber.

(See also **Advertising, Banks and Building Societies, Do-it-yourself Buying and Selling, Estate Agents, Land Registry, Local Authority and Other Searches, Mortgages, Removal Firms, Solicitors and Licensed Conveyancers, Stamp Duty, Surveys.**)

FIRST-TIME BUYERS

Well some people talk of morality, and some of religion,
but give me a little snug property.
Maria Edgeworth, Anglo-Irish novelist, *The Absentee*

Never forget that you hold one crucial advantage over other buyers: once you have arranged finance you are in almost exactly the same position as a cash buyer. You have nothing to sell and are therefore not trapped in a chain at the whim of other buyers and sellers.

Use this to your advantage; it may mean you are able to negotiate a slightly better price for a property. If you show that you are serious and have your finance in place then you will have an edge over other buyers.

If you need a 100 per cent mortgage it is worth approaching developers of new-build property who often specialize in 'starter' homes and offer high percentage mortgages.

(See also **Home Hunting**, **Joint Ownership**, **New Build**, **Shared Ownership Schemes**.)

FISHING

I shall stay him no longer than to wish him a rainy evening
to read this following discourse; and that if he be an honest
angler, the east wind may never blow when he goes a-fishing.
Izaak Walton, 'Epistle to the Reader' in *The Compleat Angler*

Fishing is Britain's most popular sport – undertaken by millions of people including the Queen Mother until she was well into her 90s. There is nothing like the babble of a river and the charm is not lost on those who don't fish but just want to sit. As a result any property with fishing rights fetches substantially more than something similar without this sporting asset. On the best fishing rivers like the Test you can pay as much as 20 per cent extra if the river runs through or along the edge of your property and you have rights to fish in it. If you fish such a property is worth the price; if you are not you are probably better off buying at a less popular fishing spot.

Remember:
If you are not a fisherman and you buy a property with fishing rights any extra value will deteriorate if the water is not fished. It is rather like buying a second-hand car. The car with a good service record will sell much more quickly and for more money than the one with no service record. Fishermen like records; fish are fickle creatures, the level of fish in any stretch of river fluctuates from year to year and they can be encouraged up or down a stream. Without records the value of the fishing deteriorates.

(See also **Flooding**.)

FIXTURES AND FITTINGS

> Suns, that set, may rise again;
> But if once we lose this light,
> 'Tis with us perpetual night.
>
> Ben Jonson, *Volpone*

Buckets of tears have been wept and many deals broken over what is and what is not included in the sale of a property. Fixtures and fittings are at the hub of such rows and it is best – both from the buying and selling points of view – to be very clear from the start.

It is generally accepted that anything fixed to a property comes within the purchase price so if you have fitted antique doorknobs, walnut-fitted bookshelves or wall lights which you intend to take with you be clear about this. Simple courtesy requires you to organize simple replacements; particularly for essential items like doorknobs. Any fitted electric appliance you take should be properly removed and wires secured so that the new owner isn't faced with the immediate possibility of an electric shock. Problems arise because of the confusion about what is a fixture and what is not.

The garden can be a minefield. Some owners not only want to take the greenhouse but half the plants as well. However, from the buyer's point of view it is sometimes the character of the garden that has persuaded them to buy and the prospect that it will be stripped bare can cause a sale to break down. Technically, plants, shrubs and trees are fixtures.

One agent tells of an owner who insisted on taking many of the plants much to the distress of the purchaser. The particular charm of the house was a rose that had been trained to ramble around the front door and some of the windows and the new owner was delighted to see the rose blooming around the door when she finally moved in – until a week later when the leaves and flowers wilted. On investigation she found that the previous owner had hacked through the plant just above the roots, dug them up and taken them with her.

Fixtures and fittings are often the focus of price negotiations. 'I will pay £122,000 instead of £120,000 but that must include the carpets, cooker, fridge and curtains,' is a common bargaining gambit.

Remember:
Buying or selling: don't lose the sale by fighting over a pair of curtains.

Selling

Make a careful list in each room of what is included in the sale and what else you are willing to part with for a price. Be particularly clear about something that someone else might consider a fixture. A living room list might read as follows:

- Included: carpets, bookshelves, door furniture, central light fitting, curtain tracks.

- Available but not included: curtains £250, pair antique wall lights £100.

- Excluded: overmantel mirror above fireplace (although not a fixture many people might assume it was).

Hand the list to your agent who will include some of the details in the property particulars sent out to purchasers and have it available when a potential buyer expresses interest in the property. It is worth keeping a copy handy for reference later on.

Buying

Once you are seriously interested in buying take a notebook and note what is in each room, confirming with the owner what is included in the sale and what is not. If there is a particular piece of furniture – for instance an oak dresser in the kitchen or a snugly fitting desk in a bedroom that you would like to purchase – always ask if there is any chance that it could be sold. If the owner is moving to a smaller or a different style of house they may be more than happy to sell it.

(See also **Brochures**, **Finances**, **Buying Checklists**, **Selling Checklists**.)

FLATS

All I want is a room somewhere,
Far away from the cold night air
Alan Jay Lerner, *My Fair Lady*

There are advantages and disadvantages to owning a flat rather than a house but it is with a flat that many of us start out our home-owning lives and it is in a flat that a number of us end them.

Flats come in two types: purpose built – from graceful brick Victorian mansion buildings to ultra-modern blocks – and conversions. If buying a conversion make sure that the services to each flat are totally separate and that a good management scheme is in operation to ensure that the fabric of the building is regularly maintained.

Flats can be extremely practical. On the positive side,

you are not responsible for organizing the maintenance of the roof, fences, drains and plumbing; that is the responsibility of the landlord or management organization to whom you pay an annual service charge. In addition, heating and hot water can be cheaper if it is run for the whole building.

On the negative side, you have less privacy because of the close proximity of your neighbours – above and below as well as on both sides – and you need to consider their needs: absolutely no late-night music. Floors almost always need to be carpeted to insulate your noise from the flat below unless you want an irate neighbour hammering at your door every night complaining about hearing you get up, go to bed, go to the bathroom or cook your supper . . . You are unlikely to be allowed to keep a pet.

Selling

Remember if you are moving from a flat to a house that your bills and personal responsibilities are going to go up including insurance, heating and general house maintenance. You will not have to pay a service charge but you will be 'servicing' your own property.

Tell a buyer about any active residents' association. If possible give buyers details of the services you get for any charge you pay. A prospective buyer also needs to know who cares on a day-to-day basis for the common parts of the building or if they will share responsibility for keeping common areas clean.

Buying
Look for:

- The longest possible lease or a share of the freehold. If you are not a cash buyer a lease under sixty years and preferably more than seventy-five years is advisable even though the 1993 Leasehold Reform Act gives certain flat owners the right to extend their leases.

- A good management structure to ensure the building is well maintained.

- Reasonable service charges. Although lifts and porters are wonderful you do pay for them.

- Good sound insulation from other flats. Spend some time quietly in the property at a busy time of the day – perhaps early evening – to see how much noise can be heard from neighbouring flats.

- If you are a pet owner check that the management allows animals; many don't.

- Good security at the entrance to the building.

Remember:
Legal charges might be slightly higher for flat purchase than on a house at a similar price because there is usually more work in checking a lease.

(See also **Conveyancing, Leasehold, Sellers' Information Packs, Service Charges**.)

FLIGHT PATHS

If God had meant us to fly he would have given us tickets.

Graffiti in a London pub from *The Dictionary of Twentieth-Century Quotations*

Today more and more planes take more and more people to more and more places. It is almost impossible to find a place in town or country where you won't occasionally see and hear aeroplanes and this situation is only going to get worse. The occasional sighting is one thing, the constant roar overhead suffered by people who live near an airport is another. In the past ten years the combined airport traffic at Gatwick, Heathrow and Stansted has gone up by a total of nearly 28 per cent.

Nearness to an airport is an important plus for some people whose working lives require them to travel but there is a difference between being close and too close. If you are buying a property within ten miles in any direction of an international airport, check how badly the plane noise affects life in that property. Among other things you should: knock on a neighbour's door and ask about flight noise in the area; ask your solicitor to make enquiries about flight paths; contact the airport authority yourself, say you are considering buying a property in a certain area and ask them to tell you where the flight path runs.

You can also find out for yourself whether any or many flight paths pass over your possible new home by contacting Virgin One account (08456 000 001) who publish a series of homebuyer's guides including one on flight paths from main airports. There are limits to how many night flights can take off from each airport and the government says it is seeking an overall reduction in aircraft noise levels.

FLOODING

STREETS FLOODED. PLEASE ADVISE.

Robert Benchley, telegram sent on arriving in Venice

It can be delightful to live near a river or by the coast, but be warned: those beautiful views bring with them the risk of flooding. It is estimated that more than 1.3 million homes in Britain are at risk from flooding but that only 5 per cent of people living in these homes take the risk of flooding seriously.

There are certain areas which are prone to flooding, particularly deep, flat valleys surrounding rivers like the Wye. Property is sometimes cheaper in these spots because approximately every ten to fifteen years there is a strong chance that the river will burst its banks or a storm send the sea on to usually dry land. You will have paid the insurance and may have a wonderful 'we won't make a drama out of a crisis' policy but don't underestimate the nuisance factor.

Tony and Peggy Roots were told when they bought their house in Staunton on Wye in Herefordshire that there was a risk of flooding but that there were only serious floods on average every twenty years. In October 1998 one of those serious floods hit – with only a few hours warning. The Roots moved their furniture upstairs and their living room lay for several days under three feet of water. Apart from the trauma of the flood and having to move out, they faced months of repair work. Although their insurance company dealt with everything from drying out the property to replacing the cooker, it wasn't until March 1999 that everything was back to normal. 'It has been a long and slow process to complete the repairs as everything had to be replaced,' said Mr Root.

Repairs to property flooded as a result of the torrential rains of October and November 2000 – the worst flooding Britain has seen in forty years – are still being undertaken. Homes were flooded from Yorkshire to Kent and from Sussex to the River Severn. The financial and emotional toll was extremely high with even hospitals and old people's homes in the worst affected areas having to be evacuated. Stephen King of Robertsbridge in East Sussex was flooded five times in the space of ten months; his home is on the edge of the flood plain of the river Rother. In December 2000 he estimated that the insurance bill for ruined carpets and furniture stood at £36,000. Camping on the top floor of his house which was built in the 1970s he said, 'When we bought the house in 1987 we paid £70,000. It should be worth £200,000 now but who is going to buy it? I'm thinking of cutting my losses and asking my mortgage lender for the money to buy a small three-bedroom house. We can deal with selling this one later.'

Living under the threat of flood, Stephen King and others like him pay higher insurance premiums than people on higher drier land. Expect to be charged approximately 35p extra a year for every £100 worth of contents if you live in an area where there is a risk of flooding. If you live on a flood plain this could rise to £2.35 per year for every £100 of contents insured. Most insurance companies base their charges on sums they have had to pay out in recent years so they can vary enormously. One underwriter for Royal and Sun Alliance warns, 'In extreme cases premiums can double.'

Selling

Don't assume your property is unsaleable; major floods do not normally happen sufficiently frequently for buyers to be put off. The day after major floods hit Leamington Spa in 1998 – resulting in television news coverage of ducks swimming down the main street – local agent Mike Gardiner of Loveitts (whose basement was two feet under water) reported business as usual. 'Funnily enough, I had just closed a deal on a house on Maundy Thursday. The following morning the house was flooded and I thought the buyer might have had second thoughts. Not a bit of it. He realized that what had happened was unusual and went ahead with the purchase regardless. People are quite sensible about this sort of thing.'

When potential buyers view your property, point out any measures you have taken against flooding.

Buying
If you are tempted to buy by the sea or along a river bank, check out if or when the house was last flooded and the current cost of insurance.

(See also **Insurance**.)

FOOTPATHS AND RIGHTS OF WAY

No written law has ever been more binding than
unwritten custom supported by popular opinion.

Carrie Chapman Catt, American feminist, 'Why We Ask for the
Submission of an Amendment', speech to the US Senate, 1900

Sometimes your home is your castle and sometimes other people have the right to cross it – not through the house but possibly your garden. A footpath can mean less privacy, less security and more prying eyes.

Many footpaths are rights of way dating back hundreds of years; in some ways they belong to a different era when walking was the most common way for people to get from A to B. Footpaths may run right across people's land and sometimes through their front gardens so if you are using them do not step off the track; one foot either way and you are technically trespassing.

As the owner of a property with a footpath, it is up to you to ensure that the way is clearly marked and illegal to block the footpath or divert it without permission. It is extremely time consuming, difficult if not impossible and usually very costly to get a footpath diverted. You have to apply under the Highways Act (1980) giving an alternative route.

Sarah Smith had a footpath running through her West Sussex front garden. It didn't worry her for thirty years as only two or three people used it a week. But a new housing estate and supermarket suddenly turned it into a popular daily thoroughfare for local residents. She applied to have it diverted but the Ramblers Association objected on principle. Three and a half years and several thousand pounds later the council agreed to divert the path round her garden and along the edge of a field she owns.

Selling

If there is a right of way across your land – an ancient footpath or just a right to access a field or garage – don't try to hide the fact; tell prospective owners how often it is used. Don't let a buyer find out about a footpath or right of way from their solicitor; that is almost sure to make them suspicious that there are problems. You are more likely to clinch a sale if you play an open honest hand.

Buying

Don't necessarily be put off a property which has a footpath or right of way running across it. Find out as much as you can about who can and does use the right of way and how popular the path is. Do your own research: walk the path yourself and see where it goes to. If the path is overgrown you can assume it is used only infrequently, if wide and clear it may be busy. Even if the current owner says it is unused, be prepared for someone to start using it.

Any rights of way on to or across the property, if they haven't been discussed before, should come to light when your solicitor receives draft contract details. A footpath or right of way running through a property, particularly if it is within sight of the house, will devalue it slightly.

(See also **Accessibility**.)

G

GARAGES

The slogan of progress is changing from the
full dinner pail to the full garage.
Herbert Hoover, 31st President of the USA, speech, 1928

One of today's biggest property assets – whether you live in the heart of London or the further reaches of Cornwall or Wales – is a garage. There are several major advantages:

- You always have somewhere to park adjacent to the house.

- You can usually reduce your car-insurance premium.

- Extra storage space. Even with a car inside most garages have room for other things.

- Better security.

Garages or garage spaces in busy cities and popular towns sell for a premium, even without a house or property attached. In central London agents boast of selling garages for between £50,000 and £150,000. But not only Londoners look for a place to park their car and are prepared to pay for the privilege. Three years ago an estate

agent in the popular Cornish fishing village of Polperro
sold a garage for more than £15,000 and a parking space
for £10,000. Gone are the days when garages were converted into extra living space; it is now the garage that
commands the premium price.

Buying
Check out the garage:

- Will it comfortably accommodate your car? Garages
  built some years ago are often much smaller than those
  built today.

- How easily do the doors open?

- Is there electric power?

- What is the condition of the garage itself, the driveway
  and the approach to the garage?

- How clear is the visibility on to the road?

Remember:
If there isn't a garage and you want to put one up you will
have to apply for planning permission.

(See also **Parking**.)

GARDENS

If you would be happy for a week take a wife;
if you would be happy for a month kill a pig; but if you
would be happy all your life plant a garden.

Seventeenth-century proverb

Gardens used to be reserved for country houses. A view, a terrace to sit on, a tree to climb, sweeping lawns, scented beds of roses, hollyhocks, delphiniums and daisies were part of the country house dream. But now outside space is top of the list – whether you are buying a tiny flat in Birmingham, a terraced house in Leeds or a cottage in Devon.

A power shower and stainless steel and granite kitchen are no longer enough; a desirable apartment has to have plant space. The fashionable dream is a decked terrace, patio or balcony where you can sit among the potted greenery sipping chilled Chardonnay and nibbling nuts on a sultry summer's evening. Flat hunters can even be swayed by a Juliet balcony with standing room only for two. The trend has been led by television. Suddenly a garden isn't just somewhere children can kick a ball and grandad can entertain himself pruning roses; it is a lifestyle statement.

But the key to enjoyment is the size of the garden. Too big and complicated and it ceases to be a delight consuming too much spare time or too much money or the need for a professional pair of hands to take care of your plot. Unless you are an enthusiast, a garden should never stretch to more than two acres even around a manor house. Half an acre is plenty around a cottage.

Remember:
It takes between two and three hours to mow an acre of lawn properly, or an hour on a ride-on motor mower. Gardening equipment alone can set you back several thousand pounds.

Selling
The garden can be the major selling point so mow the lawns, tidy up the flower beds, clear away any unsightly rubbish, broken garden furniture and rusty bikes. If your garden is looking dreary, buy a couple of trays of colourful annuals and plant them in tubs, along borders or in window boxes.

Buyers rarely pay a premium for an attractive garden or balcony but it does add huge appeal to a property and will probably help it sell more quickly than similar properties with less attractive outside space. The current fashion is for small-scale kitchen gardens, so if you have a herb patch, fruit trees, a few rows of lettuces or a greenhouse full of tomatoes make sure everyone sees it and that the agent puts it on the particulars.

Buying
A garden can be a real pleasure but ask about upkeep:

- Does the current owner have a gardener; if so for how many hours a week; how much does it cost them and is the gardener willing to stay on if you buy?

- How much time does the owner spend looking after the garden?

- Who is responsible for fencing?

- Ask if the owners plan to take any plants or anything else in the garden – a fountain, statue, sundial or greenhouse – with them.

Make a note of the area of lawn to cut, hedges to trim and borders to be weeded; some gardens are laid out for easy care, others are not. Watch out for trees too close to the house whose roots could damage the foundations or the drains. It is worth checking whether any permanent garden furniture is included in the sale. Ask about security. A garden can provide privacy but it needs to be secure from prying eyes.

(See also **Land**.)

GAZUMPING

Some people have suggested that gazumping should be made illegal but sometimes a seller may be justified in accepting another offer. We think it would be more useful to speed up the whole process and so reduce the time when gazumping and gazundering can happen.

Department of Environment, Transport and the Regions statement made on the DETR Internet site 1998

To gazump: to accept another, higher offer having previously accepted an offer. The gazumper is the seller; the
buyer the victim. The gazumper wants the best price for
the property and the other buyer is prepared to pay more
to push you out of the running. If they succeed, then
you've been gazumped.

In a boom market and with particularly desirable properties – those with light airy rooms in established areas
within good reach of trains and buses, shops and restaurants – gazumping can assume epidemic proportions.

Two partial solutions have been found to the problem
of gazumping:

- The Conveyancing Standing Committee set up by the
  Law Commission has recommended a pre-contract
  deposit agreement. Under this agreement each side
  pays a preliminary deposit of 1.5 per cent of the
  purchase price to a stakeholder and agrees to exchange
  contracts within four weeks. If one side withdraws
  without good reason (a disastrous survey for instance)
  both deposits are released to the other.

- An informal method used by some solicitors where the
  seller gives the buyer the exclusive right to buy in
  return for a fee – say £1,000 – and on condition that
  contracts are exchanged within a certain period of time.
  The buyer only loses the money if the sale doesn't
  proceed within the set time.

Selling

Try not to get into the gazumping game, tempting as it is;
you could regret it. Buyer number one could be well down
the conveyancing route and in a good position to buy
whereas buyer number two, who is offering you more,
might suddenly duck out and go elsewhere. If you are
really not happy with the offer that has been made be
honest and say you will accept it but you will continue to
show the property in case you get any higher offers. If
another interested buyer comes along ask both parties to
put in sealed bids on a certain day at a certain time.

The government is not planning to make gazumping
illegal in their current proposals for property buying and
selling legislation.

Buying

Your main aim is never to be gazumped. There are several
ways of minimizing the risk in a boom market:

- Ensure you are ready to move. Have your financing in
  place and appoint a solicitor before making an offer.

- If you are in a boom market and the property is highly
  desirable don't quibble – offer the asking price.

- Ensure your solicitor moves with speed.

- Make your offer conditional on an anti-gazumping
  contract (consult the Royal Institute of Chartered
  Surveyors) where both parties agree to abide by the
  deal for a specified time, or to a lock-out agreement.

- Get the survey done quickly.

- Call the seller or agent almost daily and ensure they know you are keen to buy and that things are moving forward. This way if there are other offers around you should find out.

- Be amenable to any reasonable demands of the seller; if they particularly want the front door knocker and to move on a certain day, try to fit in.

If the seller says he or she would like a higher offer but has accepted yours just move as swiftly ahead as you can. They obviously want to move quickly or they would not have accepted your offer in the first place. If another buyer appears and you want to match the higher offer do so, but don't keep bidding up. Appeal to the seller's better nature but don't get cross. If the other buyer makes a still higher offer suggest the property goes to sealed bids.

Sadly there is no infallible answer to gazumping. If an owner is willing to keep on changing buyers and someone else is determined to pay more, then you might lose. But knowing your financial limits is more important than fighting over bricks and mortar.

(See also **Contract Races**, **Home Hunting**, **Lock-Out Agreements**, **Queue Jumping Without Gazumping**, **Sealed Bids**, **Sellers' Information Packs**, **Viewing**.)

GAZUNDERING

Damn it all, you can't have the
crown of thorns *and* the thirty pieces of silver.

Aneurin Bevan, in *Aneurin Bevin*

To gazunder: as the deal reaches exchange the buyer suddenly says they will not go through with the purchase unless several thousand pounds are knocked off the price.

As nasty a habit as gazumping, gazundering usually occurs in a slow market when people are concerned that house prices might be moving downwards.

To gazunder someone is really mean and here is a true story from 1995, a sluggish year for property. A young couple with two children wanted to move from London to Hampshire and planned it to take place over the summer holidays so their children could start their new schools in September. A third child was due in November. Their London house didn't sell immediately (slow market) and the couple arranged to keep the children on at their schools for a further term. In the early autumn they found a house to buy and a buyer for their house. Everything was arranged: the move was to take place four weeks after the birth of the third child and two weeks before Christmas. Their buyer, at exchange just after the baby was born, offered several thousand pounds less. Put under greater financial stress than they expected at a difficult time they saw no option but to accept.

There is little advice to be given except move as quickly as you can once an offer has been made and, in a sluggish market, do as much as you can to accommodate the buyer. Ultimately be prepared to pull out of the sale if the lower offer is going to put too great a stress on your available finances.

(See also **Gazumping**.)

GHOSTS

> you want to know
> whether I believe in ghosts
> of course i do not believe in them
> if you had known
> as many of them as i have
> you would not
> believe in them either
>
> Don Marquis, American poet and
> journalist, *archy and mehitabel*

However strongly one doesn't believe in ghouls and ghosts and three-legged beasties it is not easy to be told your home is haunted. Childhood nightmares and terrors resurface. Tales of sad Molly who died when she was sixteen of a broken heart and roams the attics looking for her lost lover or Thomas the tailor who was crossed by his partner and occasionally storms across the landing banging doors make us nervous.

Almost every large country house is supposed to have some sort of ghost; some owners chuckle at the tales, but others, quite seriously, tell you stories of sad wraiths who roam through their rooms. One agent tells the tale of selling a property that included as part of the fixtures and fittings a group of ghostly French nuns who haunt a vegetable garden. Another house was said to be haunted by two elderly women who were murdered by their butler and hidden in the cellar.

Most people just don't like the idea of ghosts. A house that should take six weeks to sell might take six months to change hands if it is haunted. Believe in them or not, ghosts put many a buyer off.

Selling

The question is whether you are legally bound to reveal you believe your house is haunted. Not according to Elizabeth Pewsey, who sold her haunted house in Somerset in 1998.

On the day of her move into the property in 1994 one of the removal men passed an old lady in a white-sleeved shirt as he carried furniture to an upstairs bedroom and asked Mrs Pewsey who she was. Nobody she knew, confessed Mrs Pewsey. She subsequently discovered the elderly ethereal resident went by the name of Mavis but never herself saw her. She was worried about what she should say to people viewing the house when she put it up for sale four years later. At the time a Derbyshire couple whose life had been made a misery by things that went bump in the night in their eighteenth-century cottage, were pursuing a civil action against two sisters who had sold them the property.

Mrs Pewsey consulted her solicitor who consulted the local trading standards officer. With the wisdom of Solomon he proclaimed that (in that corner of Somerset) there was no obligation to mention the ghost in the particulars of the property but, if Mrs Pewsey was asked by prospective purchasers whether the house was haunted, she was legally bound to say yes.

Mrs Pewsey sold her house to Hilary Carter and her family. Mrs Carter did find out about the ghost but was not in the least spooked; she doesn't believe in ghosts.

GRANTS FOR HOME IMPROVEMENT AND RENOVATION

If it moves, salute it; if it doesn't move,
pick it up; and if you can't pick it up, paint it.
Anon, army saying from the 1940s

If you are improving or renovating an old (particularly an historic) house, converting a newer one for use by someone who is elderly or disabled, or need to carry out major repairs to your property but cannot afford to do so, do not ignore the possibility of a grant.

Many people feel that they are entering a time-consuming minefield from which they will probably get nothing; but if you don't ask you don't get. Grants are normally administered by local authorities though they are primarily financed by the government. All grants are discretionary and in some cases your finances are taken into consideration when deciding what sort of grant to award and over how long a period. Grants are often made dependent on other work; you will be given a 50 per cent grant for tiling the roof but must agree to replace the guttering and repair the chimney.

A number of pamphlets have been produced by the Department of the Environment giving guidance on grants and how to get them: 'House Renovation Grants', 'Disabled Facilities Grants' and 'Home Repair Assistance'. They are usually available through your local authority. Information on grants for repairs to historic buildings and buildings in conservation areas is available from English Heritage and also on their website: www.english-heritage.org.uk.

Be prepared; some authorities are more sympathetic than others but it is an avenue worth investigating, particularly if you are facing alterations because one of the family has become disabled (this sometimes applies to elderly people who find, for instance, that they can no longer make the stairs) or you are renovating or repairing a listed house or live in a conservation area.

Grants fall into four main categories:

- House Renovation Grants are for essential works to a property. They do not cover second homes, homes built or converted less than ten years before the application (unless the application is for disabled facilities) or council tenancies.

- Disabled Facilities Grants are for improvements or alterations to a home to make it more comfortable for a disabled person.

- Home Repair Assistance is available to most private sector tenants and home owners – even houseboat and mobile home owners as long as they can prove they have been in residence for at least three years. Assistance is available to people in receipt of income-related benefits, those over sixty years of age, the disabled or infirm. This grant can cover minor repairs and improvements and is limited to £2,000 per application or £4,000 over a three-year period.

- Listed Building Grants. If you live in a listed building then you may be able to get grants to carry out essential structural repairs and to repair or retain a particular architectural feature – this can be as insignificant as re-tiling a garden path. These grants are available from the local authority but are sometimes also given by English Heritage for buildings of outstanding interest.

Remember:
All grants are entirely at the discretion of the authority handing them out; no one has a right to any grant.

(See also **Listed Buildings, Wrecks, Ruins and Redundant Properties.**)

H

HEATING AND INSULATION

The English have adopted Central Heating like some sort of
cargo cult . . . All the English seem to know is they're supposed
to have these sharp-looking metal objects scattered around
the walls – they're not interested in heat. But what can one
expect in a country where a plug on an electrical
device is considered an optional extra?

Lucy Ellman, 'Banana Split' from *Sweet Desserts*

Never underestimate the importance of good heating and
insulation, well-sealed and well-insulated windows and
doors. Wasting heat is considered almost a crime in today's
environmentally conscious world. It is also expensive.
These days the ideal constant house temperature is around
25° Celsius – winter, summer, spring or autumn.

One of the first things you should enquire about when
you become interested in a property is the heating system:
how effective it is and how much it costs to run. You
should also check out the insulation in the roof and how
well the doors and windows fit.

Selling

On anything but a hot day, put the heating on so that people feel comfortable when they view your home. Make sure your boiler has been recently serviced and is in good condition. Explain how you heat the house, particularly if you don't have central heating. Most people will want to know how much annual fuel bills are and will want to know about any back-up system if there is a power failure.

Buying

Central heating is expensive to install so check out the current system thoroughly:

- If it is not already on, ask for the heating to be put on so you can feel for yourself how effective it is. If it is summer you could ask the surveyor to check the system

- Ask about the annual costs of heating.

- Ask about the age of the boiler and if there is a service record.

- If oil-fired find out where the tank is and how often it needs refilling.

- Check out the number of solid fuel and gas fires

- If you are seriously interested in buying look at the positioning and size of the radiators. Consider whether they should be changed for smaller, modern, more effective radiators.

Ask your surveyor to report on the insulation of the property. Correcting a badly insulated roof and ill-fitting windows and doors could be expensive in the short term but ultimately you will save on heating bills and your life will be more comfortable. The Association of Building Engineers (ABE) publishes a free leaflet on family efficient buildings.

Remember:
You may be able to get a grant to install central heating as part of a comprehensive improvement plan for the house but the central heating will have to be combined with other essential work.

As well as being costly it takes about two weeks to install a new heating system. To get the names of qualified contractors call the Heating and Ventilating Contractors Association.

(See also **Grants for Home Improvement and Renovation**, **Services**.)

HOME HUNTING

Mid pleasures and palaces though we may roam
Be it ever so humble there's no place like home.

J. H. Payne, American actor, playwright and songwriter,
'Home Sweet Home' from *Clari* or *The Maid of Milan*

So you have decided to move. Home is not home any more and you need a new one. Before deciding on where to look write down a list of the reasons why you are moving and what you want to get out of the move. Most people move because they want one or several of the following:

- a different size or type of property: bigger/smaller/ easier to maintain

- a different quality of life: country/town

- convenience: work/family/friends/shops

It is important to remind yourself periodically of these aims. It is all too easy to get carried away by the delights of a property which is not however in the right place or the right size. Sometimes there are mitigating factors – the house can be extended or is so wonderful that the extra commute is worth it – but not always. The important thing is to recognize what you are willing to compromise on.

Having decided why you are moving the next step is to work out the travelling essentials in your life (work, family/friends, schools, shops, clubs/hobbies, church) and the availability of transport. Use a map to determine possible locations for your new home. (See also **Accessibility**.)

Now that you have decided why you are moving and where you want to be, the next step is to consider how much you have to spend. This depends on the capital you have or can realize (possibly by the sale of another property) and the amount of money you can take out in a loan. (See **Finances**.) Be careful and remember that banks and building societies make cold calculations based primarily on your income.

Now you have the guidelines start the search. First drive or walk around the selected area(s) thoroughly and make a list of the streets or villages that you particularly like. Then contact local estate agents and property shops, look for 'For Sale' signs, scan the local press and the Internet property sites and if you have friends or family in the area let them know about your search. If the area you are considering is limited consider a private letter drop. (See **Do-it-yourself Buying and Selling.**) If your time is limited it is worth considering getting in touch with a relocation service.

When you reach the property viewing stage it is important to be ready to move. This means you have sorted out your finances, put your own property on the market if you have one to sell and appointed a solicitor. As you go around each property ask questions and make notes of any major problems you foresee.

If you decide you are interested in a property, visit it several times at different times of the day. One experienced estate agent once told me that a property should be visited on a cold dark wet day during rush hour; if you like it under those conditions it is probably the home for you. Your second visit should be made on a different day of the week at a different time and in the company of someone impartial. Look at how the property could meet your future needs as well as your immediate needs: if you have a young family you need to consider if there is room to extend; if you are retiring it is important to note if there is a bathroom downstairs, or room for one, and a ground-floor room that could be turned into a bedroom. If you are really serious then go through the house again, much more carefully.

Before making an offer you need to cost all the things that need to be done to the house: rewiring, fitted cupboards, new bathroom or kitchen, replastering, new roof, central heating, etc. Subtract the cost of these things from the total of what you have to spend and also the other costs involved in moving: Stamp Duty, building survey, solicitor's fees, etc. You also need to consider longer-term expenses which may increase or decrease: fares to work, Council Tax, water and fuel bills, insurance, service and parking charges, etc.

Remember:
Most properties look wonderful on a sunny Saturday afternoon.

(See also **Accessibility**, **Do-it-yourself Buying and Selling**, **Estate Agents**, **Finances**, **Internet**, **Mortgages**, **Solicitors**, **Buying Checklists**, **Selling Checklists**.)

HOUSEBOATS

There is *nothing* – absolutely nothing –
half so much worth doing as simply messing about in boats.
Kenneth Grahame, *The Wind in the Willows*

For the Rattys of this world, there is something very romantic about the idea of living on a houseboat. A small number are moored along our waterways and some have been there for more than fifty years.

They are not as difficult to buy or sell as you might think. There are magazines that specialize in buying and selling houseboats and companies which provide loans or 'mortgages' to people wanting to buy a houseboat. But there are surprisingly few residential moorings in Britain; the British Waterways Board has issued only 330 residential houseboat licences. With this licence you can live permanently on your boat; without it you are only allowed to stay on the boat at weekends and for holidays up and down stretches of canal. There are however 1,500 boats registered as being continuously on the move on Britain's waterways. Many residential houseboats are firmly fixed and, even though you pay for a mooring, you are hardly going to be able to up anchor one day and cruise down the river to a different spot. Weekenders who buy canal boats as houseboats are more likely to travel.

Selling

Tell whoever is in charge of your moorings. They often have a list of people wanting to buy houseboats in the area and many moorings have extremely long waiting lists, particularly in London. There is a waiting list of between three and five years at Little Venice, and at the Cumberland and Paddington Basins. You can advertise your boat with special ist magazines like *Canal and Riverboats*, *Canalboat* and *Waterways World*. *Exchange and Mart* is another popular choice for the sale of boats. Don't be shy; put your own 'For Sale' sign on the boat and list it on one of the property Internet services. Although houseboats regularly come up for sale, they are quirky enough to attract quite a lot of interest.

As with preparing any property for sale, spruce your boat up with a bit of paint and possibly some plants. Visitors, unless they have owned a houseboat before, will want to know about insurance, upkeep, costs and delivery of fuel or power to the boat.

You will probably attract some people who are not really considering buying but are just curious to see the inside of a houseboat, hear how it works and what its value is.

Buying

Approach as many moorings as possible and ask the keeper if he knows of any houseboats for sale. Search the Internet. Look through the pages of the boat magazines noted above. It is well worth contacting the British Waterways Board who can provide you with a list of moorings around Britain and will tell you what they cost, what facilities are available and if there is a mooring free.

British Waterways advise potential buyers to spend time on a houseboat or canal boat before buying as they can be dark, dingy, cold in winter and claustrophobic. They have their own Internet site – www.britishwaterways.co.uk – or can be contacted on 01923 201120. They ask potential buyers to note that it is illegal to live on a houseboat without a licence to do so and without being registered with the local authority.

You can obtain financing to buy a boat but the maximum loan will usually be over a shorter period than that offered on a house – maybe just 10–15 years – and you may have to pay up to 4.5 per cent above the base rate. You should get the boat properly surveyed which will cost you about £300 but make it easier to get both your mortgage and insurance. Few houseboats have the investment potential of land properties, but for some people it is the only way to live. They start out with a small boat and buy their way slowly up to a craft sleeping as many as eight people with a large salon and respectable kitchen.

Remember:
You will still have to rent your moorings, usually for a four-figure annual sum, and you should check this out first. Expect to pay a premium for a mooring in somewhere like central London; mooring charges reflect property prices.

HOUSE TYPES

I wonder what it is like to be a tortoise. Not a barrel of laughs, I shouldn't imagine. You can't be frivolous or facetious if you're a tortoise, can you? And think of the danger of being turned into a pair of hair-brushes. But you do have a home to go to.

Keith Waterhouse, *Jeffrey Barnard is Unwell*

Each type of house has its own advantages.

Open plan

Space – how we use it and how much of it we need – varies hugely from person to person. There are people who love living in barns and find thirty-foot-high ceilings liberating; others yearn for the cosiness of low beams and small rooms.

Open-plan houses clearly appeal more to lovers of space and are becoming more popular. Open-plan reception areas provide plentiful entertainment space and an inclusive social environment. The big eat-in/live-in kitchen is a feature much in demand particularly when it opens on to the living room, study or playroom.

The disadvantages of open-plan design are: less personal privacy and the need to be very tidy to maintain the sense of space; clutter can not simply be hidden behind a closed door. Dream as you may of wide open spaces it is worth seriously considering how well this fits in with your needs and the needs of those that you live with. Open-plan areas are sometimes more difficult to insulate and more expensive to heat.

Terraced houses

There are far more terraced houses in Britain than there are semi-detached or detached properties. They are the norm in cities and towns and provide for good compact living with your own front door and back garden.

Terraced houses are generally cheaper than semi-detached or detached alternatives in the same neighbourhood and you are well insulated against the weather on two sides of the property. In addition, the proximity of neighbours can add to the sense of security. They are often surprisingly spacious inside and space is used well with few 'blank' areas.

On the other hand, noisy neighbours can be a real nuisance (you need to be aware of noise levels in your own household, particularly when you are in the garden), off-street car parking and garages are rare and external improvements must conform to the character of neighbouring properties.

Semi-detached

One up from a terrace and one down from a detached property, the endless suburbs of England are filled with semi-detached properties. They offer a side wall and outside entrance from the street side of the house to the garden, but you still have a party wall with neighbours on the other side.

Semi-detached houses are reasonably secure as your neighbour in the other half of the building is very close. Moreover there is no loss of heat through the party wall so your house is better insulated against the cold.

There are, however, disadvantages. You can't totally let your hair down; noise can be a big problem, particularly in the garden. Bad neighbours this close can be a disaster; if possible check them out before you buy. Side access to the property means less security than in a terraced house.

(See also **Boundaries**, **Listed Buildings**, **Neighbours**, **Period Properties**.)

HOUSING ASSOCIATIONS

It's easier to love humanity as a whole
than to love one's neighbour.

Eric Hoffer, American philosopher, *New York Times*, 1959

Housing associations are non-profit-making organizations whose main aim is to help people who otherwise would otherwise not be able to do so, to buy property. The majority are charitable organizations and most have a specific set of guidelines within which they have to operate.

Different housing associations have different criteria which they use to allow people on to their lists so it is worth approaching a number; contact your local authority or the Housing Corporation to find out about housing associations in your area. Some give priority to single people, some to families, some to local residents; there are also sheltered schemes for older buyers.

Selling

Under most schemes the housing association will ask you to offer the property back to them first before selling on the open market. This enables them to maintain a stock of properties to offer to other buyers.

Buying

Housing associations sell you a portion of the property and you rent the rest; as a result the overall cost of the property is usually dramatically lower than similar houses in the same area. Schemes are variable: under some you gradually acquire more and more of the property; under others the housing association retains a portion of the property.

However unlikely a candidate you think you are and however long you are told you have to wait it may well be worth putting your name down. You can suddenly find yourself at the head of the queue if a couple of occupiers of the type of property you are looking for suddenly decide to move on and those ahead in the queue have found themselves alternative accommodation or are not able to move.

(See also **Joint Ownership, Shared Ownership Schemes**.)

I

INSURANCE (BUILDING AND CONTENTS)

The Act of God designation on all insurance policies: which means, roughly, that you cannot be insured for the accidents that are most likely to happen to you. If your ox kicks a hole in your neighbour's Maserati, however, instantaneous.

Alen Coren, *The Lady from Stalingrad Mansions*

Building insurance

Essential, and anyone giving you a mortgage will make it a condition of the loan that the property is properly insured. Most lenders will suggest companies who can provide insurance cover, but by law the lender must let you choose your own insurance company. If you are prepared to shop around you will probably find something much cheaper than that suggested by the lender. In such a case the lender will want to check the policy to ensure that there is sufficient cover for their investment. They will charge a small fee, £20–£30, for approving the insurance. Many mortgage deals are tied up with insurance deals so check everything out carefully.

The building insurance will not be for the bought value

of your house but for 'reinstatement'. This is the cost of completely rebuilding your home from scratch and includes an allowance for things like central heating and double glazing. You should never be underinsured as this could land you in trouble if an accident occurred. If reinstatement of your property would cost £100,000 but you were insured for £75,000 and half the property was damaged by fire, you would need £50,000 but the insurance company would only pay half of what you had insured the property for: £37,500.

To work out roughly what building insurance will cost on the property you are thinking of buying contact the Association of British Insurers or look them up on the Internet: www.abi.org.uk. They issue free information leaflets on building insurance which give approximate details of reinstatement costs on different types of houses. Another source of information is the Insurance Ombudsman Bureau which also has a website: www.theiob.org.uk. Your surveyor will, for a small fee, give you an estimate of the reinstatement costs of the property you are buying.

The cost of reinstating your home is constantly going up with inflation. You do not however need to regularly have your house re-assessed and a new insurance agreement drawn up. Most insurance companies issue index-linked policies so that the sum insured is linked to the house rebuilding index and changes automatically. Your premium will change in line with the increased index rating on the renewal of the policy.

Remember:
If your house is an older building, is listed or is in a conservation area, reinstating it so that it fits in with the other buildings around it will probably cost considerably more than reinstating a modern house and so insurance costs could be higher.

It is particularly important to establish who is paying the building insurance between exchange and completion as this varies. Ask your solicitor.

Contents insurance

There are two types of contents insurance:

- Indemnity, where your contents are insured for what they are worth now. Your television is valued as being second hand.

- New for old, where your contents are insured for what it would cost to replace them. Your television would be valued as new for replacement purposes.

Be careful to insure all your furniture, carpets and belongings. Keep receipts for any particularly expensive items: jewellery, a new washing machine, a racing bike or an antique mirror.

Remember:
The more secure your property, the more likely it is that you can negotiate a discount on your insurance premiums.

Check that your insurance company covers the contents of your home while it is being moved from one property to another. They are usually happy to provide this for a small fee if the removal is being undertaken by a professional removals company. Cover will be for loss, damage (but not minor scratches and dents), accidental breakage, etc. Rather like car insurance you may be expected to pay the first £50 or so of any claim.

If you have a complaint about an insurance broker or mortgage adviser contact The Corporation of Insurance and Financial Advisers (CIFA).

(See also **Banks and Building Societies**, **Mortgages**.)

INTERNATIONAL PROPERTY BUYING

They say travel broadens the mind;
but you must have the mind.
G. K. Chesterton, 'The Shadow of the Shark'

This is a minefield, but one that many people would like to enter. An apartment on the Costa del Sol, a villa in Portugal, a cottage in Normandy, a farmhouse in Tuscany or a condominium in Florida are dreams many people aspire too, and prices are often cheaper than they are for second homes in Britain.

Some banks now offer 'euro mortgages' to help buyers who want to own property abroad: Abbey National and Barclays Bank both offer euro mortgages; other banks and building societies will lend against properties abroad in sterling including the Norwich & Peterborough Building Society.

It is important to know that the costs of buying and selling property in Britain are generally less than in other European countries. For instance in Spain – one of the most popular places to buy a second home – buying costs around 10 per cent of the purchase price. But then again you can still buy a reasonable second home in a number of European countries for under £50,000.

A list of agents and solicitors who can help you buy a property abroad is available from the Federation of Over- seas Property Developers' Agents and Consultants (020 8941 5588).

If you are serious, first decide where you want to buy; it's best to go where you have some knowledge of the language and perhaps know one or two people who also own property in the area. Go to one of the international property exhibitions which are held in Britain every year – in London, Birmingham, Manchester and other main cities; they are usually well advertised in the national and regional press. At these exhibitions you will find the whole range of international property specialists – from estate agents to solicitors and removal companies – who can give you an idea of what you can get for your money, what your rights are and the costs involved.

Don't buy on a whim during a holiday; there is far too much money and time involved. Go to your chosen area in the low season with the specific intention of looking at property to buy and spend at least a week there.

Establish the legal position regarding purchase of land. In some countries you are only in effect leasing the property; rights to land can only be held by a national.

Don't underestimate the cost of getting to and from your property and of maintaining and securing it in your absence.

You can also look at the property section of www.globalnetwork.co.uk, the weekly *Telegraph* site.

Remember:
You are in every sense in foreign territory. Be sure you know what you are up to, and if you do go ahead expect lots of visitors.

Ensure your property abroad is correctly registered in your name. The *Telegraph* published the sad story of Mollie and Peter Day who had their £140,000 Spanish retirement villa seized and sold at auction for a fraction of its value along with all their possessions after it emerged that the house had not been properly registered in their names in 1989. The development company who had built their home had gone bust – and still legally owned the property.

INTERNET BUYING AND SELLING

Computers are composed of nothing more than logic gates stretched out to the horizon in a vast numerical irrigation system.

Stan Augarten, *State of the Art: A Photographic History of the Integrated Circuit*

Buying and selling property on the Internet is beginning to come of age. It is hard to count the number of Internet sites dealing with property – from sales and mortgages to newly built developments – that have started up in the past two years. Property Internet sites fall into three different categories:

1. Those belonging to already established agents who are using the site as a new 'shop window' where they can advertise properties for sale. Some agencies just put up a picture and basic details of properties in each area, others offer three-dimensional virtual tours of some of their most spectacular properties. Most agents have their own sites and a number have links with larger national sites containing details of properties from literally hundreds of different agencies. Some national sites used by established agents include:

   - www.assertahome.com (claims to be one of the biggest sites)

   - www.rightmove.co.uk (operated by the Halifax)

   - www.propertyfinder.co.uk (site links to dozens of small agency sites from Miller & Son in Cornwall to John Thorogood in South London)

   - www.fish4homes.co.uk (owned by the regional press this site boast more than 30,000 properties in seven regions from established agents like Your Move, Aylesfords and the Halifax)

- www.homes-on-line.com (site offering online details of properties available through 6,000 estate and lettings agencies)

- www.homedirectory.com (contains details from a wide range of agents nationally)

2. Developers' sites are used to advertise new developments and sometimes give potential buyers a virtual tour around the show home. The presentation and sales patter will be liquid smooth.

3. Sites offering a service to individuals who want to sell their own property. This type of site is growing fast. The company puts your property up on their site sometimes for free and sometimes for a small fee. There isn't usually a fee attached to contacting any of the site holders and this is done either through the company or directly. A number of good national independent sites are up and running. They include:

- www.easier.co.uk (advertising free, their mission is 'to revolutionize the way homes are bought and sold')

- www.homefreehome.co.uk (describes itself as a forum for buyers and sellers to meet and do their own deals)

- www.loot.com (advertising free, renting or buying, part of *Loot* magazine)

Most sites also offer advice on different aspects of buying. For instance www.rightmove.co.uk has how to find an agent, tips for buyers, moving terms, tips for sellers and the legal stages of buying and selling.

Selling

If you are charged a fee, be clear about what the deal includes. Check that the site gets good results as well as a good hit rate. Make sure you don't have to keep paying to keep your property on the site. Don't put a telephone number or your full address on the site; you don't want to invite criminals posing as potential buyers into your property.

The effectiveness of Internet selling has not yet been established but the Internet is being used on a daily basis by an increasing proportion of the population. It can only become more important.

Buying

The Internet is a good way of finding out what sort of property is available in an area but it will not list all the properties for sale. Some sites try to give the impression that they will solve all your house-hunting needs in a specific area but they rarely do. They can only tell you about the properties on their books or those they have been given to advertise.

Be aware that many companies are not very good at updating their sites so you may fall in love with a property that has sold. However well updated a site is, direct contact with the agent running a site is better than a regular site check. Ideally you want to know about the best house on offer before the agent gets around to putting it up on the site.

Most large agencies now have a website so that you can check what is currently on their books. There are also a number of websites that bring together properties on offer by several agents. These are opening up all the time.

(See also **Do-it-yourself Buying and Selling**, **Home Hunting**, **Preparing Your Home For Sale**.)

INVESTMENT

The necessities were going by default to save the luxuries
until I hardly knew which were necessities and which luxuries.
Frank Lloyd Wright, *Autobiography*

For most of us the house we live in is the major investment we make in life and it is obviously important to choose wisely and well. As more and more people work on contract or for themselves and don't have the long-term security of a job for life and a pension to go with it, homes become even more important investments: capital that many hope to realize in later life in order to support their retirement.

Position is everything when considering the investment value of a property. The better sited a property is the faster it rises in a buoyant market and the less likely it is to fall when things go flat. It is also important to consider the size of the property in relation to the plot it sits on. Large houses in small gardens always do badly and few people buying a cottage want more than an acre of land. The overall attractiveness of the exterior of the property is important; interiors can be dramatically changed but altering the exterior is very often impossible.

In the country the best location for a property is one which is convenient for access to a major town or shopping centre; in a generally attractive green environment offering good privacy (on the edge of an unspoilt village is considered by many agents the ultimate); not overlooked; away from road, rail and air traffic noise or any industrial development. The prettier the position and the overall appearance of the house the better.

In a town or city the best position for a property is within a conservation area or near facilities like a park, river or garden square; convenient for public transport access to the centre of the city; not on a main road or overlooking a railway line; in a low crime area with attractive local shops and restaurants.

Many people who find themselves with extra cash decide to invest it in a second property which they then let out – either through a holiday company or on an annual lease. If you decide to go down this route take the advice of an estate agent who deals with rentals in the area who can advise you on the type of property they find easiest to let and the best way to get the maximum rental for your investment. Or you can talk to a holiday letting company who will be happy to give you an idea of the types of property that let well in their area and for what. If you have found a house you are hoping to buy, a good agency will happily view it for you and tell you what they would hope to get from renting it and what you would have to do to make it lettable.

(See also **Second Homes, Tax**.)

J

JOINT AGENCY AGREEMENTS

The business of everybody is the business of nobody.

Thomas Babington, 1st Baron Macaulay, 'Hallam'
in *Essays Contributed to the Edinburgh Review*

When selling, most agents will try to persuade you to give them sole agency. This is the cheapest method of selling through an agent as they will probably charge you a lower percentage of commission – say 2 per cent instead of 2.5 or 3 per cent. But the wisdom of going the sole-agency route is dependent on the market. If you want to move quickly in a slow market it is often better to put your property jointly with two or three agencies at once. This will give you a greater number of prospective buyers.

The assumption is that it is always better to sell your house comparatively quickly – within three months of it being launched, while it is fresh on the property shelves. If it hangs around too long it goes stale. Although the house hasn't changed, potential buyers' perceptions of it do. 'What an interesting house' becomes 'Why hasn't it sold, what's wrong with it?' Even if an agent says there is nothing wrong with a property, the simple lack of interest from other buyers is enough to put people off in a soft market.

Whatever the state of the market, if you do decide to have a sole-agency agreement, most property experts would strongly advise you to limit the terms of this agreement to a short period of time, no more than six weeks.

(See also **Do-it-yourself Buying and Selling, Estate Agents, Internet Buying and Selling**.)

JOINT OWNERSHIP

Everything has been thought of before . . .
the difficulty is to think of it again.

Anon

Many properties are in the joint ownership of couples who buy and live in them together. There is also an increasing trend for friends or siblings, unable to afford a property on their own, to buy together. Why not? They all then have a stake in the property market which will help them to move forward in the future.

The problem is that friends and siblings rarely want to spend the rest of their days together. Living together is not easy – as anyone who has shared a flat knows – and it can be complicated further when you both own part of the property. Problems are no longer confined to the washing up and the cleanliness of the bathroom but also include what does and doesn't need repair and significant financial matters. Nevertheless people can and do buy together successfully. There are two ways to do this:

- A Joint Tenancy Agreement. Joint tenancy is when two or more people own a property together and wish the share of anyone who dies to pass automatically to the survivor. This agreement is primarily used by married or committed couples.

- A Tenancy in Common is used in almost all other circumstances. This means that if one of the tenants in common dies, his or her rights pass to their next of kin or whoever is nominated to receive the rights to the property in their will.

If when you supply your names to the Land Registry you do not say whether you are joint tenants or tenants in common the Land Registry will assume you are tenants in common. If you go down this route it is advisable to draw up a legal contract about who owns what proportion of the property; it doesn't have to be even thirds or halves, someone can own 50 per cent and two other people 25 per cent each. You will also need to make a decision on how refurbishment, maintenance and decoration costs are divided and who will purchase shared equipment for the property, from the living-room sofa to the fridge and cooker.

It is also highly advisable to have a legal agreement drawn up about what will happen in the event of someone's girlfriend/boyfriend wanting to move in and someone wanting to move out. Although in the euphoria of deciding to buy somewhere together such things may seem trivial or easily resolvable, they aren't. Rather than having a bitter argument based on small misunderstandings it is better to make a legal agreement at the start.

Many solicitors who carry out conveyancing work now have experience of this type of agreement. A Declaration of Trust and Cohabitation Agreement sets out who owns what percentage of the property and can include every detail about the property, for example even the ownership of the cooker. One of the most important things is to ensure that the agreement stipulates that the portion of the property owned by any person wanting to move out should first be offered to the other owners sharing the property. However a time limit should be set for the other owners to pick up this option or find someone else to buy the share of the property.

If you decide to buy with friends you should also be aware that as a group of two or more individuals buying together you might find it harder to get the mortgage you want. Also the mortgage company is within its rights to pursue you for your friend's half of the mortgage if they jump ship. If you buy out a fellow owner's share of the property and have the deeds of the property changed you will be liable for Stamp Duty on the entire value of the property. Stamp Duty is for just that: stamping a document. Deeds will have to be stamped after names are taken off or added, meaning you can pay it twice or more if you keep changing the names on the deeds.

Other problems that have to be addressed by families or groups who buy a second home for shared use include:

• who can use the property and when

• how bills are to be apportioned

- whether people other than those purchasing can use the property

- whether any of the parties involved can let out their weeks at the property

- what happens when someone moves out

(See also **Housing Associations, Mortgages, Shared Ownership Schemes, Solicitors.**)

K

KEYS

All the world's a stage,
And all the men and women merely players:
They have their exits and their entrances

William Shakespeare, *As You Like It*

... And most of our exits and entrances require keys.

Selling

Make sure you find them all – including the one to the garden shed – and label them. You will need to give one set to the agent or solicitor to hand over on completion and you must tell your buyer where you are leaving the other sets.

A purchaser may ask for access to a property after exchange to measure up and the temptation is to let them have a key at this point, particularly if the property is empty. You would be well advised not to do this but if you do, get a signed agreement that the key is for viewing purposes only. A better alternative is to ask estate-agency staff to take them around.

Buying

Even if you are pretty sure you have received all the keys, change the main lock on the front door as soon as you can. Although few people hand out whole sets of keys to their property, the key to the front door does get passed to the cleaning lady, the babysitter, various relatives and visiting friends and even the window cleaner.

(See also **Completion**.)

KITCHENS

We don't talk fancy grammar and eat anchovy toast.
But to live under the kitchen doesn't say we aren't educated.

Mary Norton, *The Borrowers*

Time was when the British dining room was second only to the British drawing room in domestic ranking. But in the 1990s the dining room has been replaced by designer eat-in kitchens. Informal eating is fashionable and most people spend more on doing up their kitchens than on any other room in the house. And it's not just a country fad. Even in sophisticated Kensington, Edinburgh or Bristol, the kitchen has become the centre of the house. Cooking is no longer consigned to a cold dark room at the back of the house – at today's informal food feasts you talk to the chef, taste the sauce and help wash the salad. Confirmation that large kitchens have taken over comes from the fact that few developers are now building homes with a separate dining room. The demise of the dining room has also inspired the revival of the back kitchen or scullery for washing vegetables and storing dirty pots and pans.

Selling

A large eat-in kitchen is a major selling point and should be made much of in the sales particulars of your property, but whatever the size of your kitchen make as much of a feature of it as you can. Make sure it is tidy and looks inviting with large bowls of fresh fruit on the table and all equipment gleaming. There are few things less inspiring than a bowl of dirty washing up. If your kitchen is small and you have given some thought to enlarging it, share your thoughts on this with whoever is viewing the property; you have had plenty of time to think of the pros and cons and you might have come up with the perfect solution.

Don't invest any money in altering the kitchen if you are planning to move beyond giving it a good clean and polish and possibly the walls a coat of paint in a plain colour if they are looking very grubby. Everyone has their own ideas on how a kitchen should look. A good kitchen will add to the attractiveness of your property and could add a modest amount to the price but you will not get the full price back if you decide to sell immediately after significant alteration work has been done.

Buying

Think of how you would use the kitchen space and how you could extend it. However, extensions and new kitchens are expensive. If either is necessary, take into account the fact that a modest but good extension will probably set you back between £20,000 and £30,000. Kitchen costs vary enormously depending on whether you plan to have something specially fitted, go to somewhere like IKEA or choose from the vast range of semi-fitted kitchens in between. You are unlikely – with equipment – to pay less than £5,000 and can easily spend more than £50,000.

Think carefully about your priorities. Sometimes it is worth putting up with the existing kitchen until you are able to afford to refit and/or extend it to the standard you want. If you are looking to the future and to increasing your investment in the property, the potential of a property is often more important than what is immediately before you.

When viewing a particularly attractive kitchen talk to the owner about whether the equipment is for sale – the range cooker, the fridge freezer, everything that is fitted in to it. Nothing ruins the look of a kitchen more than wrong-sized equipment forced into the space left by a departing cooker or fridge.

(See also **Brochures or Property Details**, **Extensions**, **Finances**, **Preparing Your Home for Sale**.)

L

LAND

What between the duties expected of one during one's
lifetime, and the duties expected from one after one's death,
land has ceased to be either a profit or a pleasure. It gives
one position and prevents one from keeping it up.
That is all that can be said about land.

Oscar Wilde, *The Importance of Being Earnest*

The ideal plot for a cottage is 0.5 to one acre, for a small
country house one or two acres and for a good-sized
country house between three and five acres. Only those
looking for a farm or sporting estate want more than fifteen
acres; faced with acres in double figures, the rest of us
scratch our heads and wonder what to do with it. But land
attached to any country property is an asset that gives you
privacy and protects your view. If you don't want to
manage it yourself you can:

- Rent fields as paddocks to a local stable.

- Rent fields to a local farmer.

- Exchange the hay (which a farmer will cut and bale) for
  upkeep of the gates and hedges.

- Buy a small flock of sheep (six to an acre) and create your own Capability Brown pastoral scene. Contract a local farmer to look after, sheer and dip them.

- Excavate a lake and stock it with fish – this could attract an income from anglers.

- Create a woodland.

Selling

If you are selling with a lot of land explain how you manage it or whether you know a farmer who is interested in renting it.

Buying

If the property you are buying is surrounded by open land, establish who owns it and whether it is in agricultural use or just vacant. There are few things more depressing than buying something with a glorious view of the countryside and finding two years later that a development of fifty houses is being built smack in the middle of that view.

(See also **Farms**, **Gardens**.)

LAND REGISTRY

The great and chief end, therefore, of men's uniting into commonwealths, and putting themselves under government, is the preservation of their property.

John Locke, English philosopher, *Second Treatise of Civil Government*

Most property in England and Wales is registered and when you purchase the property you are given a Land Certificate. This certificate is a copy of the information held by Her Majesty's Land Registry which is a government department responsible to the Lord Chancellor. You will also receive an official site plan of the property showing exactly where all the boundaries run.

The function of the Land Registry is to record land ownership in England and Wales. All property has to be registered and when you purchase a property the title is transferred by the Land Registry into your name. Information about land registration is available on the Land Registry's website: www.landreg.gov.uk. This website also monitors the value of property sales in each district.

Buying

For a small fee you can obtain information about the exact land rights of a particular property and who owns it. When there is some doubt about the ownership of part of the property this information can sometimes help resolve the problem.

It is now compulsory in Britain to register all land so if you buy a property that is not registered you as the new owner will be obliged to do so. You or your solicitor has two months in which to register the land after completion of purchase and the registry will then record the changes and send you the new Land Certificate.

When you buy property a Land Registry fee has to be paid. The fee is the same whether it is a new registration or a transfer but is on a variable scale according to the price of the property you are buying. It ranges from £40 for a property valued up to £40,000 to a maximum £800 for property valued at over £1million.

(See also **Accessibility**, **Conveyancing**, **Neighbours**, **Solicitors**.)

LEASEHOLD

And life is given to none freehold, but it is leasehold for all.

Lucretius c.91–55 BC, Roman poet, *De Rerum Natura*

Property can be bought either freehold or leasehold.

A freehold property is one that you own and have a title to; you will not pay any rent or service charge and maintenance of the property is your responsibility.

However, a few houses and almost all flats are sold on a lease. This means that you have the title to the property and own it for the number of years specified on the lease; after that ownership reverts to the landlord who owns the freehold of the site and to whom you pay ground rent every year.

Under new laws some leaseholders have the right to buy an extension to their lease or the freehold of their property and it is an increasingly popular practice for flat owners to get together and buy the freehold of the property. The government is now looking at ways in which to extend and clarify these rights.

For more information about leasehold properties, extend-

ing a lease and details of current legislation contact the
Leasehold Enfranchisement Advisory Service. Reports on
new government proposals are on their website: www.
lease-advice.org.

Selling
You need to be very clear about how the property is
managed. Point out the advantages of not having to organize the cleaning of the hallways, the painting of the windows, repairs to the roof and all other joint responsibilities.

Buying
When buying a leasehold property it is important to:

- Get as long a lease as possible. Unless you have a lease
  of at least sixty years you may find it difficult to obtain
  a mortgage.

- Check out the management and maintenance of the
  property; this is important whether you own a share of
  the freehold or not. There are unscrupulous
  management companies and landlords who charge over
  the odds for repairs and services. Residents who take
  management of a property into their own hands can
  also have problems with repairs and improvements.

- Ensure that the service charges are reasonable. Look at
  what you are getting for the annual service charge.
  Don't forget to include this sum when working out the
  costs of living in the property.

- Check whether there has been any serious dispute between the tenants or leaseholders and the landlord or managing agent in the recent past. If this dispute has not been satisfactorily resolved do not buy.

- Ask at the outset whether it is going to be possible to either buy a share of the freehold or to extend the lease, and enquire how much this will cost. The 1993 Leasehold Reform, Housing and Urban Development Act gave some leaseholders the right to extend their lease or to buy the freehold. Check whether these rights apply to you.

Remember:

The conveyancing fee charged by your solicitor may be higher if you are buying a leasehold property because of the extra work involved in checking through the lease, often a lengthy document. Your solicitor must also check that service charges and ground rent on the property are paid up to date.

Ground rent is usually a token amount and is payable annually to the freeholder. It is technically the rent for the ground the property sits on. The lease you have bought is the right to occupuy that land for a specific period of time.

It is worth noting that for a few buyers a short-leasehold property is a good option: for instance, if you have cash and are not interested in the long-term investment possibilities of a purchase. A property in a prime position on a short lease will cost dramatically less than one that is freehold or on a long lease. You can – for a short term –

buy more for less and in many cases could find that you will be able to purchase an extension to the lease after several years.

(See also **Accessibility**, **Common Parts**, **Flats**, **Neighbours**.)

LISTED BUILDINGS

> This [Buckingham Palace] isn't ours. It's a tied cottage.
> Prince Philip, Duke of Edinburgh, in *Royal Quotes*

These are properties – from castles to cottages and telephone boxes – that are deemed to be part of Britain's architectural heritage. They are listed Grade I, Grade II* and Grade II and there are in all about 380,000 listed properties. The great majority of them are old and all buildings constructed before 1700 which survive in anything like their original condition are automatically listed. Buildings have to be at least ten years old before they can be considered and are listed for one or several of the following reasons:

- architectural interest

- historical interest

- close historical associations with nationally important people or events

- historical or architectural interest as a group of buildings

- outstanding quality or design

- the pinnacle of building fashion or standards of a particular moment

The most important buildings or structures in Britain are listed Grade I and include places like Buckingham Palace and Warwick Castle. There are nearly 9,000 of these buildings. Nothing can be done to alter the structure of these buildings, no extension may be built and all repairs must be carried out in keeping with the property – even if that means rebuilding a wall with daub and wattle or having wooden nails made to hold floorboards or beams together. Because these buildings are so important grants are sometimes available from English Heritage to carry out any repairs.

The next classification is Grade II*. There are just over 20,000 buildings and structures that come under this category including such oddities as the penguin pool at London Zoo. Again no structural changes may take place.

Grade II is the commonest listing and there are approximately 350,000 of these. Again you have to get special consent to make any changes but there are fewer rules; you may well be able to put on a conservatory and there is unlikely to be a problem about minor internal works, for instance accommodating a new kitchen. But if in doubt, don't do it. Contact your local planning office or English Heritage as it is a criminal offence to alter any listed

building without planning permission and any breach of
this law is punishable with a five-figure fine.

Current listings include several ponds, the burial place
of a dog called Tippo who was the lone survivor of a
shipwreck, a telephone kiosk designed in 1935 by Sir Giles
Gilbert Scott and a red-brick icehouse in Braxted Park.

If you know of, own or are buying a building that you
think should be listed you should contact English Heritage
who will tell you if your case is a good one. The case for
listing has to be put forward in a proposal to the Department of Culture, Media and Sport.

Sadly, English Heritage say that at the moment 1,600
listed buildings are at risk and are not being properly cared
for.

Selling

Don't underestimate the added attraction a listing will give
to your home. Many people feel it is a privilege to live in
such a building, and are willing to deal with the planning
restrictions. Tell the agent and give them as much history
as possible about the property: when it was built, who by,
who else has lived there, etc.

Buying

Listed status may add to the value of the property you are
buying but you will have trouble making any alterations
to the building. The basic rule is that no listed building
should be altered or extended in any way which would
affect its character as a building of special architectural
interest. You must apply for listed building consent from

your local planning authority in order to alter the property. This can be done at the same time as obtaining planning permission to carry out any alterations.

On the positive side you will be buying a piece of acknowledged history. If repairs are needed there are grants available from English Heritage for the repair of buildings of outstanding architectural or historical interest. The application must be made before work begins. Information about grants and services is available on their website – www.english-heritage.org.uk – or from their information service.

Local authorities also give grants towards repair work on buildings of special interest in their area. You may also save on VAT which is zero rated for improvements or approved alterations to listed buildings.

The Department of Culture, Media and Sport can provide owners and occupiers with a free guide to what listing means.

Remember:

The same restrictions to development of a property apply if you live in a conservation area.

Within conservation areas trees are protected and subject to preservation orders. The conservation order will also cover dividing walls and outbuildings.

(See also **Conservation Areas, Grants for Home Improvement and Renovation, Planning Permission, Trees.**)

LOCAL AUTHORITY AND OTHER SEARCHES

Books will speak plain when counsellors blanch

Francis Bacon, 'Of Consel' in *Essays*

Property searches should be undertaken to ascertain that what you are buying is what it purports to be and that a main road or bypass isn't about to be built next door. Part of the buyer's solicitor's job is to undertake searches to uncover these things. Searches are made between your offer being accepted and exchange. A lot of time can pass waiting for the results. However, under proposed government legislation, local authorities will be required to reply to requests for a standard search within ten working days. Other organizations receiving search enquiries, such as water companies, will be asked to meet similar targets.

The local authority search should reveal information about future plans for the area, particularly information about new roads and road systems or plans for new housing developments. There is a standard form of questions and a fee is charged by the local authority for providing written answers. This is usually between £80 and £140 but can be more in London. Sometimes this fee is included in the solicitor's fee to you as a buyer or seller.

It is important to remember as a buyer that the local search will only produce information about the house itself; it will not show information about nearby property and land. If you are concerned about an empty field next to the house ask your solicitor to check in case there are plans for development.

Your solicitor will also make a number of other searches on your behalf, dependent on where the property is. For most properties there will be a water search: a standard set of questions is sent to the local water authority about the property. Other searches are made when and where necessary. If you are purchasing a property in a mining area your solicitor should conduct a search for past or present mining activity close to the property.

Under legislation currently being put together by the government, the seller rather than the buyer will become responsible for carrying out the search.

(See also **Conveyancing, Finances, Solicitors and Licensed Conveyancers**.)

LOCATION
Hot spots and spotting hot-spot potential

Filthy old house – fashionable Chelsea – preserved
as of Architectural Interest – God Knows Why. Providing
you have enough patience and cash wld make: 3 bedrms.
27ft L-drawing r, a dining room, 1 or 2 bathrms., kit.
The horrible patch of weed, refuse-infected earth
behind wld make a lovely – Gdn – maybe.
Roy Brooks, advert in 'Mud, Straw and Insults'

Most agents will tell you that location is everything if you want your property to appreciate in value. Never mind the house, think of its location. It is also vital to your happiness to live in the right spot. As a general rule people gravitate towards areas where like-minded people live: families cluster around schools and parks, singles and couples often value being near public transport, wine bars and cinemas, older people appreciate being within easy distance of health and shopping facilities.

The top locations or 'hot spots' are the areas where most people would live if they could afford it. Prices are higher, houses move faster and even in a falling market they lose their value much more slowly. The downside is that you get less for your money; growing families might have to leave a hot spot in order to get more space for the same amount of money. The most desirable hot spots combine:

- a beautiful environment (an attractive square or conservation area in a town or city, an unspoilt village in the country)

- easy access to a major city

- no blight in terms of road, rail or air-traffic noise.

They range from the graceful Georgian terraces of Bath for townies to the desirable estuaries around Dartmouth in Devon for the sailing community or the delights of the countryside around the Victorian spa town of Harrogate with its easy access to York and Leeds. There are hot spots everywhere and we all know where they are in our area.

If you can't afford the best look carefully at the rest.

Areas become hot spots and to spot a potential hot spot is to do yourself a great favour. Just as the unsympathetic development of an area can destroy its desirability, so positive new development, new road systems, schools, businesses and improvements in rail services can bring an area up. One very basic way of spotting an urban area on the up is the presence of one or more wine bars or restaurants and a delicatessen; sure signs of upwardly mobile movement. In towns and cities another mark of an improving area is the number of skips you see in a road. But it takes time. People who cannot afford to move right into a good environment find they can buy on its edge, and so that area then begins to increase in value as the houses are restored. This ripple factor is particularly prevalent in towns and cities. Keys to up-and-coming country area are new access routes, bus and train services, attractive new developments and a pleasing environment.

According to one national estate agent a good location can add value to the property as follows:

- easy access to main commuting routes + 15%

- within twenty minutes of good schools + 15%

- fashionable village situation + 10%

- well sited (edge of village) with right amount of land for property size + 5%

- good views + 5%

Value is reduced by:

- motorway, flight path or railway noise − 20 to 30%

- close to industrial or council estate − 15 to 20%

- large house with inadequate land − 10 to 15%

- no view/overlooked/poor situation − 10%

An area can move down because of a new road system creating traffic and road noise and the closure of a 'honey-pot'. Factories, businesses and schools all attract people into a community; if they close people move away, too many properties come on the market at once, prices drop and the area might take some time to recover.

It is not always worth moving to a hot spot. To squash yourself or your family into too small a house in a fashionable area for investment reasons may not be a sensible decision. Your lifestyle may suffer.

Here are a few examples of up-and-coming areas according to one national estate agent. These are areas which they believe will see the greatest growth in value in the first five or ten years of the new millennium in the British countryside.

Berkshire
Newbury and areas close to it because of the expansion of Vodafone. Villages including Donnington, Inkpen, Highclere, Burghclere, Curridge, Shalbourne and Ham are increasingly popular. Villages further along the M4 corridor are in demand because of Microsoft at Reading, Motorola at Swindon and Vodafone.

Somerset/Devon

South Molton and Barnstaple because of good access on the comparatively new North Devon Link Road A361 combined with proximity to fashionable parts of Exmoor, good beaches and schools in Tiverton.

West Midlands

Jewellery Quarter within Birmingham city centre has good interesting sites with traditional buildings being converted into loft-style apartments.

Gloucestershire

North of Cirencester due to the new link road with the M4/M5 access

Warwickshire and the Cotswolds

Anything within five miles of Banbury because of good M40 access and improved rail services to London Marylebone. The tract of land to the west and north-west of Banbury contains the pretty unspoilt villages of the Tysoes, Brailes, Cherington, Adderbury, Warmington, Hornton and Horley.

Hampshire

The area west of Winchester and particularly the Test Valley is expected to see the greatest growth with its concentration of unspoilt countryside and living villages with shop, pub and garage.

Remember:
Don't expect an area to change overnight; the move from cool to warm to hot spot can take twenty years.

If you do buy in a cool spot be very sure that you are comfortable within it and don't mind its downside.

All predictions are guesswork.

(See also **Accessibility**, **Assets and Liabilities**.)

LOCK-OUT AGREEMENTS

> But, as the world, harmoniously confused:
> Where order in variety we see,
> And where, though all things differ, all agree.
> Alexander Pope, 'Windsor Forest'

A lock-out agreement gives the buyer a chance to do essential checks and put his funding together in preparation for exchange without the threat of someone else coming along and snatching the property from under his nose. The seller knows that she will be able to accept without guilt another offer if things don't move swiftly forwards. Under a standard lock-out agreement the seller agrees that for a period of (usually ten) working days she will:

- not allow any other potential buyer to inspect the property

- not advertise the property

- not negotiate for the sale of the property with any other potential buyer

- not accept any other offer for the sale of the property

- not issue any other draft contract

- ensure any agent instructed by the seller is aware of the lock-out agreement

- instruct a solicitor to send the draft document and other necessary documents to the buyer's solicitor

- permit the buyer's surveyor and valuer access to carry out any necessary survey and inspection

The buyer agrees to:

- take all reasonable steps to exchange contract for the purchase of the property within the lock-out period

- without delay instruct his solicitors to deal with the draft contract

- arrange for any survey or valuation required to be carried out as soon as possible

- keep the seller and her agents advised on the progress of the survey

- notify the seller immediately if for any reason during the lock-out period the buyer decides not to proceed

- not negotiate or make any offer for any other property.

Lock-out agreements are designed to reassure both sides and avoid gazumping but it is interesting to note that the government has decided not to make these agreements a part of their new property buying and selling legislation. They say: 'Lock-out agreements still don't guarantee that the sale will go through. The seller can wait until the end of the agreement and then accept a better offer. The buyer may be in a "chain" and unable to guarantee to be ready before the agreement expires, or they might just pull out of the deal.'

(See also **Queue Jumping Without Gazumping, Sellers' Information Packs**.)

M

MOBILE HOMES

The only possible way there'd be an uprising in this country
would be if they banned car boot sales and caravanning.
Victoria Wood, performance at the Strand Theatre, 1990

Mobile homes do not have the same rights of protection as
other properties because they are not considered permanent structures, but they are protected under the Mobile
Homes Act 1983. Although they are difficult to move they
have the same legal status as caravans. You rent the site on
which your mobile home sits.

Selling
As with any other home make sure everything is in reasonably good order. Ensure that you have a good long-term
agreement with the site owner. Find out if the site owner
expects to receive a percentage of the proceeds if you sell.

Buying
Study carefully and take legal advice on the agreement
between the mobile home owner and the site owner which
you will take over with the home. Check the site regulations, services and how much they cost and any agreement

about transferring the property on. The site owner might expect to receive up to 10 per cent of the value set on the property.

MORTGAGE BROKERS

The difficult we do immediately;
the impossible takes a little longer.

US Armed Forces, late nineteenth century

Mortgage brokers can guide you through the mortgage jungle and they particularly come into their own in four instances:

- When mortgages are in short supply and banks and building societies are closing their doors to all but regular customers or those with specific financial qualities.

- You are buying an unusual property that the high-street lending institutions see as too high a risk, anything from a listed barn which you plan to convert into a house to a terraced town house with a sitting tenant.

- You need a very large loan.

- You have been self-employed for less than three years and are finding it difficult to acquire a loan.

A mortgage broker's job is to find you a mortgage and for this you either pay a fee – usually 1–2 per cent of the loan – or they get a commission from the company that finally sells you a mortgage, in this case usually an endowment or pension mortgage. Ensure you are dealing with a professional; anyone can use the title mortgage broker. Insurance brokers have to be registered with the Insurance Brokers Registration Council. The British Insurance and Investment Brokers' Association or the Corporation of Insurance and Financial Advisers will give you a list of members in your area. A list of independent mortgage brokers is available on the Internet through: www.mortgage-brokers.co.uk.

(See also **Banks and Buildings Societies**, **Mortgages**.)

MORTGAGES

*Money is used to pay bills and
credit is used to delay paying them.*
Sir Alan Walters, *Observer*, 1989

The great majority of privately owned property in Britain is first bought on a loan of some sort, usually a mortgage. Technically a mortgage is a deed that is held by the bank or building society that lends you the money to buy the property. It acts as security for the loan and legally prevents you from reselling the property without paying this loan off. If you default on your payments the lender (mortgagee) can go to court and get a repossession order on the property in order to sell it and recoup their losses. The lender usually hold the deeds to the property until the loan has been repaid. There are two key issues that govern the extent of any mortgage: your income and the value of the property.

Income

The amount of money you can borrow is based on your income. The basic formulae used by most lenders are:

- **Single person**: 2.5 to 3 times annual income before tax.

- **Couple who are both earning**: either 2.5 to 3 times the higher income plus 1 to 1.5 times the lower income *or* 2 to 2.5 times the joint income.

- **Self-employed**: the same scales as above but based on your average income over three years. The lender will want this verified by your accounts and/or your tax assessment.

In all cases you may be allowed to borrow more if you take the loan out over a longer term. However, if you are buying a leasehold property, the length of the lease may limit this.

Remember:
The lenders' calculations don't take into account the horse you keep in the country, the allowance you pay to a dependent relative, school fees, going skiing twice a year or a passion for collecting paintings. Going for the

maximum mortgage may mean dramatic changes in your lifestyle.

Value of the property

No one will give you a mortgage for more than the value of the property and few (except new-build starter homes) will give you a loan for 100 per cent of the value. The maximum that most banks and building societies will lend against a property is between 75 and 90 per cent. It is important to remember that this percentage is based on the value the lender puts on the property, not on what you are paying for it. Be warned; very often the valuer employed by the lender will value the property below the price you have agreed to pay. They will always play very safe, even in a soaring market.

There are plenty of different mortgage products on the market and they are constantly being changed and updated in order to attract customers. It is like buying a suit, essentially the same product but dozens of styles and sizes to suit different needs – your age, lifestyle and type of employment are all factors to consider and there are bargains if you can find them.

The Internet means that you can browse through some of the mortgage options at home. No longer do you have a long trek around high-street banks and building societies to find out what is available; you can make an initial selection through the Internet and often get the lending organization to send you details.

The *Telegraph* has recently opened up an internet site –

www.money.telegraph.co.uk – which provides advice on mortgages and immediate access to mortgage companies. After entering the site go to personal finance which included a mortgage section. Other established mortgage 'supermarkets' online include:

- www.charcolonline.co.uk – operated by John Charcol carrying four hundred mortgage deals from forty-five lenders.

- www.creditweb.co.uk – allows searches of every lender on the market, giving access to more than 4,500 mortgage products. Online applications cannot be made.

- uk.eloan.com – calculates monthly repayments on different mortgages. Features 1,700 loans from five hundred lenders.

- www.ftyourmoney.com – quotes from twenty-four different lenders.

- www.moneygator.co.uk – to search out and buy mortgages. Has helpful guides but you must register first to access these.

- www.mortgage-brokers.co.uk – lists independent mortgage brokers.

- www.virginmoney.co.uk – offers a selection of mortgages.

Despite the variety of mortgages available they fall into two distinct groups: repayment mortgages and interest-only mortgages. You are more vulnerable with an interest-only mortgage because your mortgage repayments vary with interest rates, but these mortgages are better value if interest rates are low – less than 10.5 per cent – and you want life cover. You are less vulnerable with a repayment mortgage as there are now plenty of fixed-rate deals. You also pay off the capital you have borrowed year by year.

Repayment mortgages

- Could suit: anyone taking out a loan which does not stretch their finances.

- Unlikely to suit: those taking out a large loan on a fixed income who need more security.

- A repayment mortgage is when you repay the loan and the interest over the mortgage period (usually 20–25 years). When you move house you pay it off and start again.

- How much you pay each month depends on how much you have borrowed, the length of the mortgage period and the current rate of interest set by the Bank of England.

Interest rates can vary dramatically from as little as 4 per cent to as much as 14 per cent in 1990 and 1991 when many borrowers found themselves unable to repay their mortgages and faced repossession of their homes. As a result and in order to help buyers in the first, usually most demanding years of a loan, lending institutions came up with fixed-rate schemes.

Fixed-rate mortgages

- Could suit: anyone on a fixed income taking out a large mortgage.

- Unlikely to suit: those able to afford the risk of fluctuating interest rates.

- Under a fixed-rate repayment mortgage you agree to pay the lender interest at a specified rate for a certain number of years, usually between two and five but it can be as many as ten years. At the end of this term the rate reverts to the then current rate of interest as set by the Bank of England.

- The advantage of fixed-rate schemes is that however high the interest rate goes your repayments stay the same for the fixed term.

- The possible disadvantages are several. First, there are high penalties if you decide to change to a different scheme within the set period. Second, interest rates may go down; you will therefore have paid more than if you had chosen a variable rate repayment mortgage. Third, the possibility the lender will insist as part of the package that you buy other property-related services from them like building or contents insurance.

There are a number of variants of this basic scheme (new ones are appearing all the time) including capped- and discounted-rate mortgages.

Capped-rate mortgages
- Could suit: borrowers on a fixed income during a boom economy taking out a large loan (so needing a fixed rate) but who believe interest rates might fall.

- Unlikely to suit: anyone who can afford the risk of fluctuating interest rates.

- A capped-rate scheme is where you have a fixed-rate mortgage but if the Bank of England rate falls below a certain level your payments will also drop.

Discounted-rate mortgages
- Could suit: first-time buyers and those buying an older building and renovating.

- Unlikely to suit: young couples and families whose costs are escalating.

- With a discounted rate you pay less for the first few years but pay more later.

Interest-only mortgages
These are mortgages where you do not pay back any of the capital until the end of the mortgage period. Instead, you pay interest only on the loan throughout its term. This is variable and depends on the current rate of interest set by the Bank of England. You also pay premiums on an investment, life insurance or pension policy. These are not variable and at the end of the term of the mortgage the capital is paid off by the proceeds of this policy. You can take this mortgage with you when you move house.

Again, there are variants. The following are the most common.

Endowment mortgage

- Could suit: those who move regularly and want to take their mortgage with them; those looking for life cover.

- Unlikely to suit: the older, those on a tight income, people who may wish to repay their debt ahead of schedule

- This is when the mortgage is linked to an endowment life-insurance policy. The endowment policy is timed to mature at the same time as your mortgage period ends. The capital is then paid off by the endowment policy. Life insurance is automatically included so the mortgage is paid off if you die. Payments are an estimate based on investment returns; when these are high endowment policies look extremely good value, when they are low the policy when matured may have insufficient funds to pay off the money borrowed.

- With this type of policy what you pay depends on your age and health; the older and less healthy you are the higher the premiums.

There are a number of different types of endowment policy:

- Non-profit endowment simply aims to pay off the full amount borrowed – no more, no less.

- With-profits endowment aims to pay off the full amount borrowed plus a share in profits made by the company through investing your premiums.

- Low-cost endowment guarantees to pay off a percentage of the capital (usually about half) and uses any profits made from investing your premiums to pay off the rest. If there is a recession there is a real worry that the profits won't meet the additional costs which you would then be asked to pay.

- Low-start low-cost endowment allows you to defer paying all or some of the interest and premiums for the first few years. The downside is that you will have to pay substantially more in later years.

The Office of Fair Trading has criticized these mortgages for their high cost and inflexibility. The Financial Services Authority, the mortgage industry's official watchdog, has decreed that home buyers wrongly advised to sign up for an endowment mortgage must be compensated. However they point out that most people who maintained payments into endowment policies over the past ten years are actually better off than if they had chosen repayment mortgages.

Pension mortgage

- Could suit: self-employed, older borrowers.

- Unlikely to suit: buyers under the age of thirty who might find it hard to find a lender.

- Pension mortgages are very similar to endowment mortgages but here you pay into a pension plan which is timed to mature at the same time as your mortgage term comes to an end. The main advantage is tax relief on the contributions made to a pension plan.

- As some of your pension is being used to pay off the mortgage you should consider having a second top-up pension policy. There is a maximum amount of pension investment on which you can receive tax relief. Your lender will probably insist on your taking out life insurance cover to repay the loan if necessary.

Individual Savings Account (ISA) or corporate bond

- Could suit: high-rate taxpayers

- Unlikely to suit: lower-rate taxpayers

- The ISA has replaced the PEP (personal equity plan). Under this scheme as well as paying interest you also pay into an ISA or a corporate savings plan. This scheme carries an element of risk as the fund may not build up enough to pay off the mortgage and so you are often asked to pay mortgage protection insurance.

Pure interest-only mortgages

- Could suit: older buyers looking for a low-cost mortgage which is a small percentage of the value of the property.

- Unlikely to suit: lenders looking for a mortgage to cover a high percentage of the value of the property.

- With this type of mortgage only the interest is paid; the capital is not repaid until the house is sold or the purchaser decides to repay it. It is rare for a lender to agree to this sort of scheme unless a relatively small percentage of the capital value of the house is being borrowed.

Remember:

If sorting your way through the massive selection of mortgages is too much to get your head around then you could go to an independent financial adviser. Ask friends to recommend one or go to the Independent Financial Advice Bureau who will give you the names of a financial adviser in your area specializing in property matters. You will have to pay for an adviser's advice but they should guide you through the mass of information that mortgage lenders now deluge potential clients with.

(See also **Banks and Building Societies, Mortgage Brokers**.)

N

NEGATIVE EQUITY

On the outskirts of every agony
sits some observant fellow who points.
Virginia Woolf, *The Waves*

Negative equity is when things don't just go wrong, they go so badly wrong that you end up owing more money than your property is worth. In early 1993 there were 1.8 million householders, the great majority of them first-time buyers, with negative equity. By 1995 this had dropped but city analysts estimated that there were still two million households with insufficient equity to move. More than a third of all mortgaged properties in Britain were essentially frozen. In the first half of 1995 more than 25,000 homes were repossessed.

This is a sobering story and a warning to us all. In the mid to late 1980s the property market skyrocketed with central London house prices at one point almost doubling in a year. The ripple was felt around the country; even depressed areas of Wales and far corners of Cornwall beleaguered by unemployment experienced a property boom. Gazumping was rife and buyers often had to pay over the asking price in order to secure their future home.

Banks and building societies, confident that things would continue on the up, were happily handing out 80 per cent and 90 per cent mortgages.

But the property rocket ran out of fuel and dropped like a stone. Prices tumbled and those who had bought in the boom very quickly found they were bust. Our television screens were awash with tearful young families who had bought a starter home for £60,000 in 1989 at the peak of the market with a 90 per cent mortgage. In 1992 they wanted to move on to something slightly larger but their home was now only worth £45,000 – and they had a £54,000 mortgage.

In an attempt to help buyers trapped in this way, particularly those who for job reasons need to move from one part of the country to another, some lenders have introduced schemes to transfer the negative equity from one property to another. But this is not a complete answer because lenders are unlikely to loan you the extra money you need to purchase the new property.

It is a warning not to get too excited during a boom market and never to borrow more than you can afford.

(See also **Banks and Building Societies, Finances, Mortgages, Repossessions.**)

NEGOTIATING

Let us never negotiate out of fear.
But let us never fear to negotiate.

John F. Kennedy, 35th President of the USA,
Inaugural address, 1961

The English usually hate to bicker over price, but this reserve seems to disappear when it comes to property. This is one of the few commodities for which we don't expect to pay the asking price. A deal isn't a good deal unless we have managed to pay less. Negotiating is the key to ensuring that you get the best deal; the cleverer you are at negotiating the more likely you are to succeed in this two-hand game where no one with any skill ever lays all their cards on the table.

Selling

If you haven't overpriced your property it is essential to remain calm during the negotiating process. If you have found the property you want to buy, keep cool but don't play too hard a game. You may need to reassure the owner of the property you are buying that you are in a position to move and there is no better pitch than being able to tell them you have sold and will soon be a cash buyer.

- Don't let any potential buyer know that you need to move within a certain time.

- Don't accept the first offer unless it is for the full asking price – most people offer slightly less than they are prepared to pay. Don't accept any offer too quickly; a twenty-four-hour wait is acceptable and makes the buyer worry whether they have offered enough.

- Behave as if you have all the time in the world.

- Find out the buying position of the person who has made the offer. Have they sold their own property? Are they cash buyers? Are they still trying to sell their property?

- Give the agent a guide as to what you might accept in a slow market; the agent is working for you and should try to persuade a potential buyer to go beyond this figure.

- Ask the agent's opinion of the price you are asking and the demand for your sort of property.

- Be prepared to negotiate over carpets, curtains, etc. It is worth leaving a few things like this out of the asking price so that they can be part of the bargaining process. If you are offered less than you want you can always say yes but exclude some items. The buyers might then increase their offer in order to get these items if they are in reasonably good condition.

- Be prepared to go to best and final offers if necessary and to stick by this decision.

Buying

You've seen it – the flat, the house, the walls you want to call home. You've checked and know the price is roughly right. Now you need to negotiate the deal. Nobody wants to pay too much but nobody wants to lose out because someone else offers an extra £1,000. The better prepared you are the more smoothly and successfully you will be able to negotiate.

Before making a bid:

- Ensure your financing is in place and approach a solicitor who is willing to act for you.

- Look at the extras like curtains and carpets that could be used in negotiating. Ensure you know what is already included but remember; it's the property you are buying, not the present owners' furniture or lifestyle.

- Don't forget the agent is working for the seller not the buyer.

Negotiating tactics are dictated primarily by the state of the market, but the popularity of the area, the condition of the property, the size of rooms and attractiveness of layout will give you more or less scope to negotiate. The better the property the better negotiator you must be; no matter what the market everyone is looking for the right property with no drawbacks.

Once you have made the decision to buy:

- Put your offer in to the agent on the phone, subject to survey.

- In a fast-moving market if you really want a property, know it is something special and other people are after it offer the asking price.

- In a slower market offer 85–95 per cent of the asking price; more if you think the property is special, less if you feel the house is overpriced and/or you will have to do a lot of work on it. Don't make a silly offer – more than 20 per cent below – unless you are sure there is some reason it might be considered.

- Follow up your offer immediately with a letter. Confirm your offer and that you are ready to move, have financing in place and give the address of your solicitor. Whatever the market and whatever the price you have offered this makes you look like a serious and efficient buyer; the owner who might have thought your offer was marginally too low might just be impressed enough to reconsider.

- If the agent doesn't come back within twenty-four hours, hassle.

- If your offer is refused, go up by 2–4 per cent of the purchase price but do not let the agent know you might go any higher. Be prepared in an active market to pay more or to go to sealed bids, which is when you have to put your best and final offer in an envelope. When the envelopes are opened the highest wins.

- When you are making a second raised offer ask for one or two extras: perhaps the carpets if these were not included in the original price or the cooker and dishwasher.

- Once your offer is accepted ask for all agents handling the sale to be told that the property is not on the market. Ask for details to be removed from any websites and from any agents' windows.

Remember:

In a quiet market it is sometimes wise to wait a day or two before putting in a second offer. If there isn't another buyer around the seller will worry that they have lost your bid and may be more keen to accept a slightly higher offer.

Statistically, most houses are sold for 95–98 per cent of the asking price.

(See also **Estate Agent**, **Fashion in Property**, **Finances**, **First-time Buyers**, **Fixtures and Fittings**, **Gazumping**, **Location**, **Lock-Out Agreements**, **Queue Jumping Without Gazumping**, **Relocation Agents**, **Buying Checklist**, **Selling Checklists**.)

NEIGHBOURS

Living next to you is in some ways like sleeping with an
elephant. No matter how friendly and even-tempered the
beast, one is affected by every twitch and grunt.

Pierre Trudeau, on relations between Canada and the USA
in a speech at the National Press Club, 1969

Neighbours used to be people from whom one borrowed
some sugar. But today they are too often strangers. It's not
always easy to love your neighbours but some people
don't even try. They seem to believe that there is an
invisible impenetrable soundproof wall between their
house and lives and the lives of those around them. It is
not that they set out to be nasty, it is just that they do not
take their neighbours into consideration when they turn
up the volume on the stereo or light a bonfire in the back
garden minutes after you have hung up your washing.

A recent survey by the Alliance and Leicester uncovered
the sad fact that 6 per cent of people move for no other
reason than the fact that they can't stand their neighbours.
Most disputes between neighbours are about three things:
lack of consideration – noise being a classic; ownership of
inches of property; party walls and fences.

Remember the eighteen-year dispute between Bernard
Stanton and Michael Jones over a leylandii hedge which
finally ended in 1999? It started in 1971 when Mr and Mrs
Jones moved into a newly built house on the Bournville
Village Trust estate in Selly Oak, Birmingham. The Stan-

tons had previously enjoyed a view of a field and decided to block out their new neighbours by planting a hedge on the border between the two properties. Eight years later the leylandii was thirty-five feet tall and casting gloom into the Jones' garden and living room. Words were exchanged: the Stantons said they allowed the hedge to grow so high because Mrs Stanton thought Mr Jones was spying on her. Mr Jones said his wife, an ex head teacher, used binoculars only to study an albino starling.

Mr Jones lost his cool in 1989 and took a chainsaw to the top of the hedge. Mr Stanton sued for damages and trespass and the legal battle began. Finally, in 1994, two law lords ruled that Mr Jones could trim the hedge. Mr Stanton retaliated by planting a second row of leylandii. That came down in 1998 when the Bournville Village Trust issued a writ against Mr Stanton threatening further court action under a 'nuisance annoyance' covenant. Mr Stanton was by then ninety and in hospital without the energy 'to chop a twig'. Mr Jones has started an anti-leylandii help group called Hedgeline with 2,000 members.

Tales of unneighbourly behaviour are commonplace but the minimal effort involved in keeping on good terms is worth its weight in gold. On a practical level neighbours can:

- Hold keys to your house if you get locked out.

- Take in parcels while you are out.

- Keep an eye on your house while you are away on holiday, feed the cat and water the plants

- Share lifts to the station, commuter and school runs.

Good neighbours also improve the ambience of a street: security is better with ten or twenty eyes and ears watching rather than four and you are more likely to hear about plans for road changes in the area, new shops and restaurants, good babysitters, gardeners, cleaning ladies and window cleaners. The golden rule to being a good neighbour is to do as you would be done by.

Selling
Don't forget to tell your neighbours of your planned move and, once you know, who will be moving into your property. It is against the law not to inform your agent if there is a dispute of some sort between you and your neighbour.

Buying
Don't forget to ask about relations with the neighbours. Ask if there has been any dispute; you do not want to inherit any bad feeling. If you share any facility with the neighbours it may be worth talking to them before you make an offer on the property. See what sort of reaction you get.

(See also **Accessibility, Boundaries**.)

NEW BUILD

Americans have been conditioned to
respect newness, whatever it costs them.

John Updike, *A Month of Sundays*

For some buyers there is nothing more exciting than the prospect of a brand new house where they will be the first inhabitants, but for many people, modern houses simply do not compare to their historic counterparts. Nothing can beat a Georgian or Queen Anne country house set in the lush countryside of Berkshire, Hampshire, Sussex or Hertfordshire. History has value. But things are changing. The gap between old and new is narrowing for two reasons: the development of extremely high-quality, architect-designed new homes and the lack of good older property.

In every village there are only one or two good substantial old houses and a handful of pretty cottages. Supply is short and gets shorter when you weed out those ruined by ugly extensions or insensitive modernization which saw old fireplaces, fixtures and fittings, original doors and windows all consigned to the dump. New roads and industrial sites too close for comfort reduce even further the supply of 'good' old houses.

Some buyers are now opting to buy the perfect plot of land with an ugly house and pulling it down to build something newer and much better. Developers have spotted the market for stylish, high-quality homes. They are mixing styles and materials to ensure that new developments harmonize with one another and with their environment and also have individuality, privacy and the best views.

The demand for high-quality new homes was in part stimulated by architects like Quinlan Terry in the 70s and 80s who showed that traditional quality and style could go hand in hand with new development. The House Builders' Federation promotes new-build homes and can provide you with a list of builders operating in your area and a leaflet: 'Why buy a New Home'. Information is also available on their website: www.hbf.co.uk.

A new house has the major advantage of conforming to modern standards of security, heating, lighting and plumbing as well as kitchens and bathrooms boasting every mod con. But new build is not a guarantee that the building is sound. Don't assume that you won't need a survey. One *Telegraph* reader tells the following tale about trying to sell her new-build house.

She had bought it in 1992 but soon discovered the land under her house was slipping and the property was suffering from subsidence. By the year 2000 the property had been underpinned by the developers twice, unsuccessfully, and a third underpinning was planned. Fed up living with the nightmare of her own leaning tower of Pisa she decided to move and asked the developers to buy the house back at an 'unblighted' price, but because the developers are continuing to try to resolve the problem she can take no legal action to force them to do this. Although, if the problem is not resolved, she will eventually be able to sue the developers for recovery of the full purchase price, she meanwhile has to stay put while the ground slips away beneath her.

Selling

Only developers sell real new-build houses but sometimes as a seller you are in the position of selling on a reasonably newly built home.

If all properties on the development have not yet been sold or a similar development is being sold nearby it is worth telling the developer that you want to sell on. If they have greater demand for your type of property than they can meet they may well send prospective buyers around to you.

Buying

Make sure you buy a property built by a company which is a member of the National House Building Council or the Zurich Municipal Scheme. Almost all reputable builders and developers belong to these schemes which set standards for property development. Under the NHBC and Zurich schemes the building of the property is insured against the developer going bankrupt, so you won't be left with a half-built house and major defects found in the first two years will be put right by another builder. Few lending institutions will give you a mortgage on a property that has not been built by an NHBC or Zurich builder or under the supervision of a qualified and properly insured architect or surveyor.

If you are looking for a new-build home and there is a particular style or quality of home you like and have seen, contact the developer who can tell you if and where they are putting up similar properties. Scan the pages of local papers in the area you want to buy as well as the nationals for notices and adverts of new developments.

The Internet is also a great place to spot new-build property. But be aware that the pictures you see may be of similar completed developments, not the one they are selling. On the screen it all looks complete and quite beautiful, in reality it is a muddy building site. Each developer sets their own standard of finish. Some provide painted walls, carpets, fitted kitchens and chrome fittings in the bathroom. Others give you a shell.

The National House Building Council suggests you work your way through the following checklist when you are looking for a new-build home:

- Check the builder has a good national or local reputation; ask to look around houses they have built before.

- Is the builder a member of NHBC or Zurich? If so the property gets the council's ten-year Buildmark Cover after completion. Find out more about this cover by ringing freephone 0800 688 788 and leaving your details.

- Visit the site. If it seems tidy and well managed this gives you a clue about the attitude of the builder and his commitment to quality.

- Note a 'Pride in the Job' award stamp on site boards; this is a sign that the new home will be built with quality workmanship.

- Before completion your solicitor should check that the property has received its final certificate from NHBC.

- Consider getting a structural or home-buyer's survey done.

- If any problems are spotted within two years of completion put your complaint in writing to the builder and keep a copy.

The NHBC will provide you with a moving-in checklist to ensure the builder has properly completed the job. This includes everything from checking that the brickwork is clean and free of major chipping to verifying that paint hasn't splashed on to the windows and that the loft is insulated. They also provide a guide: 'Running in your new home'. You can consult their website – www. nhbc.co.uk – for information.

If you are buying off plan (before the property has been built) make sure you have in writing exactly what you are getting for your money. The following could be included or excluded: bathroom fittings, kitchen fittings, cupboards, internal and external decoration, carpets and floor coverings, electric sockets and fittings, garage and landscaping. You can negotiate; sometimes a developer who excludes certain things from the initial price may later agree to include them in order to close the deal.

Developers may tempt you by offering to pay solicitors' and estate-agents' fees and offering you a 100 per cent mortgage. This is particularly enticing for first-time buyers.

Take a close interest in the property as it is being built if it is still under construction when you buy. This way you can ensure it is meeting the standards you agreed on and expect. Don't complete until you are completely satisfied with the work that has been done, right down to the fitting of the front door. Apart from the obvious delight of being the first people to live in a house the advantages of buying something newly built include:

- Major repairs and redecoration should be unnecessary in the first few years.

- The property will be under NHBC or Zurich guarantee.

- If the house is still under construction you can sometimes influence certain features: bathroom and kitchen fittings, where the electric sockets go.

- A bigger mortgage is often available and can be easier to get as many developers arrange mortgage facilities for a whole estate.

But there are disadvantages:

- The property may take longer than scheduled to be completed. Many developers' timetables are based on wishful thinking; you should be prepared for an extra wait if you are buying off plan on the basis of a show home. To guard against this get the builder to agree to an absolutely final completion date, with a penalty clause in the form of some sort of compensation payable to you if he doesn't complete on time.

- A number of new-build properties suffer teething troubles: cracking plaster and sometimes settlement of the property.

- You might find yourself living for some time at the centre of a building site if you have bought early on in a scheme.

- The garden will probably be a raw plot of earth though more developers are now carrying out basic landscaping around new-build properties.

- The major disadvantage is that buyers usually pay a premium for the privilege of purchasing a brand new property. If you sell within a few years you might lose money, even in a rising market.

Remember:
It might be worth being the second rather than the first owner of a new-build home. You lose the thrill of being the first to take a bath, cook a meal and sleep in the property, but you pay less, don't have to deal with teething problems, probably won't be living in a building site and might have some sort of garden around you.

(See also **Builders, Extensions, First-time Buyers, Internet Buying and Selling**.)

O

OUTBUILDINGS

*Itching for what you want doesn't do much good;
you've got to scratch for it.*

Anon

From a garden shed to a block of Victorian stables, out-buildings can be the saving grace or disgrace of a property. On the one hand they offer enormous potential; on the other they can clutter up an otherwise pretty garden or property with ugly and useless structures.

On the positive side, if an outbuilding has some sort of foundation it is ripe for conversion – not just to a granny annexe or holiday cottage but also to a games room, office, workshop or studio. There is almost no limit to what a building can be converted to; it depends on what the planners will allow. A recent winner of the *Daily Telegraph* Home Building and Renovating Awards converted a stone-built Victorian laundry in the garden of his Scottish manse into a very beautiful two-bedroom home. If you are planning to convert stables or outbuildings into accommodation you will need planning permission but extra living space is a significant plus if you ever come to sell the property.

On the negative side, it is better to have no outbuildings than to have ugly structures which encroach on the main house or destroy aspects of the garden. There is often a temptation to keep something – just in case it is useful – but if it is an odd shape or in very bad condition it is probably better just to get rid of it.

Remember:
Outbuildings with foundations are a fixed part of the property and should not be moved when the owner sells the property. Outbuildings without foundations – like a lot of greenhouses and wooden summerhouses – are not fixtures and can be taken by the owner when they go.

(See also **Builders, Extensions, Garages, Planning Permission.**)

P

PACKING

Don't be frightened; I am recalled.
Pay, pack and follow at convenience.

Sir Richard Burton, English explorer, a note to his wife
on being replaced as British Consul to Damascus

Packing up to move house is when you find those school
reports you had forgotten and that pea-green and purple
vase given to you by a distant aunt for your twenty-first
birthday. You also discover lots of rubbish.

There are three basic ways to go about packing up to
move: you can do it all yourself, do part of it yourself or
leave the packing of every last tea bag (literally) to the
removal company. If you decide to do the whole move
yourself be sure you know how to lift heavy objects so as
not to injure your back; the last thing you need is to be
laid up with a bad back in your new home. The essentials
are:

- Stand straight in front of the object you plan to lift and
  close to it.

- Bend your knees to pick up; do *not* bend your back
  which you should keep straight; do not twist.

- Hold the object you are carrying as close to your body as possible.

- When putting an object down, bend your knees *not* your back.

Whether you plan to move everything yourself or have someone else do the bulk of the work, there are preliminaries that must be undertaken to ensure that everything arrives in the right place in your new home. It is no use leaving the packing to the removal company only to discover you are unpacking the cases you don't need first and in the wrong place because you haven't worked out a system. There are five stages to packing:

- Go round each room and remove everything you don't want and consign it to the dustbin, give it to a friend, take it to the rubbish dump or donate it to a local charity shop.

- Now go round again with colour-coded sticky labels and plan where all the furniture is to go in your new home using a colour for each destination: pink for the living room, yellow for the kitchen, blue for the master bedroom, etc. Don't put sticky labels on polished wood surfaces; tie a piece of string around a leg of the object and attach the colour coding to it. Remember to give your code to the removal men.

- Pack valuables that you don't want anyone else to handle, ready to transport them to the new house.

- Either leave it to the professionals to do on the day or start to pack up all the smaller items yourself, room by room.

A good removal firm should supply you with packing boxes and, even if they are not moving you, some will sell them to you. Supermarkets and off-licences are usually the best places to acquire extra cardboard boxes. If the removal firm has not supplied you with packing paper, arm yourself with piles of newspaper, several rolls of bubble wrap and some brown parcel tape. Cushion china and other breakables on a bed of crumpled paper, as well as wrapping them. Mark which way up the boxes go. Write FRAGILE in capital letters in red on relevant boxes and don't forget to code each box to show which room it should go into. Note on the side of the box the items that you have packed inside; it is easy to forget what is in each.

The advantage of packing yourself is that you end up sorting as you go. You can also label the boxes so you know what to unpack first and can store less urgent things in a garage, cellar or corner of a room.

- Prepare an emergency box for your arrival containing kettle, instant coffee, tea bags, milk, some robust mugs, a knife, a spoon, washing-up liquid, a packet of biscuits and a tea towel. Keep out your overnight bag for toothbrush, etc.

Remember:
Be careful to keep screws and fittings of furniture that has been dismantled for the move in separate labelled bags.

(See also **Removal Firms, Moving Timetable**.)

PADDOCKS AND PONIES

Go anywhere in England where there are natural,
wholesome, contented and really nice English people:
and what do you always find? That the stables are the
real centre of the household.

George Bernard Shaw, *Heartbreak House*

A move to the country often includes the Thelwell dream of a plump pony grazing in a post-and-rail fenced paddock at the end of the garden. Country-house agents estimate that over 30 per cent of their country house applicants request land for horses. Riding is part of the country scene but there never seem to be enough properties with paddocks to go around.

However, you can buy the right property for a pony without the paddock and stables. If the property includes a piece of agricultural land or an orchard this can be turned into a paddock without planning permission and a garage converted into a stable. If this is your intention make sure that the putative stable is not too close to the main house. Stable yards and all the paraphernalia of keeping horses can be unattractive and messy, even if the smell of hay and horse manure is perfume to your nose.

Remember that ponies are expensive animals; a good pony can cost anything from £700 and a competition horse as much as £50,000. Day-to-day expenses doing it all yourself – keeping a pony in your own paddock and stable – work out at about £200 a month plus competition entry fees and lessons broken down as follows: feed £10 a week in winter, 50p in summer; insurance £35 a month; worming £10 every ten weeks; shoes £50 every six weeks; saddles and other saddlery items £25 a month; vet bills average £500 a year; hay £14 a week; straw £6 a week (winter only).

Selling

Although a paddock and stables are a great selling point, make sure that they are clean and smelling of sweet fresh hay. Untidy smelly stables are nearly as off-putting as an untidy smelly house. If you have reason to believe the buyer is interested in keeping a pony but you do not have facilities, establish whether any adjacent farm land is for sale which could be turned into a paddock.

Buying

Don't get too taken in by the Thelwell dream. Properties with proper stables and paddocks do command a premium; you might do better to look at the possibility of buying adjacent land.

(See also **Adjacent Land and Property**, **Land**.)

PARKING

The car has become an article of dress without which we feel uncertain, unclad and incomplete in the urban compound.

Marshall McLuhan, *Understanding Media*

One national estate agent estimates the value of a house with off-street parking in central London as more than the value of the house plus the purchase of a garage two streets away. In the country, holiday cottage companies say that it is much harder to let even a summer cottage if it doesn't have parking outside.

We not only need to park, we need to park outside our doors, or as near to it as possible – because we don't want a hundred-yard dash in the rain when we come home and we don't want to lug the week's shopping or our holiday luggage through the streets. There are safety considerations as well: if you have children, a less able friend or granny, car parking close to the front door is not only desirable but necessary.

Buying

Don't underestimate the importance of somewhere to park; even if you don't drive most of your visitors will. The most delightful cottage in the most delightful village can be marred by parking frustrations. Always ask the owner where they park and enquire about any residents' parking schemes and how much these cost. If the parking is not on the property itself, visit several times at different points in the day or week to ensure that there isn't a problem parking nearby.

Beware double yellow lines, properties next to or near a pub or adjacent to a popular shopping area where you might have to fight to find a parking space.

(See also **Garages**.)

PATIOS

I just come and talk to the plants, really –
very important to talk to them, they respond I find.

Prince Charles, in a television interview, 1986

Our current love affair with outdoor living – when weather
permits – has lead to a boom in patios: sit-out and eat-out
areas which are gravelled, paved in brick or slate, cobbled
in stone or decked in wood. We relish the thought of
sitting on our terrace watching the rays of a slow setting
sun and sipping a glass of ice-cold something. We have all
indulged in cedar benches, wrought-iron garden chairs or
white or green moulded plastic furniture from a garden
superstore.

You don't need planning permission to put in a patio.
They cost anything from hundreds to thousands of pounds
to have professionally laid, depending on the materials you
decide to use. Concrete slabs are probably the cheapest
option, Portland stone may well be the most expensive.

Selling
Make a feature of your patio: pot up a few begonias and
ensure that the table and chairs are invitingly out, not
stacked in the shed in case of rain. Feed the dream.

Buying
If a patio doesn't exist look at where one could go. A patio
outside a pair of bedroom doors doesn't have the same

value as a patio outside the living room or kitchen. However pretty, it isn't a place where you will take friends and that is part of the amenity value.

(See also **Permitted Development Rights**.)

PERIOD PROPERTIES

Fifty years on from now, Britain will still be the country of long shadows on the cricket grounds, warm beer, invincible green suburbs, dog lovers and – as George Orwell said – old maids bicycling to Holy Communion through the morning mist.

John Major, speech to the Conservative Group for Europe, 1993

There is something particularly attractive about living in a piece of British history. A period property – whether a thatched black and white Tudor cottage or an Edwardian semi – evokes the lives of our ancestors and the craftsmanship of the past. There are properties in Britain that date back – at least in part – to the days of the Domesday Book. All buildings constructed before 1700 are listed as of special interest but for the great majority of us living in a period property means an Edwardian, Georgian or Victorian property. Each has its attractions.

Georgian
Faced in white stucco, stone or brick, the classical proportions of a Georgian property are pleasing to the eye. A

Georgian country house is for many a dream – like living in a life-sized doll's house – and consequently anything Georgian tends to go for slightly more. During the 1980s architects like Quinlan Terry modelled their exteriors on those of their popular Georgian predecessors. Interestingly, about three years ago, one of Quinlan's houses came up for sale a couple of counties away from a Georgian country house of very similar proportions. The two properties were advertised in *Country Life* and the susceptible reader could easily have believed that they were the same. So remarkable was the spot-the-difference effect that the *Daily Telegraph* carried a news story about the houses, and also mentioned both houses were being sold for a very similar price.

Georgian style continues to be popular and one reason why modern country-house developments have become more acceptable is that many have taken their inspiration from Mr Terry and used Georgian features.

Victorian

The Victorians were prodigious builders and many of the terraced houses that are a feature of Britain's towns and cities date from the mid and late nineteenth century. Although solid houses they are not generally considered as desirable as Georgian properties. However, Victorian houses do have many benefits including high ceilings and good-sized rooms. Those considered most desirable are properties that have kept some of their original features: marble fireplaces, tiled paths and hallways, stained-glass panels in doors and decorative stonework on the exterior. Early Victorian architecture is less ornate. Although Victorian terraced houses tend to look similar there are lots of small differences: in one street of houses there are square and semicircular bay windows, different styles of tiling, different widths of rooms and minor differences command.in layout. This is because many streets were developed by a number of different builders, each adding their own mark to homes that initially appear identical and often building slightly larger or smaller homes to fit the available space.

One of the major advantages of Victorian houses is that most of them have cellars. Originally used for coal, these basements have come into their own again as storage space.

Edwardian

Edwardian houses have a certain suburban garden charm, perhaps because many thousands of them were built on the outskirts of Britain's major cities in the early decades of the twentieth century. Apart from the very best by architects like Edwin Lutyens (who sometimes worked in partnership with the landscape gardener Gertrude Jekyll) these properties are often rather unfairly sniffed at by architectural gurus as repetitive and tiresome, lacking the quality of brick, stone and tile work of their earlier Victorian neighbours.

But the Edwardians did know how to design comfortable homes and the terraced houses they built often manage to get away from the railway-carriage-corridor feel of earlier Victorian terraces. Panelling, tiling and stained glass are also a feature of this period, sometimes with a flavour of art nouveau and the later art deco. This was the time when England's garden cities were laid out.

PERMITTED DEVELOPMENT RIGHTS

I have a cunning plan.
Baldrick, *Blackadder*, 1987

There are a lot of things you can do to a property without planning permission but it is worth knowing just what these are before you start knocking walls down and putting others up. What you can and can't do in a home is regulated by the General Permitted Development Order 1995 which covers the following area:

1. The enlargement, improvement or alteration of a house. Extensions to houses are permitted provided the extension does not exceed:

    - 50 cubic metres or 10 per cent in the case of terraced housing and housing within National Parks, areas of outstanding natural beauty or conservation areas

    - 70 cubic metres or 15 per cent (whichever is the greater) in other cases to a maximum of 115 cubic metres

    - the height of the highest part of the roof of the original house

- 4 metres in height if it is within 2 metres of the boundary

- 50 per cent of the ground cover area of the original building

The extension should not be nearer the road than the original property or less than 20 metres from it whichever is the nearest. Development should not involve alterations to the roof.

2. Altering the roof in order to enlarge the property. The development should not:

- exceed the height of the highest part of the existing roof

- extend beyond the plane of the existing roof shape on to a highway frontage

- increase the cubic content of the property by more than 40 cubic metres in the case of a terraced house, or 50 cubic metres in other cases

- result in a material alteration to the shape of the house

3. Construction of a porch outside any external door. You can put up a porch as long as it:

- does not exceed 3 square metres in area

- does not exceed 3 metres in height

- is not within 2 metres of the boundary

4. Development of a leisure facility within the grounds. Development is permitted provided:

   - it does not relate to a new dwelling or satellite antenna

   - the building is no closer to the road than the original property or within 20 metres of the road (whichever is nearer)

   - it is not within 5 metres of the original house

   - it is no more than 10 cubic metres in size

   - the height of the building does not exceed 4 metres (with ridged roof) or 3 metres in any other case

   - the total area does not exceed 50 per cent of the total area of the curtilage

5. Other things you can do without planning permission:

   - Create a hard surface within the grounds of a property for any use 'incidental to the enjoyment of the dwelling house' (car parking or patio).

   - Provide a store for domestic heating oil, though the capacity of the container should not exceed 3,500 litres and it should not be more than 3 metres above ground level or nearer the road than the original building or within 20 metres (whichever is nearer).

- Install or replace a satellite antenna as long as it does not exceed 45cm if located on a chimney or 90cm if located elsewhere, and there is no other satellite antenna on the property. The highest part of the antenna must be below the highest part of the roof or, where relevant, chimney.

- Put up a new boundary fence or wall, as long as it is not more than one metre high along the boundary adjacent to a road and not more than two metres high anywhere else.

- Construct an access to a roadway, as long as it is not a trunk road or classified road.

Remember:

If you live in a listed building, an area of outstanding natural beauty, a conservation area or a National Park the rules are different and much more limiting.

Whether planning permission is necessary or not, building regulations will apply to any work that you do.

Wherever you live, if in doubt as to whether the development you plan to carry out is permitted, check with the local planning authority.

(See also **Builders**, **Listed Buildings**, **Planning Permission**, **Surveyors**.)

PETS

Love me, love my dog.
Sixteenth-century proverb

From the goldfish to the guinea pig and the golden retriever, pets have to be taken into careful consideration when it comes to moving house.

Selling

If your pet is loud, bouncy or smelly shut it in the kitchen or even the car (safely) while people are viewing your property. Open a lot of windows and clean like mad. You may be immune to the smell of cat, dog or guinea pig but the viewer may not and it could easily put them off the property.

Buying

Remember to think about your pet in the choice of your new home including any rules that apply if you are moving to a flat or sheltered accommodation. You may think the flat will happily accommodate Fluffy the cat or Billy the dog but if the lease says no pets that is what it means and some very tearful goodbyes will have to be made. (Fish are generally allowed in virtually all properties.)

If the home is more important than the pet, then you are in the difficult situation of needing to find your furry or feathered friend a new home. This may be less traumatic than you think. Your first port of call should be the vet who may know of a family looking for a pet just like yours and if not will be able to put you in touch with a reputable pet-rescue centre. Animals in rescue centres with a known history are much easier to place than those without a history or found wandering the streets. Many rescue centres operate a policy of not allowing families to take a rescued stray because they are unsure of how they will react to a family environment, so pets with a history are in demand.

If you have a pedigree animal contact the breeders who will put you in touch with whoever rescues that particular breed. There is usually a waiting list for these pets.

Moving pets

Pets will increase the stress of a move. To make things easier it is better not to have them around.

Both for your pet's peace of mind and for yours it is well worth finding someone who will take care of them on the day and possibly for a few days more while you sort things out. Organize this well in advance as it is not something you want to be worrying about the day before you move. And you certainly don't want to be hunting for a confused cat or dog and wondering where you packed its basket as you try to lock up and leave the house. Too many distressed animals get lost and forgotten during the hectic process of moving.

Once your pet arrives at a new property remember:

- Before you let a dog out for the first time make sure the garden is well fenced.

- Cats hate new environments. Shut the cat in a room with bedding, its favourite cushion or chair, water, food and a litter tray. Keep all windows closed. Leave it there while you sort out. Once you release the cat into the house keep it inside (all windows and exterior doors closed) for at least twenty-four and preferably forty-eight hours. It is probably worth giving the cat a collar with name tag for the first weeks you are in a property.

- Birds can be transported in their cages with a cover on. They are susceptible to temperature so don't put them in a draughty room in the new house or in a substantially colder room than the one they used in your previous home.

- Small furry animals need to be transported in a chew-proof box. Once they have arrived and are back in their hutch or cage with their favourite toys, water, food and clean bedding it's home from home.

- Fish don't mind moving but don't like their water being changed so put them in a leak-proof thick polythene bag with some of the water from the tank or pond they have been living in.

- Exotic pets of any variety should not be moved without consulting a specialist.

(See also **Preparing Your Home for Sale**, **Removal Firms**, **Selling Checklists**.)

PLANNING PERMISSION

Castles in the air – they are so easy to take refuge in.
And easy to build, too.
Henrik Ibsen, *The Master Builder*

Many people move with the aim of immediately extending their new home. If this is your intention, before you make an offer check with the agent and the owner that a previous application for extension has not been turned down. If this is the case you may need to look elsewhere for a property. Remember that development of listed buildings or properties in conservation areas, National Parks and areas of outstanding natural beauty is heavily restricted.

After purchase, if there appears to be no reason in principle why you should not put on an extension you will need to apply for planning permission, unless your plans come under permitted development rights. Before applying, talk to your neighbours and anyone else who might be affected. They will find out anyway because the planning authority will approach them for their views. It is much more neighbourly to forewarn them and seek their views on what you plan to do.

Extending a home takes time: months, even a year or more. Appoint a surveyor or architect to draw up the plans you need to apply for planning permission which can take some weeks or months to come through. You can shorten your wait by applying for planning permission after you have exchanged contracts and before you have completed.

You do not have to own a property in order to apply for planning permission to change it.

Discuss your plans with the local planning authority, who will guide you as to what will and will not be acceptable. Planners are mostly concerned with significant changes to external appearance, but you must remember that however small the extension it must not affect your neighbours' light or privacy. Get hold of the booklet 'Planning: A guide for Householders' produced by the Department of the Environment, Transport and the Regions (DETR) and the Welsh Office and available at council offices and Citizens Advice Bureaux. The information is also available on the DETR website: www.planning.detr.gov.uk. It is worth contacting the Royal Town Planning Institute who publish a number of leaflets covering different aspects of planning permission. Information is available on their website: www.rtpi.org.uk.

Listen carefully to the advice of the planners; it is up to them to recommend approval or rejection of a plan that goes before the planning committee. Ignore what they say at your peril. You will need to fill in an application form for planning permission to alter or extend your property. The fee for the application is usually under £100. Find out when planning meetings are held; ensure your application is in several weeks before they meet and gets comfortably on to the agenda.

If you don't get planning permission you can appeal against the decision. However, it is worth talking first to the planning officers as there may be some minor change you can make to satisfy the planning committee. If you are still unsuccessful but feel the decision is unreasonable you can appeal against the decision to the DETR. This has to be done within six months of the decision being made by the council. Information about this is also on the DETR website.

Remember:
You are unlikely to get planning permission for any extension that increases the volume of the property by more than 50 per cent.

Whether planning permission is necessary or not building regulations will apply to any work that you do.

(See also **Architects**, **Builders**, **Extensions**, **Permitted Development Rights**.)

PREPARING YOUR HOME FOR SALE

You cannot have everything and certainly cannot dust everything. To cite Conran's Law of Housework – it expands to fill the time available plus half an hour: so obviously it is never finished . . . Keep housework in its place, which, you will remember, is underfoot.

Shirley Conran, *Superwoman*

You have decided to sell up and move – to a bigger or smaller property, to the country, to the town, to the endless lush suburbs – but before you invite an agent in to value your house, prepare it for sale. Even an estate agent is not immune to a stuffy untidy house or an unkempt garden and will not value the property quite so highly.

Inside and out inspect your home objectively and think of ways in which you could inexpensively enhance its appeal. We get used to the way things are: we cease to notice that one of the windows in the bedroom was never given more than an undercoat; we are inured to the chipped paintwork on the front door and the untidy pile of bikes and boots in the garden shed. But keep a sense of balance about what you do; it is worth repainting the front door but not refitting the bathroom or the kitchen or recarpeting the stairs.

Buyers may be put off by properties where the owners constantly point out expensive things they have just done: the new carpet on the stairs, pink tiles in the bathroom or gold and green striped designer wallpaper in the bedroom. The thought that so much money has been spent on things you would not want to live with but would think it wasteful to discard is depressing. The house with the ten-year-old orange carpet and grubby purple walls seems a better proposition; they can be ripped out or painted over without guilt. The golden rule is to clean, clear and tidy up the decor but not spend a fortune. No house or flat is the same but musts include:

- Clear the house and garden of all unnecessary clutter.

- A thorough spring clean, ensuring you get rid of cobwebs and any animal smells. Wash down skirting boards, window frames and doors. Pay special attention to the bathroom and kitchen.

- Window cleaning inside and out.

- Ensure all door handles and light switches are working.

- Check all light bulbs are working.

- Carry out all those little repairs (dripping tap, missing tile on the roof) that could take the edge off the appearance of your property.

- Clean the carpets and curtains, professionally if necessary.

- Tidy up the decor: paint the front door, give a coat of paint to any room looking dirty or shabby (use a neutral colour), paint any badly stained, chipped or cracked woodwork and restick or patch wallpaper.

- Mow grass, trim hedges, weed flower beds and if necessary brighten up the garden by planting some cheap and cheerful flowers near the house or in the window boxes.

- Ensure the garden gate works and if necessary give it a coat of paint.

Don't spend money on expensive fittings, equipment, decorative finishes, carpets and curtains and don't redecorate using strong colours. Never leave your house in a mess expecting buyers to envisage how nice it will look tidied up or appreciate its 'lived-in' atmosphere. Ask a good friend with a nice house their unbiased opinion on anything else that could be done but don't be dragged into any major expense. Once you have finished call in the estate agents, if you are using them. The more presentable your house the better price the agents will be able to negotiate for you. Ask them if there is anything else you need to do; they might notice something that has completely escaped your notice.

Most properties are sold within the first five minutes of being viewed. A minimal investment of time and money to make it look its best is well worth the effort. Think of these chores as the equivalent of polishing your shoes and wearing a clean pressed suit for a job interview. A property that looks outwardly cared for and loved gives the buyer the impression that it is structurally sound, allowing the buyer to fall in love with the house rather than first worrying about retiling the roof. Once someone loves a house retiling the roof doesn't seem quite such a problem.

Remember:
You must be prepared for buyers who want to snoop in the cupboards and under the stairs; these too need to be in an acceptable state and not stuffed full of things which tumble out when opened.

(See also **Estate Agents**, **Viewing**, **Buying Checklists**, **Selling Checklists**.)

PRICING

A toad's a beauty in a duck's eye.

Traditional Cornish saying

A special word about pricing: it's only human to believe – once we have settled into our home – that there is something a little special and unique about it.

Selling

When pricing your property take a hard look at its faults. Sellers usually look at prices in an estate agent's window to see what their property is worth and there might be five properties on view which seem similar in size, style and area but all at slightly different prices. It is natural to tend to equate your home with the most expensive, not noticing that the rooms or garden are just that bit bigger, the kitchen that bit more modern and the location a fraction more desirable.

If you want to sell your property it is not sensible to set the price above those of similar houses or to imagine it has qualities that it doesn't. Take advice from the agents; if they are reputable then they should be able to give you a very good guide as to what the property is worth. It is in their interests not to underprice the house as the more it makes the more commission they will receive.

Before selling it can be interesting to look at trends in property prices nationally. The Nationwide website –

www.nationwide.co.uk – has a monthly review of the house price index.

Buying

When buying property the aim is get the best property for the lowest price. But you have to pay for a better position, more space and a property in good condition (even if the decor is not to your taste). The most difficult situations occur when you are interested in buying an unusual or special property as comparisons with other homes do not provide a guide to price. The agent will have struggled long and hard to work out how much the 'special' is worth.

Recently one British-based international agent was faced with pricing an extraordinary property: a magnificent castle in its own walled grounds of fifty acres plus, with staff accommodation and lodge houses all in spectacularly good condition. It was sited on the edge of the city of Dublin, which has become one of the most fashionable cities in Europe, and was, in the agent's words, 'unique'. A guide price was set of £10 million plus. The agent was confident of obtaining well over the asking price as there was quite a bit of international interest in the property: £12 million perhaps? Three months later I asked the agent about the castle; it had finally changed hands for over £20 million. Never underestimate the amount people are prepared to pay if they really, really want something and there is nothing else like it.

Few of us are in the Dublin castle league but occasionally you come across the property that matches your dream. Try your best to get it, if you can afford it; your home is probably the most important material thing you purchase in life. On the other hand don't find yourself straying into a price bracket you can't afford. Examine your bank balance, your motivation and your heart.

(See also **Do-It-Yourself Buying and Selling, Estate agents**.)

PRIVATE TREATY

Probably one of the most private
things in the world is an egg until it is broken.
M. F. K. Fisher, *How to Cook a Wolf*

This is when a property changes hands without appearing in an estate agent's window or in an advertisement. No brochure will be printed and no sign will appear outside the house. Unless you are a friend of the owner you probably won't know they are selling until the moving vans arrive.

Private deals have advantages and they are most prevalent at the top end of the market. 'Selling a property privately appeals to owners at the top end of the market or someone who is in public life because they often place an extremely high value on privacy. As soon as a property is on the market, anyone can establish the value of their property, view it and speculate about the reasons for their move. They shy away from that invasion of privacy,' says one agent who carries out a high proportion of private deals every year. Selling your house privately means that you avoid the idle and curious, in fact all but the most serious of applicants.

But it is not only the rich and famous who prefer to deal privately. A lot of properties change hands privately during a sluggish market because their owners don't want to put the property on the open market and risk it not selling. A private deal allows them to test the water and back out if the right buyer doesn't appear. However, in a booming market, most agents would suggest to all but the most reclusive clients that they will get the best price if a property is openly marketed.

Selling

Unless you happen to know of someone interested in buying your property, you can only decide to go down this route if your house or flat comes into the highly desirable category. If it does then take one of two routes:

- Approach one or two of the top agents in the area or a top national agent. Speak to one of the partners and explain that you might be interested in selling but do not wish to have the sale publicized in any way. They will value the house and tell you if they think they can sell it for you. Most agents are happy to keep property deals confidential when asked; they would prefer to make the deal rather than lose it because of a breach of confidentiality.

- Approach a major property search company. Contact the Association of Relocation Agents and look up national agents or those working in the area where you want to sell. They are always on the lookout for good properties for their clients and may well have just the person to purchase your home. You should get your property independently valued as relocation agents work for the buyer not the seller.

(See also **Do-It-Yourself Buying and Selling, Relocation Agents**.)

PROPERTY MISDESCRIPTION ACT

A completely honest answer always gives you the advantage of surprise in the House of Commons.

Jonathan Lynn and Sir Anthony Jay, 'The Tangled Web' an episode of *Yes, Prime Minister*

Honesty is the best policy. Not that long ago a house which was just old could be described as historic, a garden could be described as fifty feet long, even when twenty of that was a tiny side passage, and inappropriately flattering adjectives were scattered like grains of pepper to spice up property sales particulars.

The Property Misdescription Act 1991 came into force in 1993 and outlawed such practices. The Trades Descriptions Act further defined the rules to be applied to property particulars. Now agents are at pains to ensure they don't step out of line. The phrase 'believed to be' usually means the agent is not absolutely sure of his facts.

If after you have purchased a property you think you have been seriously misled by the agents, you may claim against them or the seller under the Property Misdescription Act. But it is better not to be fooled in the first place. To avoid disappointment always ensure that the proper checks on the house have been carried out by a surveyor.

(See also **Estate Agents**, **Surveyors**.)

PROPERTY SHOPS

> Years ago a person, he was unhappy, didn't know
> what to do with himself – he'd go to church, start a revolution
> – something. Today you're unhappy? Can't figure it out?
> What is the salvation? Go shopping.
>
> Arthur Miller, *The Price*

A property shop is exactly that; it is where details of houses and flats including a photograph are displayed. As the seller you pay a set fee to have your details displayed and available.

In pre-Internet days these were the coming thing. Today, except in Scotland, they are less so as more and more people wishing to carry out their own sale turn to the Internet. The most successful property shops are often run by firms of solicitors who establish an estate-agency department and add the actual buying and selling of property to the legal requirements of a purchase or sale. The solicitor undertakes the sale for you. The fee you are charged is based on the sale price of your house and has the major advantage of including the conveyancing. Property shops are well established in Scotland where solicitors are generally much more central to the sale and purchase of property.

Selling

If you are planning to sell your house yourself then it is worth approaching a property shop in your area. You will be a given a form to fill in about the flat or house you are selling. When this is completed and returned with a non-refundable fee, details and a photograph of your property will be displayed. Some property shops match sellers with buyers and provide a list of potential buyers for you to contact. Then you are on your own.

The advantages of property shops is that you are fully in charge of the sale and of setting the price. You also, of course, cut out the estate agent's fee. On the other hand, a property-shops' potential buyers may be fewer in number than an estate agent could provide. You also have to do everything yourself: deal with the enquiries, show everyone around your property and there is no one to help you with negotiating when someone finally makes an offer.

Buying

Potential buyers browse in the same way as they would through the window of an estate agency, but having obtained details of the property contact the owner directly to view and to take negotiations further. Bargains are probably to be had but at the same time you could find yourself paying over the odds for a property.

(See also **Do-it-yourself Buying and Selling, Internet Buying and Selling, Scotland.**)

Q

QUEUE JUMPING WITHOUT GAZUMPING

An Englishman, even if he is alone,
forms an orderly queue of one.
George Mikes, Hungarian-born writer, *How to be an Alien*

There is condemnation of gazumping by all but those who do it; it is at best an aggressive way to push yourself to the front of the queue. But there are other, less unpleasant, ways to put yourself in front of other buyers, sometimes even if your competitors are offering a slightly higher price for the property.

The ultimate is to be a cash buyer: you are in the GO position on the real-life Monopoly board with lots of money, able to buy whatever you land on. There is technically nothing to stop you writing out a banker's draft for the asking price and receiving the keys to your new house within an hour or two of seeing it. During boom times agents tell stories of just how quickly a property can change hands; a twenty-four-hour handover is by no means unique.

But not everyone can be a cash buyer. Most people need mortgages and a good percentage of buyers have homes to sell at the same time. There are other reasonable ways to push yourself up the queue so that when the perfect property floats on to the agents desk you are the first person the agent calls and are in the best position to move. Most importantly you need to:

1. Get your financing in place and appoint a solicitor before you start to look.

2. Focus on estate agencies and websites which are prime dealers in the type and price of property you want. Go into agents' offices, make name and face contact with their salespeople. Keep a daily watch on the websites; find out when they upload new information – all the time, once a day, twice a week?

3. Impress upon the best agents your readiness to move: you've done the research, you know what you want, the finance is ready, you have appointed a solicitor. Be very clear about what you are looking for and where; tell them the 'musts' on your list. Be realistic; you rarely get exactly what you want. Be keen; give them your work, home and mobile numbers. Be charming and interested in what they have to say; we all prefer to deal with people who are likeable and efficient. If you have made the right impression you will have pushed yourself up their calls list.

4. Phone all the other agents in the area just in case the property of your dreams ends up landing on their books. Proceed as above.

5. When you see or hear about a property that might suit you make an appointment to view immediately. You are at an advantage if you are first.

6. Make notes as you go round of good points, bad points and layout.

7. If you cannot keep an appointment or are late call the agent or seller immediately. If you arrive at an appointment and realize before you go in that it is not for you, tell them straight away.

8. If you really like a property, be enthusiastic and make an appointment to view a second time (preferably with a friend) within the next twenty-four hours.

9. Call the best agents daily to find out about new properties that have come in.

Remember:
The golden rule is to keep your cool and your charm. Don't get cross or impatient: the less stressed you are the more people will want to deal with you.

(See also **Contract Races, Estate Agents, Gazumping, Gazundering, Home Hunting, Sealed Bids, Solicitors and Licensed Conveyancers, Buying Checklists, Selling Checklists**.)

R

RELOCATION AGENTS

The theory and practice of gamesmanship or
the art of winning games without actually cheating.

Stephen Potter

Twelve years ago everyone wondered what a relocation agent was. The idea that you would pay someone to find a house for you seemed absurd unless you were seriously rich. Surely you would still have to view the property and make the final decision so why employ a middle man?

But in the 1990s, in the post boom and bust market, good properties were hard to find as many people struggled with negative equity and others simply decided to stay put. Those needing or wanting to move found that there were too few people out there playing the property game. For some it seemed they were constantly getting to the right house just too late, or spending their lives viewing properties that were perfect in the brochure but turned out to be too small, beside a motorway or railway, under a flight path or next to the local bus station. Tired and frustrated buyers needed help and relocation agents had found their niche.

For a fee – which varies from hundreds to thousands of pounds and is sometimes based on a percentage of the price of the property you buy – relocation agents carry out the search for you and argue that they are in a better position to do so for a number of reasons.

- They know the area intimately.

- They are buying agents so selling agents in the area are keen to notify them of properties coming on to their books or already on the market.

- Anyone wanting a private deal will tell them in order to tap into a number of potential buyers.

- Their professional skills enable them to carry out price negotiations to your advantage; as a buying agent they act for you the buyer and not the seller.

These are convincing arguments and the relocation industry took off. The best belong to the Association of Relocation Agents which was founded in 1986. Members must abide by a set of rules. A list of members and rules is available by post or on the association's website: www.relocationagents.com. They also publish a guide for people moving to the UK from overseas and give education, taxation and health advice.

Many relocation agents are former estate agents – gamekeepers turned poachers – and, increasingly, larger estate agency firms are opening their own relocation division. Although the major appeal of relocation agents is still to people spending over £500,000, if you do find you are pushed for time and want to move it may well be worth contacting one. Most will spend several hours talking to you in your home about the sort of property you would like to purchase and some have an uncanny knack of knowing exactly what you want.

If you go down this route, check out the agency thoroughly and get some personal recommendations. Don't part with any money until you are sure the relocation agent understands what you are looking for and can meet your needs.

(See also **Estate Agents**, **Location**.)

REMOVAL FIRMS

There is in all change something at once sordid and
agreeable, which smacks of infidelity and household removals.
This is sufficient to explain the French Revolution.

Charles Baudelaire, *Journaux intimes*

Most of us acquire piles and piles of useless and not so useless paraphernalia that as years pass become an invisible mountain; hiding at the top of a cupboard or in the cellar is everything from the exercise bike you only used for a month three years ago to the fondue set your godfather gave you for your eighteenth birthday. However ruthlessly you weed out the rubbish, you are going to expend a lot of energy hiring a van or truck and moving everything yourself or you are going to have to get in the professionals: a reputable removal firm who will pack up and take your belongings from A to B.

As you are moving your worldly goods it is better to get a good experienced firm with solid insurance backing in case anything goes wrong than to go bargain hunting; the deal may be good but the move could end in tears. To find a good firm first ask friends, family and colleagues who they used, why and what the service was like. If you can't get a good recommendation call the British Association of Removers (BAR) and ask them to give you a list of reputable companies in your area (they also have a website: www.barmovers.com). If the removal firm you use is a member of BAR it is worth remembering they operate the OXBOXX scheme, taking bags and boxes of things you don't want any more to Oxfam. You will be supplied with OXBOXX labels by the removal firm. They also provide a range of useful leaflets about moving pets, plants and a checklist for planning your move and moving. BAR also operates a care line for when things go wrong which will help you to find an emergency plumber to fix a leak or legal assistance if the previous occupier of a property has not moved out.

Call up three or four selected removal firms and ask them for an estimate in writing. The cost usually depends on the amount of stuff you are moving and how far you are going. When someone comes to do the estimate make sure you discuss pictures, antiques, audio equipment and anything fragile or special to you – and don't forget things stored in the garage or attic. If some items have to be picked up from somewhere else or there is more than one delivery address, make this clear.

When you get the estimate, check whether it includes insurance. If not, establish whether your home-contents policy covers removals or if you need to get special insurance. Check what the removal company will do if any of your goods are damaged. Also find out if you are being charged on an hourly, half-day or daily rate and ask if you can leave drawers complete with clothes or other contents. You can cut removal costs by packing everything or most things yourself but remember that if you've packed it the removal firm will not be responsible for it being damaged in transit. It will also be cheaper if you move smaller things yourself in several car loads, do all the unpacking yourself and return the cases to the firm, and move on a certain day of the week; some companies charge less for unpopular removal days. Friday is the most popular day. Packing and car runs are seriously time consuming and exhausting but doing your own unpacking suits many people as it allows you to decide where to put things in a more leisurely fashion.

Don't necessarily chose the cheapest firm; chose one you trust. When you have decided, telephone the company to discuss finer details. Most firms will send you a contract to sign and return – be careful to read the small print. You will be expected to book a firm date for the job and could be charged a cancellation fee if you move it without reasonable notice.

Leaving your old home

- First show the foreman around the house – including cellars, lofts and garden sheds – indicate everything that is to be moved and also explain any labelling system.

- If you are leaving the carpets make sure that the movers put something down to protect the carpet in the entrance hall and up the stairs if it is a wet day.

- Leave them to it but don't forget to offer cups of tea and stay on hand in case they can't work out how to dismantle something which needs to be taken apart for the move.

- Before the van leaves check the house, cellar, cupboards and grounds to make sure everything has been loaded on to the van. Make sure the driver knows where to go and make arrangements about what to do if they arrive first – a mobile number or central contact number.

Arriving at your new home

- Make sure the hall and stair carpets are protected.

- Make sure the removal men understand your labelling system; put coloured stickers on the doors as a reminder.

- Be in the room when particularly heavy pieces of furniture are brought in so you can tell the movers exactly where to place them.

- More tea.

- When they have finished unloading, check the van to see that everything has gone.

- It is normal to tip the men carrying out the removal for a good job done. Ten pounds to each removal man per day would be reasonable. The easiest option is to give all the money to the foreman or woman and ask them to ensure it is shared out.

(See also **Fixtures and Fittings, Buying Checklists, Selling Checklists**.)

RENTING

And my parents finally realize that I'm kidnapped and they snap into action immediately: they rent out my room.
Woody Allen, in *Woody Allen and His Comedy*

Most people have lived in a rented flat or house. For many this happens at university in a shambolic and draughty house with a bunch of other students; or you move away from the parental home to take up a job and share a flat with others in a similar position. Although most people ultimately move on to buying their own homes there are times when you once again become tenant or landlord: you might get a temporary job in another country or another part of Britain; your house may be uninhabitable due to building works; you might be thinking about a dramatic change – moving from country to town or vice versa – and want to find out first whether this is an option you will enjoy. This book is primarily about buying and selling but it is important to know the basics about renting and how to get the best of the deal on both sides of the renting fence if you get caught in one of the above situations.

Landlord

Before putting your property out to rent:

- Ensure all services are in good working order – heating, lighting, etc.

- Mend any dripping taps, inefficient showers, appliances that don't work properly.

- Paint any rooms that look grubby or shabby.

- Pack up and store anything sentimentally or otherwise valuable. Many people won't want much furniture anyway. Furniture you do leave – particularly sofas and beds – has to meet fire-resistant standards.

- Clean windows and have all curtains and carpets professionally cleaned.

- Ensure garden is tidy: lawns cut, hedges trimmed, etc.

To let your property either advertise it in a newspaper, magazine or a website, or approach an estate agent specializing in lettings and ask them to let it for you. If you decide to use an agent they should be registered with the Association of Residential Lettings Agents (ARLA) which has strict rules about the handling of rented property. Using an agent is the safer option as rents vary enormously and it is not so easy to establish what your house will be worth in the rental market. More importantly, using an agent gives you an added layer of security. Agents will:

- Charge you 10 per cent per annum for finding a tenant and a further 5 per cent per annum for managing the property.

- Ask tenants for 1–3 months' rent as deposit on the property and up to three-months' rent in advance.

- Check tenants' financial, employment and personal references.

- Draw up an Assured Shorthold Tenancy agreement for signature by you and the tenant which will last for six months to a year. Very few agents will take on the task of finding you a tenant for less than six months. Most agreements are for a year and are then renewable. If the agreement is renewed, the agent, even if they have not been managing the property for you, will charge you a further 10 per cent. This is usually deducted from the first month's rent.

- If managing the property the agent will deal with any problems that arise: blocked drains to a broken dishwasher.

Call in two or three agents to tell you what they expect to get for the property. You do not usually have to limit yourself to one agent as the standard fee of 10 per cent is charged in almost all circumstances. If you have a choice of tenant it is preferable to let to a family than to a group of people sharing as you are dealing with one official tenant rather than five. You should also expect the tenant to want to negotiate the rent.

Once you have agreed to let the property you will need to have an inventory drawn up of what is being left for the tenants; this should even include scratch marks on walls and furniture. Most agents insist that the inventory be carried out by a professional independent inventory clerk in order to avoid arguments at a later date. Go through the inventory with the clerk before signing to ensure it is correct and nothing has been missed. It is a good idea to take photographs of rooms and particular pieces of furniture. Even if you haven't left any furniture it is necessary for someone neutral to go through the house and garden and note its condition. Although as landlord you are responsible for general wear and tear, there is a lot of difference in the way different families treat a property and it is best to allow the professionals to deal with this side of things.

Meet the tenant; it is useful to know who will be living in your home and they will normally appreciate information about local shops, restaurants, walks, transport, etc. They may want to know about your cleaning lady or gardener.

Remember:
Agents normally take their fee out of the first month's rent.

Tenant

The first thing you have to remember is that you will have to put up with someone else's taste. Decide on your priorities: a modern easy-to-run property or one described as full of character – which can mean anything from creaking stairs and odd-shaped rooms to bizarre decor and layout. If you are renting someone's home it is worth meeting the landlord who can tell you about the quirks of the property and, more valuably, about local transport, shops, etc.

If a property is furnished but you have your own furniture ask if the landlord's furniture can be removed. Most landlords are happy to do this. Ensure that a careful inventory is made of the property by a professional inventory clerk before you move in; you do not want to end up paying for damage that was already there.

Remember:
It is unlikely that you will be able to rent a property for less than six months.

Before you move in you will usually be expected to pay three-months' rent in advance plus a further three-months' rent which will be held as a deposit against any damage to the property.

A cautionary tale

It is a particularly good idea to let out your home and rent somewhere else if you are moving from one area to another and you are not absolutely sure it is a permanent move or you will like it. This story featured in the *Telegraph* illus-trates the pitfalls.

The family lived in London. Father was made redundant but found a job in Brighton. This seemed ideal: swopping London fumes for fresh air and sea views. The family sold their south London house and moved but one week after their arrival father lost his Brighton job. He then found another job back in London.

They decided that, having just moved and the children having just settled into new schools, they would stay in Brighton and father would commute to London to work. But commuting doesn't suit everyone; he hated the journey and found he had to leave so early in the morning and was back so late at night that he saw little of his children except at weekends. A sociable couple, they also found he was too tired to do anything but eat and go to bed during the week and was busy doing things around the house at weekends. No one was happy; life was not what it was; the family missed their London friends and the access to theatres, art galleries and museums. The family decided that for the happiness of them all they would move back to London.

This was 1997 and London prices were moving up fast, Brighton's rather slower. They could no longer afford to move back into the area they had moved out of just a year before, and had to buy further out.

(See also **Estate Agents**.)

REPOSSESSION

Annual income twenty pounds,
annual expenditure nineteen nineteen six, result happiness.
Annual income twenty pounds, annual expenditure
twenty pounds nought and six, result misery.
Charles Dickens, *David Copperfield*

Don't, please don't let this happen to you. This is the Mr Micawber moment and is one of the reasons why it is never worth mortgaging yourself beyond the limits set by banks and buildings societies. You can press them into giving you more but unless you have some extra income to support this extra expense it is always an unwise move. Remember that in 1995 25,000 homes were repossessed.

Selling
If you are having a problem paying your mortgage, some building societies and banks will help you over a difficult patch by deferring payments; it is worth talking to them. The Building Societies Association/Council of Mortgage Lenders produces a fact sheet on arrears and repossessions which is available free by calling their consumer information line. Don't despair; there are lots of different ways of rescuing the situation if you are prepared to do so.

One mother featured in the *Telegraph* told of how they managed when her husband lost his job within weeks of her giving birth to a second child. She immediately registered her home with an agency offering bed and breakfast accommodation, tidied up two of the three bedrooms ready for paying guests and even prepared the living room with its sofa bed as a third letting possibility. Within a week the family were living in one bedroom, one bathroom and the kitchen with amazing good humour. It was more than a year before her husband managed to get another job, but they survived and paid the bills. They also discovered they quite liked having paying guests and have since moved to a bigger house where both they and the guests can be more comfortably accommodated.

Another possibility is to remortgage your home – perhaps over a longer term – in order to reduce your outgoings. If you can't find a way to rescue the situation and your finances don't start to recover quite rapidly then you have no alternative but to think about moving out before you are moved.

Remember:
Avoid repossession if at all possible as it could affect your chances of getting another mortgage when things do improve financially.

Buying
There is something almost morbid about buying a repossessed property. Viewing can be a depressing experience as repossessed houses may have been damaged by the embittered former owners. Vandalized kitchens, doors without knobs and lights without switches can be expected.

This does devalue the property but be aware that the bank or building society is under an obligation to get the best price possible. This means that although they may technically accept your offer they will then re-advertise the property to ensure they cannot get a higher offer from someone else. They might even suggest offers are made by tender or a contract race is entered into. Keep your cool and don't be persuaded into making a higher bid; hang on, they are duty bound to come back to you if a higher offer does appear. Another downside of buying a repossessed property is that although the lenders are the owners of the property, they won't be able to tell you about the quirks or delights of what you are buying. If you go ahead you should make sure early on that the locks are changed and have a very good survey done of the house as you will have no comeback against the previous owner.

Remember:

You are not pushing someone out of their home, they have done that themselves. By buying the property you are ultimately helping to resolve a difficult financial situation.

(See also **Finances**, **Mortgages**, **Negative Equity**.)

RETIREMENT
Equity release schemes, sheltered accommodation and retirement homes

Old age takes away from us what we
have inherited and gives us what we have earned.
Gerald Brenan, British writer, *Thoughts in a Dry Season*

Many older people want to maintain their independence
but either need more retirement income or want to move
to some sort of accommodation that has on hand someone
who can help in an emergency.

Equity release schemes

These are schemes which allow older home owners
to release capital or income from their homes without
moving. Some schemes have been criticized for tying
owners to their property and making it difficult for them
to move into sheltered accommodation or a home if that
becomes necessary or desirable. Help the Aged produces
a guide to the schemes called 'Capital Release Plans'
which explains the pitfalls as well as the advantages. Age
Concern produces another – 'Raising Capital or Income
from Your Homes' – which briefly explains the main
systems in use and lists without recommendation companies offering these schemes. Both these guides are
available free of charge. Age Concern also publish a comprehensive guide to capital release: *Using your home as*

capital by Cecil Hinton at £4.99. There are two main types of scheme.

Home reversion

This is when you effectively sell your home or part of your home to a private company called a reversion company. In return you receive a cash lump sum and/or a monthly annuity income. You can remain in the house rent-free or for a nominal monthly rent, for the rest of your life. When the property is sold, usually after your death, the reversion company receives the proceeds or a percentage of the proceeds of the sale.

It is worth remembering that the reversion company will *not* pay you the full market value of the house as you will continue to live in the property. You may get as little as 35 per cent of the market value of the property and rarely more than 60 per cent.

Home income or mortgage annuity plan

Under this scheme you receive a monthly income for life while still owning and living in your home. You take out a mortgage loan against your home up to a maximum of 75 per cent of the property value. The loan is used to buy an annuity which pays you a regular income. Interest payments on the loan are deducted from the monthly income or in some cases rolled over and added to the capital you owe. The capital is repaid from the proceeds of the sale of your house after you die.

Sheltered accommodation schemes

Sheltered property complexes are dotted all over the country and vary in expense, standard of accommodation and level of service. The more you pay the more you get but they all have quite high service charges. Before buying check:

- How the service charge is worked out. What is included in it?

- Who is responsible for repairs and maintenance?

- What happens if you want to sell the property later on?

- What happens if you become frail and need more care?

- Will someone care for your plants and make sure the pipes don't freeze if you are away?

Sheltered housing is nearly all privately built and once the properties on the development have been sold the scheme is run by a separate management group. You should only buy from a builder who is registered with the National House Building Council and is covered by their Sheltered Housing Code. The most attractive of these developments are often the newest but they are usually the most expensive.

If you are considering this type of property, choose somewhere within easy distance of friends, family and a local centre; you do not want to feel isolated inside the property. Also ensure that you have some control over the cost of the services you are getting and make sure you know what is included in and excluded from the service charge. If you have friends or family who might like to come and stay ensure they will be welcome and that there is room for them in your flat or guest facilities elsewhere on the development. Other things to consider include the alarm system; how does it work and is there twenty-four hour cover? You should also check out any communal facilities (lounge, laundry, etc.) and whether social events are organized.

Help the Aged provides advice on moving into sheltered housing in their free booklet 'Housing Matters'. The Elderly Accommodation Council has a comprehensive advice service and Help the Aged Retirement Property Services is a national matching service for people buying or selling retirement housing. There is also a *Daily Telegraph Guide to Retirement Housing* sponsored by English Courtyard. It describes what to look for and how to make the right choice in various circumstances taking into account outgoings.

Retirement homes

These are homes specially designed for older people – easy to run and near shops and services – but they are not sheltered housing as they do not have a scheme manager on site. There are currently 94,000 private retirement home units in England alone.

If you want to know more about this type of property contact the Elderly Accommodation Council who can provide you with details of private retirement housing in your area.

ROOFS

I want a house that has got over all its troubles;
I don't want to spend the rest of my life bringing up
a young and inexperienced house.

Jerome K. Jerome, *They and I*

The need for a new roof is often used as a bargaining tool by buyers to bring the price of a property down. Quite rightly so as the smallest and most inexpensive new roof is going to cost a four-figure sum, and if you decide to go for slate tiles and your property is of reasonable size that figure will need to be multiplied by five or even ten.

Selling

If your roof needs patching do this rather than have a buyer's survey condemn the roof entirely, convincing any prospective purchaser that a new roof is on the cards in the near future.

Buying

If the roof turns out to be in a bad state you have scope to negotiate the price quite considerably with the owner. If they won't negotiate but you feel the property is being sold at a bargain price then it may still be worth going ahead. If you feel you are already paying a good or high price for the property, this may be the moment to seriously reconsider. There is always the concern that if the roof needs fixing other major repairs may be necessary.

The roof was one of the few things that showed up on our survey as needing replacing. We went ahead anyway and the kitchen ceiling fell down on us two months later because of a long-standing slow leak in the bathroom above. But we managed to patch the roof and it was five years before we actually replaced it.

(See also **Builders, Surveys**.)

S

SCHOOLS

We class schools, you see, into four grades:
Leading School, First-rate School, Good School and School.
Evelyn Waugh, *Decline and Fall*

Good schooling is a prime concern for all families with children and education is often at the heart of a decision to move from city to country. Parents and children are looking for a greener way of life, trees to climb, fresh air, a lawn big enough to kick a ball about on without breaking any windows – and a good school.

In a society where job opportunities increasingly depend on academic achievement, parents are concerned that their children maximize their potential through a decent education. 'We don't even interview students who haven't got a first-class honours degree,' confided an executive with a major oil company. 'There are just too many applicants; this is one way of whittling them down.'

Most cities and major towns contain some good private schools but the best state schools are in the country. And so most migrants from town to country are families and for many the location of their home in relation to a good school is a key factor in the move. Families often decide on an area which is within a reasonable commute from where they work, then find the school, then look for the house. Note that you should find the school *before* the house as a school run of more than about twenty minutes is a serious consumer of time. A ten-minute ride to and from school means you spend a minimum three hours twenty minutes a week taking your children to school. A thirty-minute trip commute means two hours lost a day. It's also a fact that the nearer to the school you are the more likely it is there will be someone with whom you can share the school run, or even a school bus. But beyond a six-mile radius of the school, you are unlikely to find either. All this means that property within easy reach of a popular day school commands a premium over its more distant neighbours. Proximity to a good school sometimes overrides a property's lack of other attractions.

Selling

Emphasize the proximity of your house to a good school; this is possibly its main selling point. If you know children at the school or your own children go or went there parents will be eager to hear about it. They will also be interested in knowing about other children's facilities in the area. Even if children have never been part of your home environment and it is by chance that you live near a good school, don't underestimate its importance if showing the house to a family with young children.

Buying

A good school within easy reach of your home makes everyone's life a lot easier. Contact the Independent Schools' Information Service (ISIS) to find out about private schools in the area where you are home hunting. They also have a School search facility on their website: www.isis.org.uk. A directory of Scottish independent schools is available from ISIS (Scotland) or the information is on their website: www.scis.org.uk.

Alternatively, go to the library and get out the *Primary Education Directory 2000* which is a directory of over 27,000 state and independent establishments providing nursery and primary-school care. The *Education Authorities Directory* lists 13,500 local-education authority schools, colleges and other educational institutions including establishments for pupils with special learning needs. You can buy these directories from the School Government Publishing Company but they retail at £48 and £66 respectively. For details of nursery schools contact the Pre-School Learning Alliance. Their website – www.pre-school.org.uk – lists pre-school nurseries in different parts of the country. Addresses of schools in Scotland – private and local authority – are available from the Scottish Education Department.

It is worth thinking about where you want to send your children to school and where you want to live well in advance. The ideal time to move is in the summer holidays, but you should start planning a year in advance.

- September and October. Think of where you want to live, consider commutability from work and look at the schools in that area. Visit the schools and find out the possibilities of getting your child in.

- November and December. Get ready to put your house on the market and enter your children, if necessary, for school entrance exams which usually take place in January and February.

- January and February. Put your house on the market and start to get details of possible properties within easy reach of the schools you are looking at. Children sit entrance exams and get their results. This will possibly narrow the area of your search.

- March and April. Having committed to a new school for next year, intensify the search for a new home and give notice to the old school (a term's notice is usually required). Hopefully make an offer and have it accepted, having had an offer on your own home.

- May and June. Exchange and get ready to move.

- July and August. Complete and move ready for the new school term in September.

Be prepared to buy a house that needs to be slightly extended. It is better to go through the disruption of building works than to find yourself living in the right-size house too far away from the school.

Remember:
You need to be ready to jump when you see the right house and to know you are moving to the right area.

If you don't have children of school age steer clear of these properties; you pay more for them. The area will probably also contain a lot of school-age families which might not be what you are looking for.

(See also: **Accessibility**, **Home Hunting**, **Extensions**, **Location**.)

SCOTLAND

Oye'll tak' the high road, and I'll tak' the low road,
And I'll be in Scotland afore ye.

Anon, 'The Bonnie Banks of Loch Lomond'

The Scottish system is the envy of many an English buyer who has suffered the trauma of being gazumped but it is not the system that the government intends to adopt in its current review of legislation. The government says: 'More sales in Scotland depend on the buyer finding a bridging loan and the seller moving to temporary accommodation – neither of which is popular in England and Wales. In the Scottish system, any buyer who puts in an offer on the property has to pay up-front costs. More failed bids would mean more would-be buyers wasting money.'

Although the stresses and general rules of moving are the same the United Kingdom over, the legal aspects are very different in Scotland. The key differences are:

- Prices advertised are the minimum acceptable. The seller is looking for offers over that price.

- The buyer puts in an offer for however much more than the advertised price he or she thinks the property is worth.

- All bids are sealed and made in writing; when a property is popular there is a closing date for offers. Verbal offers are not acceptable. It is important to remember that a written offer formalizes the bid; never send in an offer without consulting your solicitor.

- Occasionally, property is sold at a fixed price; the first person to offer that price gets the property.

Houses and flats in Scotland are primarily not owned freehold but on 'feudal tenure'. This means they are owned just as in a freehold property except that the original owner – known as the superior – may have imposed conditions on the use of the land or property. For instance the building of any extension without their permission may be prohibited. These feudal or 'feuing' conditions remain in force in perpetuity. Flats are owned on the same basis as houses.

Selling
Appoint solicitors early on, before you decide to sell. They may handle the whole sale for you or advise you through-out. They will first ensure that your title to the property is in order and carry out local-authority searches to make sure the property is not affected by any local authority plans

As the owner you will probably show most people

around your property, even if you employ an estate agent. Many agents and solicitors in Scotland charge extra for showing prospective buyers around.

Your charges will be different. You are usually charged a modest set fee by solicitors for registering your property in the local property centre plus 1–1.5 per cent commission (sometimes less) plus the conveyancing charge. Some solicitors charge a single fee – often 1.5 per cent – to carry out both selling and conveyancing. Find out what and how you will be charged before you decide which solicitors to employ. Alternatively you can use an estate agent and a solicitor as in England.

Once your property is on the books of a property shop or estate agent you wait for people to view and offers to be made. Most solicitors won't set a closing date for offers until several people have expressed serious interest in buying but you are at liberty to negotiate with the first person who declares they want to make a serious offer on the property. You are under no obligation on the closing date to accept any of the offers for the property although prospective buyers are obliged to stick by their offers. The solicitors will handle the completion of the sale and deduct their fees from the purchase price before handing over the balance of the money – usually on the day of settlement or at the latest the following day.

Buying

You will need a Scottish solicitor and these can be found through the Directors of General Services issued by the Law Society of Scotland. Things can move quite quickly and you should appoint your lawyer before you start to look for property.

The bulk of property is sold through solicitors and through solicitors' property centres, although some is advertised and sold through estate agents as in England. A list of solicitors' property centres is available from the Law Society of Scotland. If you buy through these centres the solicitor is in charge of the purchase.

When you have found a property tell your solicitor who will inform the seller's solicitor that you are interested in buying. The survey then has to be carried out before you make an offer. The offer is a formal document in Scotland and sets out the conditions under which you would like to purchase the property including when you would like to move in – normally one to two months after making the offer – and what contents you want included in the price. If your bid is successful in securing the property the rest of the conveyancing is carried out by the solicitor. You cannot now get out of the deal without paying a penalty unless your solicitor discovers something detrimental to the property through his investigations (the equivalent of searches in England).

There will be a date of settlement when your solicitor will arrange with the seller's solicitor for your handover of the purchase price (which you should have arranged in the normal way) and your receipt of the title to the property.

Remember:
Once you have made an offer for a property you cannot pull out.

Never write letters or sign any documents relating to a purchase without first consulting your solicitor. If you do you may find you have unwittingly bound yourself to the purchase of a property you cannot afford or don't want.

(See also **Local Authority and Other Searches**, **Preparing Your Home for Sale**, **Solicitors**.)

SEALED BIDS

Anyone can Win unless there Happens to be a Second Entry.

George Ade, *Thirty Fables in Slang*

In a boom market or where an exceptional property is for sale there is often more than one buyer in the chase. As gazumping is generally frowned upon a practice has developed which in some ways is reminiscent of the Scottish buying system: prospective buyers are asked to put in sealed bids. This is when an agent or seller asks all interested parties to place their 'best and final offer' in a sealed envelope to be delivered to the buyer's solicitor or agent by a certain date. The envelopes are then opened in front of a third party and the best bid wins.

Selling
This method ensures that you get the best price on offer and everyone interested has a fair chance of purchasing the property.

Ensure that you know the financial position of each of those bidding. It could be worth taking a slightly lower bid from someone who is in a better position to move – a cash or first-time buyer – rather than an offer from someone who is reliant upon the sale of their own house which is not yet under offer. The decision is yours; you do not have to take the highest bid and what you do depends on how quickly you need to move.

Buying

If you are aware that there are other buyers interested ask if the property is going to sealed bids. When deciding what to bid think very carefully about your own finances; don't be tempted over your limit to get the property. Ensure you are in a good position to buy and that the seller or their solicitor or agent knows this.

(See also **Gazumping, Home Hunting, Queue Jumping Without Gazumping, Sellers' Information Packs, Solicitors and Licensed Conveyancers**.)

SECOND HOMES

What an odd thing tourism is. You fly off to a strange land, eagerly abandoning all the comforts of home, and then expend vast quantities of time and money in a largely futile attempt to recapture the comforts that you wouldn't have lost if you hadn't left home in the first place.

Bill Bryson, *Neither Here nor There*

Close your eyes and dream of that little stone whitewashed cottage, two up, two down, large inglenook fireplace, beamed ceilings, the whole surrounded by a flower-filled garden and five minutes from the sea. It's a dream many try to turn into reality every summer packing swimsuits, beach towels, suncream and woollies before heading off into the holiday traffic for the far corners of Scotland, Wales, Norfolk, Devon or Cornwall. But holidays aren't enough for some of us. What we want is a second home: somewhere to get away to for more than two weeks a year. Second homes have also taken on a new meaning for British buyers in the past five years. They are no longer just a weekend getaway from the hurly-burly of the city; they have become a foothold for the future and are often bought with the intention that they will one day become a first home.

A survey in 2000 by one major international agent showed a dramatic increase over the past five years in second-home buying. Buyers had one of three prime motives for their purchase: weekend retreat, long-term investment or holiday home. Although a second home can fall into all three categories, it is the top priority that affects where and what you buy.

Weekend retreat

This should be no more than three hours from your first home. If it is too inaccessible it loses its purpose. Don't forget to add into journey times the fact that traffic leaving any major city is at its worst on Friday night and traffic returning on Sunday night is often only modestly better than that on Monday morning. In order for you to get the most from it, your weekend retreat must be secure and easy to maintain; you don't want to spend your weekends cleaning the house and mowing an enormous lawn.

Long-term investment

This needs to be in an area where there is high demand for rental property, probably in town rather than the country. Look for something which is easy to keep and has good facilities. Car parking and a well-equipped kitchen are more important than a garden or a pretty exterior. If you plan to let it is simpler to invest in something with no garden or at best a patio or balcony. Talk to an agent who handles lettings in the area before you buy; they should be able to give you a good idea of the sort of properties in high demand.

Holiday home

A holiday home can be much further away from your main home than a weekend cottage. Again security and upkeep are major considerations as you don't live there all the time. If you plan to partially let it through a holiday company, call them before you purchase. They can advise you on what properties will let most effectively and how the property should be equipped. You will need to reconcile your wants with the requirements of the company, and to employ someone to clean the cottage and change the sheets when one lot of holidaymakers moves out and another lot moves in. Summer letting agents charge a hefty commission, usually in the region of 20 per cent of the rent. They also usually insist that cottages are available for them to let for most if not all of the high summer season so your use of the property is limited.

If you want to buy a second home abroad approach the experts to get help. There are a number of UK companies dealing in properties in France and Spain and others selling second homes in Florida. Look out for international property exhibitions. Make sure you know where you want to go and what sort of property you want. The laws regulating the buying process and the security of your title to your property vary from country to country.

Remember:

If you let a property you will be charged tax on any profit you make.

You may need a second mortgage. This will be calculated in the same way as a first mortgage but with the amount you have already borrowed on your first home deducted from the amount available to be borrowed.

You might be able to borrow slightly more money from a lending institution if you can show them a letter from a holiday company or letting agent with a clear indication of the income you might receive from letting.

Many lending institutions now operate buy-to-let schemes which are well worth looking into.

(See also **Finances, International Property Buying, Investment, Security, Tax.**)

SECURITY

A burglar who respects his art always
takes his time before taking anything else.

O. Henry, *Makes the Whole World Kin*

There are few things more disagreeable than discovering that somebody has got into your house and stolen your worldly goods. Whether it's a ten-year-old television or the family silver the sense of personal invasion is intense. Gone are the days when you could leave your home unlocked; you need double-bolted doors, window locks and burglar alarms to secure your property and you get little sympathy from the police or that nice man from the insurance if you fail to take serious security measures to protect your home.

It is worth remembering that 80 per cent of burglaries are carried out by opportunist thieves who are looking for cash and goods that are easy to sell on. Hi-fi equipment, computers and televisions are at the top of the shopping list alongside watches and gold jewellery. The good news is that although a skilled and determined burglar is hard to stop, many opportunist thieves are put off by a thorny hedge and positively deterred by the site of a burglar alarm. There were 442,602 burglaries from dwellings between April 1999 and March 2000 according to Home Office figures. The number of *successful* burglaries fell from 57 per cent in 1995 to 54 per cent in 1997, a fact that the Home Office puts down to increased levels of home security. One agent carrying out a survey of buyers found that

69 per cent now put security as one of their top priorities whether they are buying a flat, townhouse or country house, but only 64 per cent of properties on the market offer a good security system.

Most police authorities have leaflets offering crime prevention advice. The Metropolitan Police produce a booklet called 'How Secure is Your Home?' which covers everything from the front door to lighting, alarms, securing your garden and garage and marking your possessions so that if they are taken they are more easily traceable. Such guides to home protection recommend:

- A high wall or fence and trellis at the back of a house, with prickly shrubs like berberis. Side entrances fitted with lockable gates.

- All ground-floor windows and accessible first-floor windows fitted with window locks.

- Specialist locks for patio doors.

- A visible burglar alarm from a reputable security firm.

- Locks on garden doors and garden sheds.

- Never leave a window open when the house is empty. Although you might consider the window inaccessible, a burglar could use a ladder.

- Do not hide spare keys outside the house or in the front hall. The first place a thief will look is under pots near the front door, inside the letter box or under the doormat. There has been a spate of thefts where thieves manage to hook keys left on hall tables through the letter box.

- Front and back doors of solid core construction should be fitted with a five-lever deadlock, which can only be opened with a key. Even if a burglar manages to get in they will not be able to leave through the door without a key. Do not keep spare keys in an obvious spot near the door.

- An outside light which switches on in response to movement makes it more difficult for a burglar to remain hidden near your house at night.

- Dogs can be added security, particularly if they bark when someone approaches your home.

Less conventional security methods noted by one agent include:

- An owner who deterred burglars by spreading the rumour that his house was haunted.

- Animals including geese, a flock of noisy guinea fowl and in one instance a llama herd.

- False surveillance cameras throughout a garden.

- A doormat covering a hole in the floor down which uninvited and uninformed visitors fell.

Remember:
According to the British Crime Survey over 6o per cent of burglars enter property through a door.

If you decide to install an alarm system contact the National Approval Council for Security Systems (NACOSS) who will provide you with a list of approved installers in different areas of the country. They also have a website: www.nacoss.org.

Selling

Buyers will want to know about local crime and any precautions you have taken against being burgled. Make sure any alarm system is working and that it has been recently serviced.

Buying

When you move in it is worth having the main locks changed; you don't know who the previous owner gave keys to and how many keys have been lost.

Call your local police station and ask for a crime prevention officer to visit your home for advice on security measures. Most stations are happy to offer advice but the police are under no obligation to visit your home for this purpose; it is entirely at their discretion.

Discuss security measures with your insurance broker. Most insurers offer discounts on home-insurance premiums for well-protected homes but the protection does have to come up to a certain standard, so make sure any locks and alarms you fit are approved by them. If you need to install an alarm and are in doubt as to whom to approach contact NACOSS. After any major building work always recheck the alarm system as it could have been damaged during the work or may need extending or altering to effectively cover the new parts of your property.

Remember:
The latest British Crime Survey shows that 5.6 per cent of households experienced at least one burglary (attempted or successful) last year.

Fire

Do not forget to secure your home against the risk of fire with a fire alarm and other safety precautions. Advice is available from your local fire service. There were 467,600 house fires in Britain in 1999. The most common causes of fires (in order) are: cooking, electric appliance faults or defects (not wiring), smoking. One of the fastest rising causes of fire is candles.

In the year 2000 the Home Office carried out a national leafleting campaign about fire risks and how to prevent them. The Home Office recommends that all homes are fitted with a smoke alarm. There are two types:

- Ionization alarms are sensitive to small particles of smoke produced by flaming fires but less sensitive to slow-burning smouldering fires.

- Optical alarms are a more expensive option but are better at detecting smouldering fires and less sensitive to flaming fires.

Ideally you should have both types fitted on each floor level. All smoke alarms should conform to the British

Standard and carry the heart-shaped kitemark with an S in the middle and the number BS5446 Part 1. Alarms should be tested once a month. Other recommended ways of protecting yourself and your family from fire include: keeping doors closed at night; switching off as many electrical appliances as possible at night; putting out cigarettes and candles safely and keeping matches and lighters away from children.

The Association of Building Engineers (ABE) produces a leaflet on how to protect your home from fire.

(See also **Insurance**.)

SELLERS' INFORMATION PACKS

When a little girl asked me what two and two
make I'm supposed to have answered, 'It depends if you're
buying or selling' . . . Not true!

Lew Grade, *Still Dancing*

The property buying and selling business is littered with tales of gazumping and gazundering, failed sales, disappointed buyers, tears and court cases. Clearly the present system is unsatisfactory and the government is proposing to bring in legislation to make the whole process simpler and less stressful for both buyers and sellers. Specifically:

• Sellers want a firm offer at an agreed price.

- Buyers want to find out what they need to know quickly so that they can stop worrying about losing the home they've decided on.

- Buyers and sellers want to avoid wasting time, effort and money and want to be sure, as early as they can, that nothing will go wrong.

The highest risk period for both buyers and sellers is the time between agreeing terms and exchanging contracts. The government has decided that in order to reduce this time, both buyers and sellers need to be better prepared and to do this sellers' information packs have been proposed. The sellers' packs have now been trialled with some success in Bristol, Burnley and Bradford. The pack has been broadly welcomed by buyers, sellers and the professionals involved in selling property: Sellers thought that the information in the packs improved the marketability of their property though they were concerned at the cost (estimated at £300–£500). Buyers felt the pack introduced transparency into the market and would weed out owners testing the market but not seriously intending to sell. Professionals felt the pack reduced the number of failed transactions and assisted in dissuading 'toe dippers' who clogged up the market and cost time, effort and money.

The pack

The sellers' information pack means that anyone who wants to put a property on the market is responsible for assembling a standard set of information and paperwork ready for would-be buyers. Although this would cost sellers money to prepare, those sellers buying another property would save money on their purchase. The pack would contain:

- copies of title documents

- replies to standard preliminary enquiries made on behalf of buyers

- replies to local authority searches

- copies of any planning, listed building and building-regulations consents

- for new properties, copies of warranties and guarantees

- any guarantees for work carried out on the property

- a surveyor's report on the condition of the property

- a draft contract

  For leasehold properties the pack would also include:

- a copy of the lease

- accounts and receipts for service charges

- building insurance policy and receipts for premiums

- regulations made by the landlord or management company

- the landlord or management company's memorandum and articles

Changes for Buyers

Buyers would in future have to obtain a mortgage 'in principle' before making an offer on a property. It is hoped that this would give buyers a clear idea of what they could afford and reassure sellers that a buyer's offer was genuine. The new legislation would also put pressure on other organizations involved in the long legal process of conveyancing to become more efficient. The government wants to see all local authorities stick to their target of replying to requests for a standard search within ten working days. Other organizations receiving search enquiries, such as water companies, would be encouraged to set up and keep to similar targets.

(See also **Estate Agents, Insurance, Preparing Your Home for Sale, Solicitors and Licensed Conveyancers, Surveyors.**)

SERVICE CHARGES

It is an economic axiom as old as the hills that goods
and services can be paid for only with goods and services.

A. J. Nock, *Memoirs of a Superfluous Man*

Service charges are the fees levied by managing agents on tenants of a private estate or block of flats. The money raised is used to maintain the overall fabric of the property.

These charges can provide very little – painting, decorating and essential repairs – or they can cover everything from the heating to the hall porter, an external security system and fresh flowers in the lobby. If buying a property where service charges are made be careful to ensure that the charges are controlled and cannot escalate out of hand and that you take into account the cost of the service charges in your overall calculations of annual expenditure.

Try and find out through your solicitor if the building has recently undergone any major works or is scheduled for major refurbishment of some sort in the near future. If they are about to put on a new roof or install a lift the charges could rocket. It is worth knowing at the time of purchase that not only the flat but the general fabric of the building is absolutely sound. It is advisable to see at least three years of accounts for works carried out on the site by the landlord or managing agent before you buy a leasehold property within it. Check out the company managing your property; don't assume anything. One estate agent who looked into the accounts of a block of flats off Regent's Park discovered that the cleaners appears to be on a salary of £62,000 each. Service charges in newer apartment blocks have risen in recent years to take account of the package of extras offered by developers to tempt buyers. From the sauna and the gym in the basement to the uniformed porter, everything has to be paid for.

One of the biggest bones of contention is service charges on retirement developments. Many people live in such developments for peace of mind; they do not want to be bothered with calling out the plumber or the electrician. But they can be caught by rising service charges for which they have not budgeted. The cost of running warden-controlled developments tends to rise in line with average earnings whereas the state pension tends to rise at a much slower rate.

Remember:
Ensure that the building as well as the flat is properly maintained before you buy.

Make sure the vendor has paid the service charges up to date. Failure to pay charges can result in forfeiture of lease.

(See also **Finances, Leasehold, Sellers' Information Packs**.)

SERVICES
(gas, electricity, water)

Her own mother lived the latter years of her life
in the horrible suspicion that electricity was dripping
invisibly all over the house.
James Thurber, *My Life and Hard Times*

When buying a house ensure that all necessary services are available in the new property and find out how recently the supply was updated. Services which are not in good condition are a major hazard. Buyers also need to notify service providers that they are taking over the property and that services should not be cut off. This should be done as soon as possible after contracts have been exchanged when a firm date has been set for completion.

Before making an offer ask the owners about services to the property. If there is no gas supply or drainage to a main sewer it is best to know this at the start as you will need to know about the septic tank buried on your property which needs to be periodically emptied and the calorgas tanks which need to be regularly renewed. If you want an absent mains service provided, find out how long this would take and how much it would cost. Also check the efficiency of services to a property.

Electricity

Today we expect almost every room to have at least three double sockets and often a lot more, but older houses may only have one or two single sockets per room and this may well indicate that the property needs rewiring. As a general rule electricians say that any fittings or plugs more than fifteen years old will probably need to be replaced.

Once you have made an offer on a property you can have the wiring surveyed. Names of approved electrical contractors are available from the National Inspection Council for Electrical Installation Contracting (NICEIC). The Electrical Contractors' Association (ECA) will supply you with limited advice about checking electrical equipment and have a list of approved electricians. This information is also available on their website: www.eca.co.uk. For on-the-spot advice the ECA will recommend a member company within your area. The Electrical Contractors'

Association of Scotland will provide names of approved contractors in Scotland.

Remember:
There are advantages to rewiring a house completely as this allows you to increase the number of sockets or to reposition sockets.

Water and drainage

Check whether the water supply comes from the mains. If it doesn't find out where the water comes from, under whose control it is and whether there are water charges. Check the capacity of the water tank; is it going to be sufficient for your needs? Remember that water charges vary according to the supplier and whether they are based on the rateable value of the property or, if metered, on the amount of water used.

If the property is not on mains drainage find out how the septic tank operates, how often it has to be emptied, how you organize this and what it costs.

The Institute of Plumbing will provide you with a list of members by postcode and advice on how to deal with and prevent common plumbing emergencies. Information is available on their website: www.registeredplumber.com. The National Association of Plumbing, Heating and Mechanical Services Contractors provide a list of contractors who are members of their organization but do not offer any technical advice.

Gas

You will need to arrange for a service engineer to connect any new appliances to the gas supply when you move in. The British Gas website – www.gas.co.uk – does offer some advice for people moving home.

(See also **Central Heating, Moving Timetable**.)

SHARED OWNERSHIP SCHEMES

Whereas it has long been known and declared
that the poor have no right to the property of the rich,
I wish it also to be known and declared that the rich
have no right to the property of the poor.
John Ruskin, *Unto This Last*

Shared ownership schemes are a good option if you are finding it expensive or impossible to get a first foothold on the property ladder. Offered by housing associations, there are basically four types of shared ownership scheme:

* The 'Homebuyer scheme' is where you buy 75 per cent of a housing association property and the association retains a 25 per cent stake on which you do not pay rent. If or when you decide to sell you must do so through the association and sell at the market value. You get 75 per cent of the sale price and the housing association continues to retain its share.

This scheme is generally only available to council tenants or people on housing association waiting lists. Demand is high and lists can be long but it is worth getting on a waiting list even if you are single. Sometimes an association might find they have a glut of people selling one particular size of property in one area and you could unexpectedly find yourself at the top of the list.

- 'Do-it-yourself homebuyer' is being phased out in favour of 'Homebuyer' but it is still on offer in some areas. You find a property yourself and buy it jointly with the housing association or local authority.

- Shared ownership is open to any first-time buyer. You often do not have to buy as much as 75 per cent of the property and you pay a modest rent on the part of the property you do not own. There are long waiting lists and every housing trust has its own criteria for inclusion in and progress up its list.

- The Rural Housing Trust operates a shared ownership deal for people with family or work connections in particular villages. Their aim is to keep villages for villagers and people who have work in the area. They are also sympathetic to people who want to stay in a village or would like to move back to a village to be near other family members. The trust sells an approved purchaser a 65 per cent share in a property and retains the rest. There is no rent payable on the trust's share. If you decide to sell it finds or approves a purchaser.

If you are interested in a shared ownership scheme you should call your local authority for details of housing associations operating in your area. Another good source of information is the Housing Corporation, the government body that regulates associations, which produces booklets on shared ownership schemes including homebuy. For information call the corporation or consult its website: www.housingcorp.gov.uk. The Department of the Environment also publishes fact sheets on home ownership incentive schemes which are available on its website: www.detr.gov.uk.

(See also **First-time Buyers**, **Housing Associations**, **Joint Ownership**, **New Build**.)

SOLE AGENCY

Thou shalt not covet; but tradition
Approves all forms of competition.
Hugh Clough, English poet, 'The Lastest Decalogue'

Sole agency is what all estate agents want and what sellers shouldn't necessarily give except in a really fast market.

Sole agency means that one agent has the exclusive option to sell your property for a certain period of time. You are bound once you have signed the agreement not to sell through another agent for that period. The benefit to you is that an agency with exclusive rights to your property will charge you a smaller commission (say 1.5–2 per cent instead of 2.5–3 per cent) than would be the case if other agents were also able to sell your property.

If you do opt for a sole-agency agreement, ensure that you have thoroughly checked out the local agents and the one you have chosen seems the most likely to sell your house. Also make sure that the sole-agency agreement is for a limited period of time, preferably no more than six weeks. You need to be able to move agents quickly if you are not getting the right service.

Don't unwittingly agree to allow the agent to earn a fee on the sale for a certain time after the agreement terminates, regardless of who sells the house. And don't undertake to pay commission to an agent for introducing a buyer 'ready, able and willing to buy'. If anything goes wrong (suddenly you are not moving to Southampton) you might still have to pay the agent's fee.

You should never give sole selling rights. Establish what will happen if you sell the house yourself through your own network of friends and colleagues. Some agents ask for sole selling rights (not to be confused with sole agency) entitling them to a commission even if they don't introduce the buyer. This effectively prohibits you from selling the property privately through friends.

(See also **Estate Agents**.)

SOLICITORS AND LICENSED CONVEYANCERS

Solicitors are lawyers trying to be gentlemen.

Austin Mitchell MP, *Guardian* 1990

Solicitors are like any other profession, they specialize. So put aside any thoughts of using your best friend's brother who might be brilliant in court; if property isn't his speciality steer clear, the laws associated with bricks and mortar may be nearly as foreign to him as they are to you.

To find the right solicitor or licensed conveyancer (licensed conveyancers are specialist property lawyers regulated by their own council and by the Legal Services Ombudsman) you should:

- Ask a friend, relation or colleague, preferably living in the area where you intend to purchase, who they used when they bought. A good report from them is probably the best recommendation you can get.

- If you are buying through an agent, ask their advice. They will certainly be aware of the slow ones who have lost them sales in the past.

- Bank managers and building-society managers may give you names of people they know but are often careful not to recommend anyone specifically.

- Consult the Law Society's regional directory in your local library or the National Solicitors' Network who have a website – www.solicitorsnetwork.co.uk. – which will match you with a solicitor. Or, contact the Council for Licensed Conveyancers who will give you a list of licensed conveyancers in your area.

- Make an appointment to go and see two or three and ask them how much they will charge. Some solicitors have a standard conveyancing fee but this can vary by hundreds of pounds; expect to pay in the region of £500 for a property under £100,000 without too many complications. Other solicitors charge 1 per cent of the purchase price plus VAT for conveyancing.

When you talk to a solicitor:

- Be clear about what you are planning to buy or sell.

- Explain what sort of financing you have arranged and through which company.

- Ask their advice on local problems. One advantage of employing solicitors living in the area is that they should be reasonably aware of some of the more general problems or plans for the area: the new bypass which will affect the value of property nearby or local planning restrictions which could prevent you putting on the extension you want.

- Ask them how long the searches should take. It is well worth knowing if a council is slow or highly efficient as this can dictate the pace of the sale.

- Ask for a rough estimate of how long the conveyancing procedure will take.

- Ask for a clear guide to their fee structure. What exactly will you be charged? Are search fees included or excluded?

- Find out if the solicitor you are speaking to will carry out all the paperwork themself or will they be just overseeing the conveyancing? If they only supervise ask to meet the person who will be in day-to-day contact with you.

When you leave the solicitors' office ask yourself the following questions: Were you seen quickly and treated professionally? Were they amiable and easy to get on with? Did they explain clearly how they operated – their fee structure as well as the process of conveyancing? You want to be able to say yes to all these questions. As in all things the cheapest option is not always the best. Go with your instinct. Buying a property is one of the most stressful things you can do so don't add to your problems by employing someone you don't trust or like.

Remember:
If you are buying and selling at the same time, use one solicitor so that the chain moves forward as easily as possible.

You cannot use the same solicitors as the vendor.

Cash buyers have exchanged and completed on a property at the height of a boom in less than twenty-four hours.

Normally you can expect a minimum two months from offer to completion.

If you have a complaint about the conduct of a solicitor contact the Office for the Supervision of Solicitors who will investigate complaints about poor service, negligence, professional misconduct, solicitors' bills, theft and dishonesty. If you are complaining about someone else's solicitor the office can only help if your complaint involves professional misconduct.

(See also **Conveyancing, Queue Jumping Without Gazumping.**)

STAMP DUTY

To tax and to please, no more than to love and
to be wise, is not given to men.
Edmund Burke, Irish-born politician, *On American Taxation*

Stamp Duty is the government tax on property purchase.

Buying
The land transfer or conveyance must be sent to the Stamp Office within thirty days of the date on which it becomes effective (completion). A penalty is payable if the document is late and interest is charged on any duty not paid.

Stamp Duty is payable on the purchase price of property costing above a certain figure. It is currently payable on the purchase of property over £60,000 at the following rates:

  1% £60,001–£250,000
  3% £250,001–£500,000
  4% Over £500,000

The Controller of Stamps at the Stamp Office produce a range of leaflets about everything from lost documents to the latest changes in Stamp Duty. All information needed by the public about Stamp Duty is available on the website: www.inlandrevenue.gov.uk.

Remember:
Keep stamp duty figures in mind when you are buying a property. It is very much in your interest to buy a new home for £249,750 rather than £250,250. The difference in purchase price is £500 but the difference to you as the buyer is between paying £2,479 in stamp duty and paying £6,250.

STORAGE

Pack up you troubles in a dry room.
Lisa Freedman, June 2000, *Daily Telegraph*

It happens. Things don't dovetail and you are out of one house three or four days before you can move into the next or essential repairs and refurbishment are being carried out on your new home and you can't move in for months. In either case you will need storage facilities.

Sometimes as your goods languish in a distant packing case you can forget why some of them ever seemed important enough to keep. In a recent *Telegraph* article we featured the story of Australian businessman Bruce Palling who spent £1,000 shipping fifty tea chests to a warehouse in the suburbs of Sydney in 1986. Ever since he has been paying £3 a week to keep them there. 'At the time it seemed the cheapest way to deal with everything I'd accumulated in ten years of travel, but now I am paying for suits that don't fit and books I'll never read.' But whether goods are going into storage for two days or two years you have to employ a removal firm to move your furniture out of your house and into storage and out of storage and into your new house, virtually doubling the cost of the move. If you are in this position it is important to shop around. Depending on how long you are planning to store things it can be worth your while storing furniture in a less convenient spot at a cheaper rate, but if things are only going into store for a week or two you are probably better off keeping the storage central.

Most companies will give you a storage rate per container and the size of each container is given in cubic feet. If your removal company estimates that you have 2.25 container loads find a friend or family member who will hold on to a table and a few chairs for you for a couple of months so that you don't have to pay for the third container or, if possible, take a few pieces with you to your temporary accommodation. An average container is 250 cubic feet and holds (approximately) a sofa, armchair, double bed, chest of drawers, two side tables and ten tea chests.

To find a storage company contact the British Association of Removers who will give you the names of three reputable removal companies in your area who have storage facilities. They also provide an arbitration service if things go wrong.

Remember:

Store things near your new property so that you can move in easily.

Make sure your furniture is fully insured while it is in storage and insured against any damage done in transit. In March 1992 a fire in a Watford warehouse destroyed the possessions of nearly two hundred families. Some people lost everything they owned and were shocked to learn that the warehouse had no sprinklers, smoke or heat detectors, fire walls, security guards or alarms.

Write an inventory of what is in each container particularly if you are planning to store for more than a month.

If you want to get some things out before others, tell the storage company and then these things can be put in a separate container or packed at the front of a container.

Some storage companies charge you for accessing goods while they are in storage, others don't.

(See also **Preparing Your Home for Sale, Removal Firms**.)

SUBJECT TO CONTRACT

What usually comes first is the contract.

Ira Gershwin, when asked which came first,
the words or the music, *Guardian*, 1983

Almost all property is bought and sold 'subject to contract'. This really means that you have agreed to buy or sell in principle, and solicitors are now looking in detail at the proposed sale and drawing up an agreement.

Making an offer 'subject to contract' means that you are covered if you cannot raise sufficient funds to buy the property, a negative survey decides you against continuing with the purchase, solicitor's enquiries reveal a problem like road widening or a compulsory purchase order or you simply change your mind for some other personal reason.

There should be no objection from a vendor to an offer being made subject to contract and survey.

(See also **Conveyancing, Solicitors and Licensed Conveyancers**.)

SUBSIDENCE

The winds blew and beat upon that house;
and it fell not: for it was founded upon a rock.

Matthew 7.25

Most buyers run a mile when they hear the word subsidence. It means that the property is gradually sinking or has at some point sunk into the ground and parts of the structure have cracked. Subsidence takes place naturally or is induced by man's activities. Subsidence problems are particularly prevalent where property is built on clay. This is not uncommon; there is a belt of clay running from Bristol to the Wash and there are twenty-three postcodes in Britain where your property is considered at high risk of subsidence. Subsidence induced by man is caused by everything from underground tunnelling to planting trees too close to the walls of a property. If a house is subsiding it does not necessarily mean it is going to fall down tomorrow. However, it may mean that as owner you will have to have sections of the property underpinned to strengthen the foundations.

It is worth knowing that research shows eight in ten subsidence claims on clay soil are a result of trees and shrubs and the worst-affected homes are those built between 1940 and 1970. The least-affected homes are those built with cellars and basements.

Warning signs of possible subsidence include: cracks running diagonally down walls or around door and window frames, especially if they are wider at one end; sloping floors or jamming doors; willow trees or wide leaved deciduous trees planted within twenty feet of a wall. No tree should be planted within ten feet of a wall.

Buying

If you decide to buy a house suffering from some sort of subsidence:

- You may have to face underpinning the walls or some part of the house at some time. This is expensive and messy. All houses differ but expect to pay £15,000 plus to underpin a modest detached house. Call the Association of Specialist Underpinning Contractors.

- You will probably have difficulty getting building insurance and may be forced to take over the building policy of the present owner.

- The cost of insurance may be much more than that for a similar property not suffering from subsidence – something you have to take into account in the financing of the property. Contact the Subsidence Claims Advisory Bureau (SCAB) which will help you to find insurance cover and could help if you have found cracks in your property. SCAB estimates that more than two million people are paying more than they should for insurance just because their homes are on clay soil. The Insurance Ombudsman Bureau also gives advice on insurance and subsidence.

Subsidence is the ultimate negotiation tactic if you really want a property; the owner should reduce the price to compensate for the high cost of insurance premiums. If in doubt at all, walk away; this is not a headache you want and it doesn't just go away.

(See also **Insurance, Surveyors, Surveys**.)

SURVEYORS

You should be able to read a building. It should be what it does.

Sir Richard Rogers, the Walter Newrath Memorial Lecture, 1990

You can employ a surveyor for two major tasks. First, to carry out a structural survey on the property you intend to purchase in order to ensure that it is everything it says it is and to forewarn you of any major problems you might have to deal with: everything from dry rot to subsidence. Second, to help you carry out a simple extension or conversion, of an attic for example. A surveyor can do all the practical work that an architect does but is less creative. Surveyors can tell you what is possible structurally and draw up plans for a builder to carry out the work. For a fee a surveyor will also oversee this work.

A qualified surveyor must be a member of the Royal Institution of Chartered Surveyors (RICS), the Association of Building Engineers, or the Architects and Surveyors Institute. These bodies are responsible for maintaining standards within their profession.

Surveyors' fees vary enormously from company to company and from one part of the country to another. Your agent or solicitor should be able to recommend local surveyors or call the RICS for a list of surveyors in your area. A list of surveying firms is also available on their website – www.rics.org – or buy their directory: *Search for a Surveyor*. The RICS also give advice on buying a home and resolving disputes, and publish their own concise free leaflet called 'Buying or selling your home'. The Royal Institution of Chartered Surveyors in Scotland (RICS Scotland) gives advice on surveyors there.

It is better to hire a surveyor in the locality of the property you are hoping to buy as he or she should know of any conditions in the area which might be relevant: flooding or clay soil subsidence, for example. Call at least three different surveyors and get quotes for the work you want carried out. Discuss with the surveyor a date for the survey, what type of survey would be most suitable and the fee. Ask for written confirmation of the agreed details of the inspection and the fee. Once you have engaged a surveyor provide as much relevant information about the property as you can. Mention anything that concerns you: a damp patch or crack, the condition of the window frames, etc. Tell the surveyor if you are planning to carry out any major alterations to the property; he or she will be able to tell you whether these are feasible. Also mention if you are planning to completely replace something – the central heating, for example – as this then does not need detailed inspection.

(See also **Architects, Finances, Surveys.**)

SURVEYS

*Architecture cannot lie, and buildings though
inanimate, are to that extent morally superior to men.*

John Gloag, 'The Significance of Historical Research
in Architectural and Industrial Design'

A survey tells you what you need to know about a building: not just the good points but also the problems which
will need to be dealt with in the months and years to come.
All lenders will insist on some sort of survey before loaning
you money against the security of the property. Under
current law it is the obligation of the potential buyer to
find out what is wrong, but under government proposals
it will become the obligation of the seller to provide the
buyer with a basic survey. Don't underestimate its importance, or the necessity of obtaining a really detailed survey
on a building which looks as if it might have potential
problems. A thorough survey is a wise precaution whether
you are buying a castle in Scotland, a flat in London or a
cottage in Cornwall.

Selling

There is an increasing tendency for sellers to have a survey
prepared before putting their property on the market,
anticipating the new legislation. This is an ideal way to
kick-start your sale. It also means that if any major fault is
revealed you are the first to know about it and can either
deal with it or reduce the price of the property and be

open about its faults, and it avoids a potential sale falling through as a result of a bad survey. This wastes everyone's time and money and leaves a question mark over the property.

Buying

Once the deeds are handed over you cannot get your money back. A thorough survey is the best way of ensuring that your investment is sound. Even if you know the property you are buying is not in good condition – a fact that will be reflected in the price – it is worth finding out just how bad it is. The survey will help you prioritize what needs to be done in the near future and will prepare you for major costs. Armed with a survey you are also in a better position to negotiate the price of a property.

There are three types of survey: a lender's valuation, a home buyers' survey and a building survey. Costs for all three vary enormously and depend on: the company you employ to carry out the survey, the size and condition of the property, its approximate value and its situation. As a guide here are survey costs based on a suburban property with a value of about £200,000.

Lender's valuation

If you are borrowing money for the purchase of your property the lender – a bank or building society – will insist on a valuation. This is the most basic sort of survey and will not give you a real picture of the condition of the property.

A valuation is a short inspection of the property in

which the surveyor notes its condition and, using his or her knowledge of local property prices, fixes its value. Any serious defects will be pointed out and the lender will commonly ask for these to be rectified before lending you the money.

A valuation will not tell you if the wiring is faulty or that you will need a new roof within five years. Its object is merely to ensure that the property is adequate security against the loan.

Cost: £170–£200

Home buyers' survey

This is a nine-page standard survey drawn up by the Royal Institution of Chartered Surveyors and the Incorporated Society of Valuers and Auctioneers. It covers each major section of the property. It is based on what is visible – the surveyor will not be looking under the floorboards. It will however highlight and recommend areas where further tests or investigations should be carried out. A home buyer's survey should provide an accurate snapshot of the property's condition.

Although this survey is now widely used, some companies suggest that its standard nature means that it is unsuitable for unusual buildings or those over one hundred years old.

Cost: £250–£450

A combined lenders valuation and home buyers' survey is offered by most companies and costs just slightly more than the home buyers' survey.

Structural or building survey

This is a comprehensive report and valuation, though exactly how comprehensive is open to discussion as you can ask the surveyor to check on specific aspects of the property you might be worried about: the electrical wiring, the drains, the roof, etc.

The report will be detailed and should reveal present defects and warn of potential problems. For instance it might say that the roof is currently sound but will probably need replacing within five years. It is a proper inspection not a test.

If you are seriously concerned about the condition of the property you are buying, if it is very old or run down, then this is probably the option for you. It is worth advising the surveyor of any plans to extend the house or carry out any major repairs. If you are planning to completely rewire the property or demolish a wall it is a waste of your money checking the wiring and the surveyor can more profitably use their time finding out if the wall you are planning to pull down is load bearing.

The report will include details of: the roof – everything from the condition of the slates to the gutters and chimney; the walls – everything from cracks to pointing and plaster-work; the foundations – from the damp-proof course to subsidence. The surveyor will also look at windows, floors and joinery, plumbing, drains, electricity supply and wiring, chimneys and the garden fence. It is worth asking the surveyor at the outset to give you rough estimates of what it will cost to put right any faults.

Cost: £325–£600

Once you know the problems you may well wish to reopen negotiations with the seller, particularly if you find that you have to carry out some unexpected major work.

Remember:
A recent survey showed that 25 per cent of people who had the home they hoped to buy properly surveyed were able to get the price of the property reduced on the basis of the findings.

Just because a house is newly built it doesn't mean you can avoid the necessity of a survey; it too can have serious defects.

(See also **Negotiating**, **New Build**, **Preparing Your Home for Sale**, **Sellers' Information Packs**, **Surveyors**.)

SWIMMING POOLS

Hollywood people are afraid to leave Hollywood.
Out in the world they are frightened . . . Sam Hoffenstein
used to say we are the croupiers in a crooked gambling house.
And it's true. Everyone of us thinks. You know.
I really don't deserve a swimming pool.

Gottfreid Reinhardt, in *Picture*

There is still something glamorous about having a swimming pool of your own in the cool climes of Britain where hot, swimming weather is a rarity even in the summer.

In property terms swimming pools are a mixed blessing and their value is very much determined by the extra quality of life they provide for the owner. Swimming pools need quite a lot of care and the best can be expensive to install (and heat, almost essential in Britain). You do not get your money back on a swimming pool; it is a luxury. It might add fun to family life but it doesn't add real value to a property. If you own a £200,000 house and you put in a swimming pool for £10,000 you *might* expect to get £204,000 for the house. If you want to install a pool there are three basic options:

- The cheapest option is an above-ground pool which can be anything from twelve to twenty feet in diameter and costs between £300 and £2,300. These come in kit form and if you move you can take them with you.

- The most popular type is an in-ground liner pool. You need a digger to excavate the site. A fibreglass, aluminium or concrete shell is put into the hole and given a plastic liner. These pools cost between £9,000 and £20,000.

- The top of the range is an in-ground concrete pool which is lined with tiles. These cost between £15,000 and £30,000.

For advice on pools and a list of reputable swimming-pool companies contact the Swimming Pool and Allied Trades Association. They produce an information pack called the 'SPATA Swim Pool Guide'.

Remember:
Swimming pools are an attraction for some buyers but put a larger number of people off. Families with very young children don't like swimming pools for safety reasons, and many others prefer not to own a pool seeing the upkeep as outweighing the pleasure.

T

TAX

It was as true . . . as taxes is.
And Nothing's truer than them.
Charles Dickens, *David Copperfield*

You do not normally have to pay capital gains tax on your property when you sell it as long as it has been your main home and as long as you have not used it as a place of business on which you have claimed expenses. If you have used it as a place of business or as a second home, capital gains tax is payable on the net profit of the sale of the relevant portion of the property after taking into account the cost of improvements and of buying and selling. The profit is currently based on the property's 1982 value or the price you paid for it if bought after that time.

(See also **Finances, Investment, Mortgages, Second Homes.**)

TELEPHONES

No, I don't know his telephone number.

But it was up in the high numbers.

Attributed to John Maynard Keynes, *Horizon*, 1981

Where would we be without the telephone, not just to talk to our friends but also to send emails and access the Internet?

Selling

It is kind to allow the buyer of your property to take over your telephone line if they want to. This is easily done. But you must notify your buyer if you are planning to take the line and/or the telephones with you.

You must notify your telephone company at least seven working days before you move. The number to ring appears on your phone bill and is at the front of the telephone directory, or dial 100 and they will give you the information. You must give the company the date when you want to stop renting and being charged for the line and the new address to which your final account for that line should be sent. Tell them the buyer wants to take over the line from you so that it is not disconnected, although it is ultimately up to the buyer to apply for the line.

Buying

When moving it is worth asking the seller if you can take over the telephone line so that you are not without a phone for any significant amount of time. Contact the telephone sales office of the area you are moving to. Tell them whether you want to take over the existing line at the new address or have a new line installed. Installation of new lines is dependent on availability and you may well not be given your new number until after you move in – delaying the printing and sending out of change of address information. If you do take over an existing line that is not disconnected then there is no charge from the telephone company; if the line is broken for even a day there is a reconnection charge.

Shop around for the best deals. BT is no longer the only telephone supplier and you could find you get a better deal from a cable company operating in the area you are moving to.

Remember:
If you are moving within the same area you can often take your current telephone number with you but there is a charge for doing so.

Take your phones from your old home if you own them.

TENNIS COURTS

I'm not just involved in tennis but committed. Do you know the difference between involvement and commitment? Think of ham and eggs. The chicken is involved. The pig is committed.

Martina Navratilova, *Newsweek*, 1982

Although widely believed to derive from a medieval French game called *jeu de paume*, it was an Englishman, Major Walter Wingfield, who in 1873 invented a game called sphairistike from which modern outdoor tennis has evolved. It caught on quickly in Britain, spread throughout the then British Empire and in 1877 the first championships were held at Wimbledon. Although sadly lacking in world-class players, the British still love the game and many families aspire to owning a court of their own.

Courts cost anything from £13,000 for a grey green (known as such because it is grey when dry and green when wet) to £40,000 plus for a clay court with watering system. The most popular courts for domestic use are colour-coated macadam courts which costs upwards of £14,000. Although – like a swimming pool – you won't get your full investment back, a tennis court is a greater attraction than a pool. There are three reasons:

- The English weather. Unlike an outdoor pool a tennis court is usable throughout the year as long as it is dry.

- Maintenance costs. Tennis courts are as expensive as pools to install but much cheaper to maintain.

- Safety. Again unlike pools, there are no safety problems for children attached to tennis courts.

THATCHED PROPERTIES

Season of mists and mellow fruitfulness,
Close bosom-friend of the maturing sun;
Conspiring with him how to load and bless
With fruit the vines that round the thatch-eaves run.

John Keats, 'To Autumn'

Say chocolate box, think thatch. These are the cottages that to many people are ye olde England.

There are many fewer thatched properties today than there were one hundred years ago, partly because of fears about thatched roofs and fire and partly because of the expense of re-thatching roofs and higher insurance costs. But this decline may not be set to continue. There has been a revival of interest in thatch and new-home builders are now constructing properties with thatched roofs where appropriate in the countryside. 'Thatched roofs are making a comeback,' says David Mote of the New Homes Marketing Board and one new, thatched property won a commendation at the most recent National Homebuilder Design Awards. But the charm of these roofs has to be set against additional maintenance and insurance. A thatched roof:

- needs to be re-ridged every 7–12 years

- needs to be replaced every 15–30 years at an average cost of about £8,000 for a traditional detached cottage

- is an invitation to uninvited members of the wild community including birds, rats, mice and squirrels (though wire netting can deter some of these invaders)

- adds between £5,000 and £10,000 to the cost of a new house

- adds 50p per annum per £1,000 value of the property (£100 on a £200,000 home) to insurance premiums

It is worth knowing that most thatch fires are caused by chimneys. If you own or are buying a thatched property the chimney should be regularly swept and should finish at least one metre above the thatch.

If you want to know more about buying and owning a thatched property contact the National Society of Master Thatchers or the Thatching Advisory Service. The Thatching Advisory Service is a branch of the NFU (Hungerford) Insurance company which specializes in thatch and has a website with information about thatch: www.4x4insurance.co.uk/thatch.html.

Remember:
Many older thatched buildings today are listed and you are required to maintain the thatched roof. You will not be allowed to tile.

Different styles of thatch prevail in different parts of the country; some have a longer lifespan than others because of the materials used.

(See also **Insurance**.)

TIMBER-FRAMED HOUSES

I want an old-fashioned house
With an old-fashioned fence
And an old-fashioned millionaire.
Marve Fisher, 'Old-Fashioned Girl'

There are two types of timber-framed houses: old and new.

Old timber-framed houses are often painted black and white to highlight the attractive shapes of the timber frames. They are found in the Cotswolds, in Suffolk, Staffordshire, Shropshire and Herefordshire and, more rarely, in many other parts of Britain. Many of the old timber-framed houses standing today were built in or before the seventeenth century and are therefore automatically listed. Timber-framed houses were mainly built in areas where there was no good local stone and before bricks came into wide use. The richer you were the more wood you used and people could guess how affluent you were by looking at the walls of your house.

Now you can also buy new timber-framed properties. These are constructed from brick and prefabricated timber panels and have become fashionable in recent years. They are much in demand by some buyers and there is a Timber and Brick Homes Information Council which will give you the names of registered timber-frame builders and a list of newly completed timber-framed houses in each county. Ask the council about the *Timber and Brick Homes Handbook* which will tell you about buying and owning a timber-framed house.

(See also **Grants for Home Improvement and Renovation, Listed Buildings, Wrecks, Ruins and Redundant Property**.)

TIME SHARE

> The great and recurrent question about abroad is,
> is it worth getting there?
>
> Attributed to Rose Macaulay, in *Treasury of Humorous Quotations*

This is a popular way today of owning a stake in a holiday home that doesn't tie you down to more than a couple of weeks a year. Time-share properties exist all over Britain and Europe. They are primarily advertised in magazines and newspapers and at holiday and property exhibitions. If you are tempted, ensure:

- The development or property is well maintained and a good management structure is in place in which you will have a say.

- That the annual service charge is not too high and doesn't negate the advantages of owning a stake in the flat or house.

- There are clear rules for internal maintenance of the property and replacement of everything from tea cups to carpets.

Remember:
A time-share property ties you down to returning to the same property every year for a week or two although companies increasingly offer an exchange system so that one year you can negotiate a deal to exchange (for instance) your two weeks in a Scottish castle for two weeks in a Corsican villa.

TITLE DEEDS

There is no stronger craving in the world than that of
the rich for titles, except perhaps that of the titled for riches.

Hesketh Pearson, English actor and biographer,
The Pilgrim Daughters

The title deed is the legal document that gives you 'title' over a property. It is proof of ownership and outlines exactly what the property consists of. Sometimes it will also outline your obligations as far as things like fencing or maintenance of a joint access road are concerned.

When you sell a property the title deed passes to the buyer with the keys to the house once the buyer receives full and final payment for the property.

When buying, the deed is examined by your solicitor between exchange and completion to check that it is in order.

If you have a mortgage you do not actually receive the title deeds although the property is in your name. The title deeds are held by the building society or bank that has loaned you the money to buy until the loan is repaid.

(See also **Completion**.)

TREES

> I like trees because they seem more resigned
> to the way they have to live than other things do.
>
> Willa Cather, *O Pioneers!*

In an attempt to maintain our green and pleasant land some trees are subject to tree-preservation orders. This means that you cannot lop, cut down, uproot or wilfully destroy the tree without applying to the local authority for permission. All trees in conservation areas are automatically subject to a preservation order. All types of trees are covered by preservation orders, even hedgerow trees, but not hedges, bushes or shrubs.

Although it is generally accepted that you are at liberty to lop off overhanging branches from a tree in a neighbour's garden, it is worth checking with the owner first in order to find out if the tree is subject to a preservation order. Even if a tree is not protected it is polite to notify your neighbour if you want to cut down an overhanging branch. The owner might prefer to call in a tree surgeon to carry out the work. If a branch is crudely hacked, it may adversely affect not only the appearance but also the health of the tree. If you wilfully damage or destroy a protected tree you may be fined up to £20,000 and will be obliged to replant.

An excellent website with clear information about tree-preservation orders has been produced by the borough of Tameside: www.tameside.gov.uk/corpgen1/protecttrees.htm.

Any tree-preservation orders on a property you want to buy should come to light during the local authority searches carried out by your solicitors.

Remember:
You need to get a tree-felling licence from the Forestry Commission if you want to cut down more than five cubic metres of timber.

(See also **Conservation Areas, Local Authority and Other Searches.**)

U

UNDER OFFER

I'll make him an offer he can't refuse.

Mario Puzo, *The Godfather*

This is when a potential buyer has made an offer to buy a property and the offer has been accepted. The solicitors from both sides should now be in touch and moving the purchase forward.

Most owners will not show their property after a firm offer has been made and accepted. However, if the offer is lower than the seller would like and the buyer is not in a position to move quickly, the owner may well decide to continue to let prospective buyers view in case the offer falls through. If as an owner you decide that you are still going to show the property then it is only fair to tell the person who has made the first offer and explain your reasons why, otherwise you will quite rightly be accused of gazumping if you accept another offer.

Remember:
Although no money has changed hands your buyer will already have started to plan the move, stopped looking for other property and engaged a solicitor. If you are not

totally happy with the offer you should turn it down or tell the buyer that you are continuing to look for better offers.

(See also **Gazumping, Lock-out Agreements, Queue Jumping Without Gazumping**.)

UTILITY ROOMS

Nothing grows in our garden, only washing. And babies.

Dylan Thomas, *Under Milk Wood*

Washing and the machinery that does it for us, are necessities of life best kept in a separate space. Utility rooms are a boon to most householders. Nobody likes the constant splosh and groan – however quiet – of a washing machine or the gentle whirr of a drier in their kitchen. It is much better to have these machines shut away in a room of their own with the ironing board, iron and freezer and an indoor line where you can hang clothes that can't be spun. These rooms can also be used as 'back kitchens' or sculleries where the really messy kitchen work is done away from the eat-in family kitchen which has become a popular part of today's living environment.

Utility rooms are a particularly good selling point; even if you haven't got round to doing anything about one yourself it is worth pointing out where one could go.

Remember:

A utility room doesn't have to be very big. It can be in a cupboard at the end of the kitchen, with enough room for the washing machine, a shelf above on which sits the drier and sufficient room down the side for storage of washing powders.

V

VACANT POSSESSION

So long as the great majority of men are not
deprived of either property or honour, they are satisfied.

Niccolo Machiavelli, Florentine statesman
and philosopher, *The Prince*

This is what you should get when you move into a new
house.

As a seller it means that you must ensure you have
taken everything you want or have agreed to take and left
what you have agreed to leave before completion. Before
locking a house for the last time it is particularly important
to remember to check the attic, the cellar, all storerooms,
cupboards, outbuildings and garages. If you leave something behind you technically cannot call the new owner
and ask if your bicycle is still in the woodshed and if so
could you collect it – though many people do. The new
owner would be totally within their rights to have disposed
of the bike.

Eleven months after moving into our house we were
called by the previous owners who asked if we could look
in our attic to see if their Christmas decorations were still
there. They were and we returned them but had we had

less to do in the house and used the attic more they may well have found their way onto a skip.

(See also **Completion, Fixtures and Fittings**.)

VALUATION

> What is a cynic? A man who knows the
> price of everything and the value of nothing.
> Oscar Wilde, *Lady Windermere's Fan*

It's what every estate agency prides itself on and what owners swear they know better: the value of their property.

We all have a vague idea of what properties are worth but often like to massage the figures a little in our favour – down if we are buying, up if we are selling. Most of us who keep an eye on the property pages of national or local newspapers feel that should the opportunity arise we could hazard a good guess at most property prices. Or could we? One major estate agent decided to test the valuing abilities of visitors to a national exhibition one year; out of two hundred attempts only thirty-three came within 10 per cent of the value placed on a fictitious estate in Oxfordshire.

The Insurance Ombudsman Bureau gives advice on valuations.

Selling
However you decide to sell your property – through an agent, Internet property site, property shop or privately –

it is worth getting a proper valuation done. Let a cynic who has no particular affection for your property place a value on it.

Buying
If you are buying a property privately where the owner has set the price, unless you are very sure that he or she is right, pay someone to carry out a valuation so you can rest easy that what you are buying is worth the price.

(See also **Location, Preparing Your Home for Sale**.)

VIEWS

A room with a view. And you.

Noel Coward, 'A Room With a View'

A room with a view is what most of us hanker after. Whether it is a view of a pretty garden, a river, acres of fields or rolling countryside, a good view is restful on the eye and pleasant to the heart. Consequently, properties with good views can often sell for a small premium. The better the view and the siting of the property, the better the premium.

Selling
Make a feature of it, but not too much. One memorable buyer told estate agent Roy Brooks of the delights of his flat

on Primrose Hill not far from London Zoo with 'wonderful views of sunsets thro the tracery of the trees and model girls being photographed on the hill' and the agent added '. . . and the distant mating cry of the hyena in the still of a summer night.'

Buying

Be careful to read the small print on property details. Views of the sea from the first floor might mean only from the bathroom window.

Look at ways of improving your view but remember that you may not have the option of pulling down trees at the bottom of the garden if they are subject to a tree-preservation order.

VIEWING

Education is when you read the fine print;
experience is what you get when you don't.

Pete Seeger, *Bett's Loose Talk*

Rules about viewing properties vary according to which side of the fence you are on. And there are also stories – about the woman who came with her two children and dog to see a second-floor one-bedroom flat or the elderly couple who stayed for tea.

Journalist Patrick Lay tells the story of selling his first home some decades ago, an end of terrace in North London.

'One viewer leant against a rickety shelf in her fur coat and walked from room to room with our cactus collection stuck to her back. A couple insisted on praying on their knees in every room to seek guidance, and another woman wanted to spend the night in the house to see if she would be disturbed by traffic.'

Selling

There are two schools of thought: owners should always take prospective purchasers around because they know the property best; agents should always take prospective purchasers around because buyers will be inhibited in the presence of the owners.

Both to a degree are true and it depends on your personality as to which will suit you. If you know that in your heart you only want people to compliment your house – which for all its faults has been your home for a number of years – then you are probably better leaving the viewing to the agent. If, however, you have the time and are prepared to let people wander around your home to a degree unescorted and to clearly answer any questions then you can show them around; a welcoming smile at any door gives a property a sense of home and heart.

Whether you are showing the property or not it is essential that you are prepared for the viewing. Although if you have a young family it is not easy to keep the whole house in perfect order day in and day out it is essential to make sure of the following before a viewing:

- The entrance is clear and welcoming.

- There are no dirty dishes or mucky tables in the kitchen.

- The living room should be immaculate. Make this a no-go zone if your family is messy.

- Bathrooms must be spotlessly clean. Dirty baths and topless tubes of toothpaste are unattractive.

- All beds must be made.

Flowers in the hall or living room are welcoming as is a bowl of fruit in the kitchen. The tidier you can be – inside and out – the better impression the house will give. Even if a prospective buyer is untidy they somehow seem to imagine that if they move into your immaculate home they will suddenly change their ways.

Buying

Protocol almost always means that you must make an appointment to view a property. If for some reason you are going to be late for the appointment or on viewing a house from the outside decide you are not interested, it is polite to call the agent or the owner.

When viewing be polite but ask as many questions about the property as you want. On a first viewing you should try to get a feel for the property: does it suit your needs or could you make it suit your needs? Write down the most appealing and the most unappealing factors about the property and anything you are concerned about. Look out for telltale signs of possible problems:

- Long cracks in walls or around doors and bay windows which appear to have been repaired but have cracked again could be a sign of subsidence.

- A clammy smell could indicate damp.

- Cracking or crinkly woodwork, particularly on skirting boards, could be a sign of dry rot

- Open the windows and check the noise levels.

On a second viewing think about how you would use the space in the property and where you would put key pieces of furniture. Try to ignore the property's current decor and furniture and imagine how it would look decorated and furnished by you. Take a measuring tape to check room measurements and spaces where you would put large pieces of furniture. Remember that the positioning of doors, windows, bookcases and heaters can sometimes make even the biggest of rooms quite difficult to furnish. Think also about your future in the property. Has it got sufficient potential to enable you to live in it for a number of years, or just for a year or two? Add up the costs of any alterations you want to make. If you are really interested in the property discreetly find out when the seller wants or is able to move and try to discover if others have made offers on the property.

Remember:
Visit the property at different times on different days of the week so that you can get a feel for traffic, noise and light levels in the property.

On the second visit take someone who hasn't seen the property before whose opinion you trust.

Check how far away the propety is from local transport facilities and talk to the owners about local schools, shops, places of worship and the neighbours.

(See also **Preparing Your Home for Sale**, **Buying Checklists**, **Selling Checklists**.)

W, X, Y, Z

WOODWORM

It . . . was full of dry rot. An unkind visitor
said the only reason Menabilly still stood was that
the woodworm obligingly held hands.

Daphne Du Maurier, in *Dictionary of Quotations*

If you have woodworm this is as worrying as damp and
dry rot to buyers and, more importantly, to lending organizations. It must be treated by a professional and a guarantee for the work produced. Contact the British Wood
Preserving and Damp-Proofing Association who can give
you advice on treatment and on companies who can carry
this work out for you. Information is also available on their
website: www.bwpda.co.uk.

Selling

If your property has suffered from this it is best to say so
and to show the guarantees of treatment upfront. Signs of
woodworm remain after treatment.

Buying

When viewing a property look at the woodwork: floorboards, skirting, window frames and doors. If it is showing

cracks or shrinkage there may be some woodworm and this needs to be checked out. If floors are springy make sure the surveyor checks the joists aren't wormy or rotten.

(See **Surveys**.)

WRECKS, RUINS AND REDUNDANT PROPERTY

The difference between stumbling blocks
and stepping stones is the way a man uses them.

Anon

If a building is going to wrack and ruin there are three things we might want to do with it: pull it down, save and restore it or convert it. There are blots on the landscape waiting wearily for an appointment with a bulldozer, crumbling gems that have an architectural elegance we want to bring back to life and redundant buildings that have outlived their usefulness as churches, mills or barns and are waiting to be reinvented. According to the Department of the Environment there are more than 772,300 empty properties in Britain.

Most of us appear to have a desperate desire to save crumbling cottages or redundant barns. What is it about a derelict property that attracts the English soul? Every month SAVE Britain's Heritage gets 5,000 enquiries to their website, from those desperately seeking wrecks and every day answers dozens of telephone queries from wreck hunters.

'I have often wondered what makes them all so keen. People often pay over the price for the opportunity to do a property up,' says SAVE secretary Richard Pollard. 'I think it is really the ultimate DIY project. A lot of people say they are interested in old buildings but if that was just the case they could buy an older property.'

A package of four or five pages of advice on what to do and where to go for professional advice if you take on a wreck is available on the SAVE website: www.SAVEBritainsheritage.org. Both SAVE and the Scottish Civic Trust regularly produce lists of buildings at risk. English Heritage says there are 1,600 listed buildings in England alone currently at risk.

Selling

Maybe you always meant to restore the crumbling barn in the field at the bottom of your garden, or maybe you just forgot about it.

If the building was once lived in as a dwelling it can be pulled down (if it is not protected) and a new building put on the site and sold. Alternatively, it can be sold as is. Contact organizations like SAVE who keep a list of wrecks and ruins for sale or put it with a local agent, preferably one that also holds auctions as most wrecks sell best at auction.

If it is a barn or had some other use then it is probably worth getting planning permission for its conversion before trying to sell it on; the planning permission adds enormously to its value.

Buying

If you are looking for a wreck to pull down so that you can build something new, make sure the building is not listed and that it is roughly the size and volume of the building that you wish to replace it with. Planning authorities will rarely let you replace a three-bedroom low-built house with a six-bedroom high-ceilinged mansion with turrets. If in doubt talk to the local planning officer.

If you want to buy a crumbling gem contact SAVE Britain's Heritage or the Society for the Protection of Ancient Buildings. In Scotland contact the Scottish Civic Trust. As well as listing buildings at risk these organizations also offer advice on restoring them. If you spot a crumbling gem you can find out who the owner is by contacting the local authority for the name and address of whoever is responsible for the council tax on the property.

If the building is empty and you track the owner down, don't necessarily expect them to sell. People are very strange about property. I know of one beautiful long, low granite cottage that has been slowly falling into disrepair over the past ten years since its single rather eccentric owner died. It was left to his three nephews, none of whom want to live in it or have any need for it. Two want to sell it but the third won't. So it sits, its entrance covered every year by a greater tangle of brambles. Uncared for, its value has steadily deteriorated but possession is all the third nephew wants.

When working out the costs for restoring or rebuilding add at least 20 per cent for unforeseen extras. Restoration needs a deep pocket. Old buildings don't give up all their mysteries at once and you can often find yourself in a much more expensive renovation project than you bargained for. One man who has spent a lifetime restoring timber-framed houses says it is the 'can't we just . . .' factors that escalate the costs: Can't we just tile the floor as well as the walls? Can't we put in an Aga? Can't we fit polished oak floorboards in the living room?

The Society for the Protection of Ancient Buildings runs courses for professionals and home owners on the issues they should take into account when they take on the repair and maintenance of an historic building.

Remember:
If the building is listed it will be subject to a large number of planning restrictions. You will need an even deeper pocket to comply.

You may find it difficult to borrow money in order to buy and renovate the building.

(See also **Architects, Builders, Listed Buildings, New Build, Planning Permission**.)

Buying Checklists

BUYING CHECKLIST 1

Sorting out the finances

Your first priority is to work out exactly what you have to spend (don't forget to subtract the essentials in Buying Checklist 2 and the costs in Buying Checklist 6 before you make an offer).

Many people then also need to find out how much of a mortgage they can get. This is usually quite easy to establish but the more important question is which mortgage to chose; there are literally hundreds of deals on offer and it is best to be armed with a list of questions which will help you assess what the best deal is for your circumstances. Some of your questions will be answered in the lender's literature or on their website but if you can't find the answer ask the lender when you go to see them or on the telephone, or seek advice from a professional independent financial adviser.

1. Will you be given any specific advantage/deal because you have/have not been a former customer?

2. What are the different interest rates?

   • Do rates change according to the amount borrowed?

   • For first-time buyers?

- For endowment/repayment/pension/interest-only mortgages?

- For fixed-rate mortgages (over two years, five years, etc.)?

3. What monthly payment will you have to make per £1,000 borrowed? (Compare different deals/amounts/periods.)

4. When and how will payments be made (the first of the month, within the financial year, after the first year)?

5. In what circumstances are payments, if ever, deferred?

6. What happens when interest rates change?

7. If you chose a fixed- or discounted-rate mortgage will there be an arrangement fee?

8. Can you extend or renew a fixed-rate scheme after the early years?

9. What percentage of the valuation is the normal maximum loan they will give? Are there circumstances where this differs?

10. How much more can you borrow with extra security and what security is acceptable?

11. What, if any, insurance must be bought as a condition of the loan?

12. What will you be charged if you pay off the mortgage early? (There are often different fees at different periods in the 'life' of the mortgage.)

A mortgage comparison chart

	Amount borrowed	Type of mortgage	From whom	Repayment terms	Monthly outlay
1					
2					
3					
4					
5					
6					
7					
8					
9					

BUYING CHECKLIST 2

The costs

Buying a property is not cheap and costs a lot more than the purchase price. Use the entries in this guide and information from your own enquiries with agents, solicitors, surveyors, removal men, etc. to add up the ultimate cost of buying.

Cost	Amount
Solicitor's/conveyancers fees	
Building survey	
Stamp Duty	
Land Registry fee	
Local authority searches (£50–£100)	
Other search fees and disbursements (dependent on property)	
Lender's legal fee (usually your solicitor will also act for the lender but check this out or you could be in for two sets of fees)	
Lender's survey fee	
Mortgage Indemnity Guarantee (applicable if you borrow more than a certain proportion of the value of the house)	
Mortgage arrangement fee	
Sub-total £	_____

Moving Costs	Amount
Removal van	
Reconnection/inspection charges for gas and electricity	
Installation of telephone	
Plumbing costs for disconnecting and reconnection (washing machine and dish washer)	
Redirection of letters	
New locks	
Change of address notification cards	
Any essential decorative or building works	
Total £	

All these costs should be deducted from the capital (which includes any money you are borrowing) that you have to spend.

BUYING CHECKLIST 3

The basics

This list summarizes your position as a buyer. Ensure any estate agents you approach have all this information.

- Total to spend (mortgage plus capital less 5–10 per cent for moving costs)

- Ability to move (cash/mortgage buyer, chain)

- Location required (preferred areas, streets)

- Type of property required (modern/old/detached/ terrace/flat)

- Prepared to extend or refurbish?

- Size of property required (number of reception rooms, number of bedrooms, garden)

- Your name(s), current address, day, evening, mobile telephone and fax numbers, email

BUYING CHECKLIST 4

Viewing Checklist

Make a number of copies of this list and take one with you when you visit each property. Before you arrive tick any 'must haves' and 'would likes'. As you go round the property add your comments and circle areas where the property fulfills your needs. Make a note of 'extra pluses' (superb view, walking distance to the station) and of any 'worrying minuses' (noise from nearby major road, kitchen needs complete revamping, damp patch on wall). Remember to note storage/cupboard space particularly in the kitchen and bedrooms.

Address of property:	Must have	Would like	Comments
large kitchen			
utility room			
bathrooms (number)			
bedrooms (number/ size)			
dining room			
study			
playroom			
main reception rooms (number)			
downstairs cloakroom			
conservatory			
garden			
garage			
off-street parking			
separate granny/ nanny/letting annexe			
proximity to transport (how far, which)			

	Must have	Would like	Comments
proximity to schools (how far, which)			
proximity to shops (how far, which)			
proximity to open spaces (how far, what sort)			
cupboard/storage space			
views			
privacy			

Asking price:

Date and time seen:

Agent and phone number:

General impression:

Extra pluses:

Worrying minuses:

BUYING CHECKLIST 5

Second Viewing

As in Buying Checklist 4 make copies of this list and take it with you. The answers to these questions will give you a better idea of how much you might have to invest in the property. If you have any 'Worrying minuses' from Checklist 4 now is the time to bring them up.

Address of property: _____

Why is the property being sold?

How long has it been on the market?

Have there been any previous offers on the property?

Is there anyone else currently interested in buying?

Where is the seller moving to; have they found a house they want to buy?

Is the seller in a chain?

When does the seller want to move?
How old is the house?

Have there been any major alterations in the last ten years
(extension, new kitchen, new bathroom, new roof, new
windows, rewiring)?

Are there guarantees for any work done?

What fixtures and fittings will be included in the sale? (Go through
Buying Checklist 7 if you are seriously interested and come back
for another viewing.)

What are the council tax rates?

When was the central heating installed or serviced?

What is the annual heating bill?

What are the water bills?

Are there any service charges (flats), ground rent or parking
charges?

What are the neighbours like?

Where is the nearest shop?

What is parking like in front of the house?

Local noise levels?

How long does it take to get to the nearest main town and is there
a train or bus service?

Where is the nearest school/church/leisure centre?

Any other questions concerning you

BUYING CHECKLIST 6

Specific costs on a property you want to buy
Make copies of this list for use when you are seriously interested in making an offer on a property. It will help you to see how much money you need to spend immediately and how much you will probably eventually spend to make your new home comfortable. Before making an offer deduct these costs and the costs in Buying Checklist 2 from the total you have to spend. Use the A–Z entries and make your own enquiries to help you work out these costs.

Address of property:

	Essential	Eventual
new curtains		
carpets		
redecoration		
new kitchen		
new bathroom		
building repairs		
rewiring		
central heating		
extension		
roof		
conservatory		
landscaping		
Total		

BUYING CHECKLIST 7

Making an offer

Make several copies of this list as for a hundred different reasons you often make offers on several properties before a purchase goes through. Tick the applicable column against any of the fixtures and fittings which you would like.

Address of property:

Asking price: **First offer:**   **Second offer:**

Fixtures and Fittings		Must have	Would like	Pay extra
Kitchen	stove			
	fridge			
	freezer			
	dishwasher			
	washing machine			
	drier			
	other			
Bathroom	heated towel rail			
	mirror			
	light fittings			
	other			
Living room	curtains			
	carpets			
	light fittings			
	other			
Halls/stairway	curtains			
	carpets			
	light fittings			
	other			
Bedroom 1	curtains			
	carpets			
	light fittings			
	other			

Fixtures and Fittings		Must have	Would like	Pay extra
Bedroom 2	curtains			
	carpets			
	light fittings			
	other			
Bedroom 3	curtains			
	carpets			
	light fittings			
	other			
Outside (garage, greenhouse, shed, etc.)	garden furniture			
	lawn mower/other garden equipment			
	window boxes			
	garden ornaments			

Attach a list of other rooms with any fixtures and fittings you would like to negotiate on.

Selling Checklists

SELLING CHECKLIST 1

Preparing your property for sale
Critically appraise the condition of the property and carry out the following:

Outside

- Clear garden of clutter: old bikes, broken garden furniture, garden rubbish, etc.

- Mow lawns.

- Drives and paths: weed, rake gravel, fill potholes.

- Clip hedges and repair fencing.

- Paint gate if necessary.

- Cut back climbing plants so they don't block any window light.

- Plant colourful annuals like petunias and begonias in any bare flower beds close to the house and window boxes.

- Invest in potted evergreens to hide unsightly areas: rubbish tip, heating plant for swimming pool, gas or oil tanks.

- Sweep patio.

- Paint front door (if necessary).

- Clean door furniture.

- Paint lines on tennis court and get rid of moss. Get swimming pool up and running; make sure there are no floating leaves.

Inside

- Clear out all clutter.

- Steam clean dirty carpets.

- Clean dingy curtains.

- Thoroughly spring-clean the house getting rid of any animal smells; ensure paintwork is washed.

- Clean bathrooms and kitchen until they sparkle and smell fresh.

- Clean windows inside and out.

- Touch up any badly marked or scuffed paintwork; if necessary paint a grubby or badly marked room but choose a neutral shade. White or cream offends no one.

- Ensure all door handles and light switches are working.

- Check all light bulbs are working.

- Carry out all those little repairs (dripping tap, missing tile on the roof) that could take the edge off the appearance of your property.

Do not decorate the house at great expense; the new owner will want to do that. Your aim is simply to make each room look as clean and airy and bright as possible so that viewers can get a sense of the space available.

SELLING CHECKLIST 2

Choosing an Agent

Invite round the three agents you have asked to evaluate your property and fill in the following form to help you decide which to use. Use whatever scoring system you like to rate them: yes/no; number of ticks (one = OK, two = good, three = excellent); etc.

Name and Agency:

Likeability | Quality of inspection
Knowledge of area | Qualifications

What the deal includes

Professional photos | Brochure
Local advertising | Viewing
Access to the Internet | Distribution to other offices
Suggested sale price | (how many)
 | Agency percentage charged

Name and Agency:

Likeability | Quality of inspection
Knowledge of area | Qualifications

What the deal includes

Professional photos | Brochure
Local advertising | Viewing
Access to the Internet | Distribution to other offices
Suggested sale price | (how many)
 | Agency percentage charged

Name and Agency:

Likeability

Knowledge of area

What the deal includes

Professional photos

Local advertising

Access to the Internet

Suggested sale price

Quality of inspection

Qualifications

Brochure

Viewing

Distribution to other offices
(how many)

Agency percentage charged

Rate and then choose your agency. Don't forget to haggle over the percentage they are charging or what they will include in the deal.

SELLING CHECKLIST 3

What is included in the price, what is negotiable and what is not

Give a copy of this list to your agents so they can get the property details right.

Fixtures and Fittings		Included	Negotiable	Taking
Kitchen	stove			
	fridge			
	freezer			
	dishwasher			
	washing machine			
	drier			
	other			
Bathroom	heated towel rail			
	mirror			
	light fittings			
	other			
Living room	curtains			
	carpets			
	light fittings			
	other			
Halls/stairway	curtains			
	carpets			
	light fittings			
	other			
Bedroom 1	curtains			
	carpets			
	light fittings			
	other			

Fixtures and Fittings		Included	Negotiable	Taking
Bedroom 2	curtains			
	carpets			
	light fittings			
	other			
Bedroom 3	curtains			
	carpets			
	light fittings			
	other			
Outside	garden furniture			
(garage,	lawn mower/			
greenhouse,	other garden			
shed, etc.)	equipment			
	window boxes			
	garden ornaments			

Attach a list of other rooms with any fixtures and fittings. Remember to make a list of any plants that you will take and inform the agents and any prospective buyer.

SELLING CHECKLIST 4

Preparing for each viewing

Before *each* viewing remember to check:

- The house is clean and clutter-free – bathrooms and kitchen sparkling.

- Any animals are safely confined to one room, the garage or the car during viewing.

- Children are out or quietly occupied.

- Flowers are arranged in main rooms.

- Windows have been open for at least twenty minutes so the rooms smell fresh.

- Central heating is on.

- Fire is lit on a chilly day.

SELLING CHECKLIST 5

Questions to ask when an offer is made

- Name of buyer.

- Price offered.

- Buying position (cash buyers, still to sell, property under offer).

- Timing: how quickly or slowly do the buyers want the property or will they move to your timetable?

- Does the agent consider the buyers serious? Some buyers make an offer 'just in case they don't find anything better'. Unless you are desperate, you don't want an offer from these buyers.

SELLING CHECKLIST 6

Adding up the cost

You are anticipating the nice round figure that you have been offered but even if you are selling off a second home or moving in with someone else there are quite a few costs to subtract from this sum.

Deduct from the selling price:

- Estate agents' fees (1.5–4 per cent of the price of the property plus VAT).

- Legal fees (either 1 per cent of the price of the house plus VAT or a flat fee).

- Advertising and other marketing costs, which may or may not be included in the estate-agents' fee.

- Mortgage redemption charges: up to three months' interest if you are repaying within a short period – usually considered to be less than five years.

- Moving-out costs: removal van, storage (if necessary).

- Cost of disconnecting equipment and fittings.

Moving Timetable

On exchange agree a date for moving into a property.

Six weeks before the move:

- Contact several removal firms, ask for estimates.

- Sign and return removal contract with deposit and map and address of the property you are moving to.

- Check you have insurance cover for the move; arrange if not.

- Arrange to take your phone with you, to take over the phone number at the new address or to have a new number.

- Organize change of address cards if you have all the information.

- Inform your employer, schools, key family members and friends.

- Cancel any rental agreements from the day of the removal.

- Tell gas, electricity, water and telephone companies about the change of ownership; arrange for services at your new home.

- Measure up for new curtains and carpets at the property if necessary.

- Take a builder, painter or decorator to the property and get estimates for any work you want done.

Four weeks before the move:

- Start clearing out all unwanted items, particularly from the attic and cellar.

- Make up boxes and bags to take to charity shops.

- Confirm removal arrangements.

- Book help from family and friends.

- Organize someone to look after pets and children.

- Send out change of address cards. Don't forget to notify the bank, building society, insurance company, solicitor, car registration, passport office, TV licence, doctor, dentist, optician, all clubs and societies you belong to as well as all family and friends.

- Ask the Post Office to re-route mail.

- Make a concerted effort to use up all food in the freezer and to run down your stores of tinned and dried foods.

- Arrange for parking permit (if applicable).

Two weeks before the move:

- Start sorting and packing things up.

- Plan where all your furniture is to go – draw diagrams.

One week before the move:

- Continue packing.

- Cancel papers and milk and arrange for delivery at your new home.

- Contact seller or their agent to confirm arrangements about keys, electricity, water, gas and phone.

The day before the move:

- Take children and pets to family friends.

- Get cash from the bank.

- Charge your mobile phone.

- Pack up a survival kit (kettle, mugs, teaspoon, sugar, coffee/tea, light bulbs, bin liners, dustpan and brush, hammer and screwdriver, rubber gloves, candles and matches, loo paper, change of clothes, towel, soap, notepad and things to write with, first-aid kit, cheque book and credit cards, torch, plastic cups, bottle of champagne).

- Switch freezer to maximum if it still has anything left inside it and you are taking it.

The day of the move:

- Supply whoever is moving your furniture with clear instructions about your packing system.

- Check each room, attic and cellar to ensure you have left nothing behind.

- Lock doors and leave keys at the pre-arranged address for the new owners.

- Collect keys to your new home.

- On arrival check the services immediately – gas, electricity, water and telephone – and read the meters.

- Check the fixtures and fittings list. If the vendor has taken something major they agreed to leave you can sue them for its return.

- Do essential unpacking and make up beds before you collect any children or pets.

Useful Addresses

Age Concern
1268 London Road
London SW16 34ER
Telephone 0800 009966

Architects and Surveyors Institute (ASI)
St Mary House
15 St Mary Street
Chippenham
Wiltshire SN15 3WD
Telephone 01249 444505
Website www.asi.org.uk

Association of British Insurers (ABI)
51 Gresham Street
London EC2V 7HQ
Telephone 0207 600 3333
Website www.abi.org.uk

Association of Building Engineers (ABE)
Jubilee House
Billing Brook Road
Weston Favell
Northamptonshire NN3 9NW
Telephone 01604 404121

Association of Relocation Agents
PO Box 189
Diss
Norfolk IP22 1NS
Telephone 08700 737475
Website www.relocationagents.com

Association of Residential Letting Agents (ARLA)
Maple House
53–55 Woodside Road
Amersham
Bucks HP6 6AA
Telephone 01494 431 680
Fax 01494 431 530
Email info@arla.co.uk
Website www.arla.co.uk

Association of Specialist Underpinning Contractors
Association House
235 Ash Road
Aldershot
Hampshire GU14 4DD
Telephone 01252 336318
Fax 01252 333901

Banking Ombudsman and Building Societies Ombudsman
South Quay Plaza
103 Marsh Wall
London E14 9SH
Telephone 0207 404 9944
Website www.obo.org.uk

British Association of Removers (BAR)
3 Churchill Court
58 Station Road
North Harrow
Middlesex HA2 7SA

Telephone 0208 861 3331
Website www.barmovers.com

British Insurance Brokers
 Association (BIBA)
BIBA House
14 Bevis Marks
London EC3A 7NT
Telephone 0207 623 9043
Email enquiries@biba.org.uk
Website www.biba.org.uk

British Waterways
Willow Grange
Church Road
Watford
Herts WD17 4QA
Telephone 01923 226 422
Fax 01923 201400
Website www.britishwaterways.co.uk

British Wood Preserving and
 Damp-Proofing Association
1 Gleneagles House
Vernon Gate
South Street
Derby DE1 1UP
Telephone 01332 225100
Website www.bwpda.co.uk

Building Employers Confederation,
Carron Grange
Carron Grange Avenue
Stenhousemuir FK5 3BQ
Telephone 01324 555550
Website www.scottish-
 building.co.uk

Building Societies Association/
 Council of Mortgage Lenders
3 Savile Row
London W1X 1AF
Telephone 0207 437 0655
Website www.cml.org.uk

Controller of Stamps
Stamp Offices
South West Wing, Bush House
Strand
London WC2B 4QN
Telephone 020 7438 7452
Website www.inlandrevenue.gov.uk./so

The Corporation of Insurance and
 Financial Advisers (CIFA)
174 High Street
Guildford
Surrey GU1 3HW
Telephone 01483 539121

Council for Licensed Conveyancers
 (CLC)
16 Glebe Road
Chelmsford
Essex CM1 1QG
Telephone 01245 349599

Department of Culture, Media and
 Sport
2–4 Cockspur Street
London SW1Y 5DH
Telephone 020 7211 6000
Website www.culture.gov.uk

Department of the Environment,
 Transport and Regions
Eland House
Bressington Place
London SW1E 5PV
Telephone 020 7890 3000
Website www.detr.gov.uk
Planning Division Website
 www.planning.detr.gov.uk

Elderly Accommodation Council
Third Floor, 89 Albert
 Embankment,
London SE17 7TP
Telephone 020 7820 1343

Fax 020 7820 3970
Website www.housingcare.org.uk

The Electrical Contractors'
    Association (ECA)
ESCA House
34 Palace Court
London W2 4HY
Telephone 020 7313 4800
Website www.eca.co.uk

The Electrical Contractors'
    Association of Scotland (ECA
    Scotland)
Bush House
Bush Estate
Midlothian EH26 0SB
Telephone 0131 445 5577
Website www.select.org.uk

English Heritage
23 Savile Row
London W1X 1AB
Telephone 020 7973 3000
Website www.english-
    heritage.org.uk

Federation of Master Builders
    (FMB)
14–15 Great James Street
London WC1N 3DP
Telephone 020 7242 7583
Website www.fmb.org.uk

The Forestry Commission
231 Corstophine Road
Edinburgh EH12 7AT
Telephone 0131 334 0303
Website www.forestry.gov.uk

Heating and Ventilating
    Contractors Association (HVCA)
34 Palace Court
London W2 4JG

Telephone 020 7313 4900
Website www.hvca.org.uk

Help the Aged Retirement Property
    Services
Hempstead House
2 Seldon Hill, Hemel Hempstead
Herts HP2 4TN
Telephone 0800 592605

House Builders' Federation
56–64 Lennard Street
London EC2A 4JX
Telephone 020 7608 5100
Website www.hbf.co.uk

The Housing Corporation
149 Tottenham Court Road
London W1P 0BN
Telephone 020 7393 2000
Website www.housingcorp.gov.uk

Incorporated Society of Valuers and
    Auctioneers
(now amalgamated with the Royal
    Institute of Chartered Surveyors)

Independent Financial Advice
    Bureau
549 Green Lanes
Harringey
London N8 0RQ
Telephone 0208 348 4466
Fax 0208 348 7803

The Independent Schools'
    Information Service (ISIS)
56 Buckingham Gate
London SW1E 6AG
Telephone 020 7630 8793
Website www.isis.org.uk

ISIS (Scotland)
21 Melville Street
Edinburgh EH3 7PE

Telephone 0131 220 2106
Website www.scis.org.uk

Institute of Plumbing
64 Station Lane
Hornchurch
Essex RM12 6NB
Telephone 01708 472791
Website www.registeredplumber.com

Insurance Ombudsman Bureau
South Quay
Plaza Two
183 Marsh Wall
London E14 9SR
Telephone 08456 006666
Website www.theiob.org.uk

Joint National Conservation
  Council
Monkstone House
City Road
Peterborough PE1 1JY
Telephone 01733 562626
Website www.jncc.gov.uk.

The Law Commission
Conquest House
37–38 John Street
Theobalds Road
London WC1N 2BQ
Telephone 020 7453 1220
Website www.lawcom.gov.uk

Law Society
113 Chancery Lane
London WC2A 1PL
Telephone 020 7242 1222
Website www.lawsociety.org.uk

The Law Society of Scotland
26 Drumsheugh Gardens
Edinburgh EH3 7YR
Telephone 0131 226 7411

Leasehold Enfranchisement
  Advisory Service
6–8 Maddox Street
London W1R 9PN
Telephone 020 7493 3116
Website www.lease-advice.org

National Approval Council
  for Security Systems
  (NACOSS)
Queensgate House
14 Cookham Road
Maidenhead
Berkshire SL6 8AJ
Telephone 01628 637512
Website www.nacoss.org

National Association of Estate
  Agents
Arbon House
21 Jury Street
Warwick CV34 4EH
Telephone 01926 496800
Website www.naea.co.uk

National Association of
  Plumbing, Heating and
  Mechanical Services
  Contractors (NAPHMSC)
14 Ensign House
Ensign Business Centre
Westwood Way
Coventry CV4 8JA
Telephone 024 76 470626
Website www.aphc.co.uk

National Federation of Builders
Bridge Court
Bridge Street
Long Eaton
Nottingham NG10 4QQ
Telephone 0115 9461922
Website www.builders.org.uk

National House Building Council
Chiltern Avenue
Amersham
Bucks HP6 5AP
Telephone 01494 434477
Website www.nhbc.co.uk

National Inspection Council for
   Electrical Installation Contracting
   (NICEIC)
37 Albert Embankment
London SE1 7UJ
Telephone 020 7564 2323
Fax 020 7564 2370
Website www.niceic.org.

National Society of Master
   Thatchers
73 Hughenden Avenue,
Downley
High Wycombe
Bucks HP13 5SL
Telephone 01494 443198

National Solicitors' Network
156 Cromwell Road
London SW7 4EF
Telephone 020 7244 6422
Website www.solicitorsnetwork.co.uk

Office for the Supervision of
   Solicitors (OSS)
Victoria Court
8 Dormer Place
Leamington Spa
Warwicks CV32 5AE
Telephone 01926 820082
Website www.lawsociety.org.uk

Ombudsman for Corporate Estate
   Agents
Beckett House
4 Bridge Street
Salisbury

Wiltshire SP1 2LX
Telephone 01722 333306
Website www.oea.co.uk

The Pre-School Learning Alliance
   (PLA)
69 King's Cross Road
London WC1X 9LL
Telephone 020 7833 0991
Website www.pre-school.org.uk

The Royal Incorporation of
   Architects in Scotland (RIA
   Scotland)
15 Rutland Square
Edinburgh EH1 2BE
Telephone 0131 229 7205
Website www.rias.org.uk

Royal Institute of British Architects
   (RIBA)
Clients' Advisory Service
66 Portland Place
London W1N 4AD
Telephone 020 7580 5533
   (Publications department: 020
   7251 0791)
Website www.architecture.com

Royal Institution of Chartered
   Surveyors (RICS)
12 Great George Street
London SW1P 3AD
Telephone 020 7222 7000
Website www.rics.org

Royal Institution of Chartered
   Surveyors in Scotland
   (RICS Scotland)
9 Manor Place
Edinburgh EH3 7DN
Telephone 0131 225 7078
Website www.rics-scotland.org.uk

Royal Society of Architects in Wales
75a Llandennis Road
Rhydypennau
Cardiff CF2 6EE
Telephone 029 20 874753
Website www.architecture.com

Royal Society of Ulster Architects
(RSUA)
2 Mount Charles
Belfast BT7 1NZ
Telephone 01232 323760
Website www.rsua.org.uk

The Royal Town Planning Institute
26 Portland Place
London W1N 4BE
Telephone 020 7636 9107
Website www.rtpi.org.uk

Rural Housing Trust (020 7793
8114)
Prince Consort House
27–29 Albert Embankment
London SE1 7TJ
Telephone 020 7793 8114
Website infor@ruralhousing.org.uk

SAVE Britain's Heritage
70 Cowcross Street
London EC1M 6EJ
Telephone 020 7253 3500
Website www.savebritainsheritage.org

The School Government Publishing
Company
Darby House
Redhill
Surrey RH1 3DN
Telephone 01737 642223
Website www.schoolgovernment.co.uk

The Scottish Civic Trust
The Tobacco Merchant's House
42 Miller Street

Glasgow G1 1DT
Telephone 0141 221 1466
Website www.scotnet.co.uk/sct

The Scottish Education Department
Victoria Quay
Edinburgh EH6 6QQ
Telephone 0131 556 8400
Website www.scotland.gov.uk

The Society for the Protection of
Ancient Buildings (SPAB)
37 Spital Square
London E1 6DY
Telephone 020 7377 1644
Wbsitee www.spab.org.uk

Society of Licensed Conveyancers
55 Church Road
Croydon CR9 1PF
Telephone 020 8681 1001
Website www.conveyancers.org.uk

Subsidence Claims Advisory
Bureau (SCAB)
Charter House
43 St Leonards Road
Bexhill-on-Sea
East Sussex TN40 1JA
Telephone 01424 733727
Website www.bureauinsure.co.uk
Fax 01424 731781
Email cover@bureauinsure.co.uk

The Telecommunications Industry
Association
Douglas House
32–34 Simpson Road
Fenny Stratford
Milton Keynes
Buckinghamshire MK1 1BA
Telephone 01908 645000
Website www.tia.org.uk

Thatching Advisory Service
Faircross Office
Stratfield Saye
Reading RG7 2BT
Telephone 0845 070 6050

Timber and Brick Homes
  Information Council
Gable House
40 High Street
Rickmansworth
Herts WD3 1ES
Telephone 01923 778136
Fax 01923 777275